THE INVISIBLE POET: T. S. ELIOT

HUGH KENNER

The Invisible Poet: T. S. Eliot

METHUEN & CO LTD
11 NEW FETTER LANE LONDON EC4

First published in Great Britain by W. H. Allen 1960
© Hugh Kenner 1959
First published by Methuen & Co Ltd 1965
Printed in Great Britain by Billing & Sons Ltd.,
Guildford and London

For R. B. Robinson

amicus curiae

The dogmatic critic, who lays down a rule, who affirms a value, has left his labour incomplete. Such statements may often be justifiable as a saving of time; but in matters of great importance the critic must not coerce, and he must not make judgements of worse and better. He must simply elucidate. The reader will form the correct judgement for himself.

—T. S. Eliot, 1920.

Never commit yourself to a cheese without having first examined it.

—T. S. Eliot, 1956.

CONTENTS

The quotations throughout the volume from the works of T. S. Eliot are reprinted by permission of the author and Messrs. Faber and Faber, Ltd.

Acknowledgement is also made to Faber and Faber, Ltd., for all selections appearing from *The Letters of Ezra Pound* edited by D. D. Paige, and to Jonathan Cape Ltd., for the excerpt from "Chard Whitlow" from *A Map of Verona and Other Poems*, by Harry Reed.

PREFACE

Impenetrability! That's what *I* say!
—Humpty Dumpty.

We may assume that everyone by this time knows who T. S. Eliot is, that it is no longer necessary to testify to his lucidity, that there are as many handbooks as needed, that his religious affiliation is neither a cachet nor a curiosity, that his private life deserves to remain no less private than he has chosen to keep it, and that scholarship has barely omitted to scrutinize a line (unless perhaps "jug jug jug . . ."). Yet opinion concerning the most influential man of letters of the twentieth century has not freed itself from a cloud of unknowing. He is the Invisible Poet in an age of systematized literary scrutiny, much of it directed at him.

This is partly a deliberate achievement (he is the "impersonal" poet, and also Old Possum), partly the result of chance, but chiefly a consequence of the nature of his writing, which resists elucidation as stubbornly as *Alice in Wonderland*. Though he became while still a "difficult" writer, very famous, he was for years the archetype of poetic impenetrability. It was a safe joke only a decade ago to suggest that the BBC maintain its standard of entertainment by having T. S. Eliot cerebrate silently in front of a microphone for ninety minutes. Discussion of the poems, which total fewer than four thousand lines, still slips off into *ideas,* when it doesn't begin there.

Or it is mesmerized by personality. Here Eliot himself, "a master," Marianne Moore has noted, "of the anonymous," has added considerably to the fun. He can give, for readers and interviewers alike, consummate imitations of the Archdeacon, the Publisher, the Clubman, the Man of Letters in Europe, the Aged Eagle, the Wag, and the Public-Spirited Citizen. He has also written hundreds of publisher's blurbs, many of them, to the suspicious eye, small comic masterpieces. The only role he refuses to play is the Poet. He has been described vying at anagrams with John Maynard Keynes, quoted (aged 69) as intending to take up dancing lessons, discerned composing a letter to the London *Times* on the subject of Stilton cheese, and variously decried as a snob, a proto-fascist, the nucleus of an insidious authoritarian conspiracy, and "a sick, suffering and defeated personality." It has even been hinted—again by Miss Moore—that he may write detective stories under a pseudonym.

He commands vast influence, partly through moral consistency, partly through inscrutability, partly because, in an academic context, his prose is so quotable. The details of his poetic effects, furthermore, belong to an extremely conventional category: the tradition of the turned aphorism and the weighty line. That they also subvert this tradition is a consideration that has vaguely troubled many readers, who accordingly suppose that the poet and the tradition-loving critic are two different men.

These difficulties can be evaded by the methods of the line-by-line commentary. Commentators, one of them has noted, tour the Eliot territory in chartered buses. He has innumerable "sources," some acknowledged, some covert: they can be listed. He has images that recur, and their recurrence can be noted. He has also operated, in his later work, so near the border-line of "ideas" that wherever technical commentary fails, paraphrase can readily be trundled in. And salient passages in certain of his essays have provided a generation of literary middlemen with first-rate critical gimmicks. To be sure, when a painstaking explication of one of his poems is laid before him, he is likely to reply that he was not aware of having been so clever, being mainly occupied at the time of writing with matters of assonance, cadence, and congruity; but the hint is not taken.

Let us try another method. Let us assume that the impassive, stationary Man of Letters from whom the *Collected Works* are thought to emanate is a critical myth, the residuum of a hundred tangential guesses. Let us further assume (it is a convenient fiction: biography does not concern us) a man with certain talents and certain interests who wrote poems intermittently, never sure whether his gift was not on the point of exhaustion, and reviewed countless books because they were sent him for review and (for many years) he needed the money. Let us station him for some years in the Philosophy Department at Harvard, and allow weight to what passed through his mind there. Let us endow him with a mischievous intelligence, and set him to work reviewing for the *Athenaeum*. Let us simultaneously put him in touch with Ezra Pound, and make him, for good measure, the invisible assistant editor of *The Egoist,* which "ended with 185 subscribers and *no* newsstand or store sales"; all this in London, 1917, at the pivot of an age. Install him then, heavily camouflaged, in the very citadel of the Establishment, the *Times Literary Supplement*, where, protected by the massive unreality of his surroundings, a man who has mastered the idiom can deftly affirm fructive heresies about Donne and Marvell. Then let us consider the *nature* of what he wrote and published in those early years, examining as minutely as we like what we are under no compulsion to translate or "explain": and then see whether the subsequent career to plays, *Quartets,* and celebrity does not assume intelligible contours. There has been no more instructive, more coherent, or more distinguished literary career in this century, all of it carried on in the full view of the public, with copious explanations at every stage; and the darkness did not comprehend it. Yet never comprehended, an American was awarded the Order of Merit and became England's most honoured man of letters, not in fulfilment of ambition but in recognition of qualities, real and valuable, which he had come to personify.

In 1941 Eliot sent the *Times* a supplement to their ungenerous obituary of James Joyce. This they declined to print; and he reported the episode in *Horizon* under the enigmatic title, "A Message to the Fish." He was alluding to Humpty Dumpty's poem:

> I sent a message to the fish
> I told them "This is what I wish."
> The little fishes of the sea,
> They sent an answer back to me.
> The little fishes' answer was
> "We cannot do it, Sir, because—"

This sums up the milieu in which he condemned himself to operate: this, and certain lines of his own:

> Now a Possum who lives in a Pye
> Is doing himself Very Well.
> There was only one thing wrong with the Pye
> And that one thing was the Smell.
> There was nothing exactly precisely wrong,
> It wasn't too mild and it wasn't too strong,
> There was nothing you'd want to subtract,
> Only something or other it lacked. . . .

In 1917, himself recently settled in London, he wrote that Turgenev was "a perfect example of the benefits of transplantation; there was nothing lost by it; he understood at once how to take Paris, how to make use of it. A position which for a smaller man may be merely a compromise, or a means of disappearance, was for Turgenev (who knew how to maintain the role of foreigner with integrity) a source of authority, in addressing either Russian or European; authority but also isolation." He also noted, in connection with Henry James, the advantages of coming "from a large flat country which no one wants to visit." Ten years later he was a naturalized Britisher, but always The Stranger, impeccably camouflaged, a role congenial to his temperament, to which expatriation afforded scope. The method of the poems requires of their writer a detachment from the milieu to which he is apparently committed, a detachment easier to manage abroad. Perhaps the Unreal City finally got the better of him, a risk inherent in the method and not our business anyhow. Our business is with a phenomenon, for the tracing of which such copious evidence is seldom available: the development and course of a unique instrument of poetic apprehension. To this inquiry considerations of rank, of scale, of personality, of belief, of influence are irrelevant; and save for local corrective effect we shall not touch on them again.

Ten years ago Marshall McLuhan and I planned an "Eliot book" and spent some weeks reading through the poems and essays, conversing and annotating as we went. Though this book is very different from the one we projected and abandoned, it owes more than I can unravel to those weeks of association.

At my one meeting with Mr. Eliot, I offered to complete a book on his literary career without pestering him. In the preceding decade he had, I thought, contrived enough answers to inquiries to fill a reference book; it was time someone gave him a rest. This was not as self-denying as it sounds. The oracle's responses to most of these queries had achieved circulation, in print or otherwise, and so were available for my use. I am not, for instance, the "mid-century inquirer" mentioned in the text. He did supply three pieces of information which I am glad to be able to acknowledge. One was a summary of the contents of the *Ur-Waste Land,* so far as he could remember them. The second was a gloss on the word "lot" in *Whispers of Immortality*. He said it meant "kind," not "fate," and conceded that it perhaps violated the diction of that particular poem. The third had reference to cheese.

Mr. Eliot has been a vastly more prolific writer than is

commonly supposed. To his millions of published words, and the chronology of the interests they reflect, Mr. Donald Gallup's *Bibliography* is the indispensible key. I owe him thanks for numerous courtesies. The collection of manuscript material in the Houghton Library at Harvard I was unable to inspect. Mr. Robert Lowell, however, largely nullified this difficulty by putting me in touch with Mrs. Henry Ware Eliot, the poet's sister-in-law, who very generously made available her late husband's digests and annotations of this collection. I am also indebted to conversations with Mr. Charles Tomlinson, who helped me understand Laforgue, Mr. John Reid, who clarified my handling of the plays, and Mr. Carl Zytowski, who identified the sources of the songs in *Sweeney Agonistes*. Mr. C. A. Lyon of the London Transport Executive supplied valuable details about the layout of the Gloucester Road tube station.

A grant from the American Philosophical Society made possible the collection of material, a Fellowship from the Guggenheim Foundation gave me leisure to write most of the book, and aid from the Committee on Research of the University of California at Santa Barbara financed the typing of the manuscript. Mr. Robert Porter and Miss Genevieve Sullivan of the Peterborough, Ontario, Public Library assisted me in locating the odd things a critic frequently wants.

This book incorporates portions of articles written for *Poetry* and the *Hudson Review,* and chapters have been published in *Prairie Schooner* and *Spectrum*. I am grateful to the editors of these journals for permission to revise and reprint.

University of California   HUGH KENNER

For this new edition I have corrected a few errors of my own and a number of the compositor's. The remarks on page 38 about the unpublished thesis have been allowed to stand, though of course it has recently been published. This book preceded by less than a year T. S. Eliot's death in the early days of 1965. He elected to have his ashes interred at East Coker, amid the "ideal order" of its old monuments. Let this much be deciphered on his stone, that in his end as a mid-Western American was one of Europe's perpetual, perpetually improbable new beginnings. — 1965

I. POSSUM IN ARCADY

Chronology
  Harvard Undergraduate, 1906–1909.
    Read Symons on the Symbolists and discovered Laforgue,
      1908.
  Harvard Graduate Student, 1909–1910.
    Conversation Galante, Preludes I and II, *Portrait of a Lady,*
      beginnings of *Prufrock.*
  Sorbonne, October, 1910–July, 1911.
    Read Claudel, Gide, Dostoyevsky.
    Rhapsody on a Windy Night, Prelude III. Work on *Prufrock.*
  Munich, August, 1911.
    Finished *Prufrock.*
  Harvard Graduate Student, 1911–1914.
    Prelude IV, *La Figlia che Piange.*
    Work on Francis Herbert Bradley commenced.

PRUFROCK

The name of Prufrock-Littau, furniture wholesalers, appeared in advertisements in St. Louis, Missouri, in the first decade of the present century; in 1911 a young Missourian's whimsical feline humour prefixed the name of Prufrock to what has become the best-known English poem since the *Rubaiyat*. The savour of that act had faded from the memory of the sexagenarian London man of letters who wrote to a mid-century inquirer that his appropriation of the now-famous German surname must have been "quite unconscious." There would be no point in denying that it probably was; but the unconscious mind of T. S. Eliot once glimmered with a rich mischief which for many years has been more cautiously disclosed than it was in 1911.

The query itself must have amused him, however; Mr. Eliot's dealings with people who wanted to know what he was concealing have for two decades afforded some of the richest comedy in the annals of literary anecdote. Letter after letter, visitor after visitor, he answers with unfailing lambent courtesy. After *The Confidential Clerk* was produced, a journalist, teased by implications he couldn't pin down, or perhaps simply assigned a turn of duty at poet-baiting, wanted to know what it meant. It means what it says, said Mr. Eliot patiently. No more? Certainly, no more. But supposing, the journalist pursued, supposing you had meant *something else*, would you not have put some other meaning more plainly? "No," Mr. Eliot replied, "I should have put it just as obscurely."

No other writer's verse has inspired so tenacious a conviction that it means more than it seems to. Certainly no other modern verses so invade the mind, attracting to themselves in the months following their ingestion reminiscence, desire, and speculation. Eliot deals in effects, not ideas; and the effects are in an odd way wholly verbal, seemingly endemic to the language, scrupulously concocted out of the expressive gestures of what a reader whose taste has been educated in the nineteenth-century classics takes poetry to be.

That is why they will not leave the mind, which grows bored with ideas but will never leave off fondling phrases. How much of the grotesque melancholy of *Prufrock* radiates from the protagonist's name would be difficult to estimate. It was surgical economy that used the marvellous name once only, in the title, and compounded it with a fatuous "J. Alfred." It was a talent already finely schooled that with nice audacity weighed in a single phrase the implications of this name against those of "Love Song." It was genius that separated the speaker of the monologue from the writer of the poem by the solitary device of affixing an unforgettable title. Having done that, Eliot didn't need to keep fending off his protagonist with facile irony; the result was a poised intimacy which could draw on every emotion the young author knew without incurring the liabilities of "self-expression."

This complex deftness in the title of his first long poem epitomizes the nature of Eliot's best early verse. Every phrase seems composed as though the destiny of the author's soul depended on it, yet it is unprofitable not to consider the phrases as arrangements of words before considering them as anything else. Like the thousand little gestures that constitute good manners, their meaning is contained in themselves alone. Eliot is the most verbal of the eminent poets: more verbal than Swinburne. If he has carried verbalism far beyond the mere extirpation of jarring consonants, it is because of his intimate understanding of what language can do: how its "tentacular roots," as he once said, reach "down to the deepest terrors and desires." Only a poet who came after the nineteenth century and grew up in its shadow could have acquired this understanding. Eliot acquired it early, and was able to coerce a small masterpiece into existence at a time when (according to his later standards) he understood very little else.

Prufrock exploits the nineteenth century's specialized plangencies at every turn.

> I grow old . . . I grow old . . .
> I shall wear the bottoms of my trousers rolled.

Everyone remembers these lines. They manage to be ridiculous without being funny (the speaker is not making a joke) or cruel (a joke is not being made about the speaker). Their mechanism is allied to the mock-heroic but it doesn't burlesque anything. Like a side-show mermaid, this non-sequitur of an aging Bostonian floats embalmed in dark sonorities whose cloudiness almost conceals the stitching between mammal and fish. We feel that the two halves won't conjoin at the very instant of being persuaded they do. The vowels sound very fine, the syllables are impeccably cadenced; but vaguely within one's pleasure at Tennysonian excellence there struggles an intimation of the absurd, with no more chance of winging clear into view than a wasp in a jar of molasses.

The phenomenon of sound obscuring deficiencies of sense from writer and reader is often to be observed in English poetry; the Romantics may be said to have elevated it into a method. Mr. Eliot's originality consisted in allowing the deficiency to be concealed only from the speaker. The writer is too cool not to have known what he was about, and as for the reader, his pleasure consists precisely in experiencing a disproportion difficult to isolate. The certainty that Prufrock himself understands it no better than we do checks any pursuit of "metaphysical" analogies between senility and trouser-bottoms; and as for Prufrock's mind, where the collocation is supposed to be taking place, it working are nowhere very profoundly explored. His *sensibility* is plumbed to the uttermost, but that is not what is usually meant when a poet is praised for revealing a human soul. To say that Prufrock is contemplating a young blade's gesture, or alternatively an old castoff's, rolling up his trousers because he either hasn't learnt to care for dignity or has outgrown its claims, is to substitute for the poetic effect a formula that fails to exhaust it because incapable of touching it. For the purposes of the effect, the pathos of the character of Prufrock is no more than a *donnée*. And the effect is unique, and no reader has ever forgotten it.

The Love Song of J. Alfred Prufrock most clings to the memory whenever it exploits, as a foil to undistinguished middle age, the authorized sonorities of the best English verse, *circa* 1870:

> In the room the women come and go
> Talking of Michelangelo.

The closed and open o's, the assonances of *room, women,* and *come,* the pointed caesura before the polysyllabic burst of "Michelangelo," weave a context of grandeur within which our feeling about these trivial women determines itself. The heroic sound, and especially the carefully dramatized sound of the painter's name, is what muffles these women. The lines scale down severely in French:

> Dans la pièce les femmes vont et viennent
> En parlant des maîtres de Sienne.

That the translator has caught the sense and approximated the movement is an achievement strangely insufficient for lines whose poetic mechanism, one might have thought, depended on so simple a contrast of conceptions: talking women, and a heroic visionary. But Eliot's effects traffic only marginally with conceptions. Hence—again—the elusive disproportion from which his humour arises, a delicate vapour in whose aura the lights twinkle.

Tennyson, to whom Eliot owes so much, does not smile; "He really did hold," as G. K. Chesterton said, "many of the same ideas as Queen Victoria, though gifted with a more fortunate literary style." It was in the nature of things impossible for him to realize that the peculiar medium he had perfected from Coleridgean beginnings was a totally unsuitable climate for the conducting of human thought. This perception was reserved for his friend Edward Lear, another of Eliot's mentors, whose wistful incantations—

> . . . Where the purple river rolls fast and dim
> And the Ivory Ibis starlike skim,
> Wing to wing we dance around,
> Stamping our feet with a flumpy sound,

—provide a sort of middle term between Coleridge's incantation on the running of Alph the Sacred River and

> I grow old . . . I grow old . . .
> I shall wear the bottoms of my trousers rolled.

This embryology isn't adduced in belittlement; whatever Coleridge and Lear may have been up to, Eliot has so disciplined the procedures for securing "an *air of meaning* rather than meaning itself"* that—in his later work at least--the spectacle of their operation can itself imply meaning of a still more austere kind.

Lear, however, wasn't a technical innovator; he discovered his comic method by contemplating not the state of the poetic tradition but (Prufrock-like) his own artistic futility. Tennyson remains the Victorian norm. "His feelings," Eliot has noted, "were more honest than his mind," and his feeling found continually exact expression—

> . . . but far away
> The noise of life begins again,
> And ghastly thro' the drizzling rain
> On the bald street breaks the blank day.

But he made, notoriously, attempts to *think* in this kind of verse—

> Are God and Nature then at strife?

* Miss Elizabeth Schneider's description of *Kubla Khan*.

—which are really mistaken attempts to exploit the apparent inclusiveness of his poetic world (it contains so much that it ought to contain everything) and which emphasize by their fatuity the sacrifices through which that air of inclusiveness has been achieved. A sphere is self-bounded because its surface is turning away at every instant from possible tangents.

What was bequeathed to the young poets of 1910 by their predecessors in England was a world made out of words; much of Tennyson and most of Swinburne has no more bite on the realities outside the dictionary than have the verses of *Jabberwocky*. Coherence was obtained by exploiting the sounds of the words and the implications concealed in their sounds; "A cry that shivered to the tingling stars" would be a strikingly impoverished line if the English language could be suddenly purged of the words "twinkling" and "tinkling." T. S. Eliot from the first has leaned on words in that way; it was the *name* of Prufrock that attracted him; no information about the St. Louis bearers of that name can throw the smallest light on his poem. In the few juvenilia that have been preserved we find him manipulating sounds in Jonson's way—

> The flowers I sent thee when the dew
>   Was trembling on the vine
> Were withered ere the wild bee flew
>   To pluck the eglantine . . .   (1905)

or Swinburne's—

> Their petals are fanged and red
> With hideous streak and stain. . . .   (1908)

or Tennyson's—

> The moonflower opens to the moth,
>   The mist crawls in from the sea;
> A great white bird, a snowy owl,
>   Slips from the alder tree. . . .   (1909)

Two years later he wrote *Prufrock*. It was the Tennysonian medium that he learned to use; characteristically, he took what it seemed proper to take at the time, the manner of his immediate elders. He learned to use it; he never made the mistake of trying to think in it. Aware both of its limitations and of its extraordinary emotional inclusiveness, he contrives instead to give the impression that thought is going on alongside the poetic process, that sardonic eyes are being frequently bent on the pretensions toward which rhythmic speech incorrigibly reaches, and that whole areas of human life which the sentiments of romantic verbalism have appropriated are patently, to a rational vision, entoiled in richly muffled absurdity—

They will say: "But how his arms and legs are thin!"

Such is the situation that *Prufrock* dramatizes: a muffling of rational behaviour by rhetoric. To the aggrandizement of that situation the poet brings every conceivable wile. The epigraph is a piece of calculated opportunism:

S'io credesse che mia risposta fosse . . .

"If I thought that my response would be addressed to one who might go back alive, this flame would shake no more; but since no one ever goes back alive out of these deeps (if what I hear be true), without fear of infamy I answer you."

Senza tema d'infamia ti rispondo.

From these Italian words the English speech moves forward without a break—

Let us go then, you and I . . .

—effecting a liaison between this situation and Dante's which is all the smoother for the reflective, lingering rhythm of the opening phrase. For the next twenty lines Eliot brings all his melodic resources to the incantation of a quiet *fin-de-siècle* inferno, equipped with nightmare streets that "follow" and are ominously "half-deserted," and inimical clouds of yellow fog. It is a hell neither sustained by a theology nor gradated by degrees of crime; a genteel accumulation of stage effects, nothing quite in excess. It isn't a punishment so much as a state. Somewhere beyond or around it lies the world where questions have answers, but the moment an "overwhelming question" is mentioned we are cautioned,

> Oh, do not ask, "What is it?"

Above this monotonous emotional pedal-point runs a coruscating texture of effects. For twelve lines the word "time" reverberates, struck again and again, while (punctuated once by the startling precision of "To prepare a face to meet the faces that you meet") portentousness overlays mere sonority:

> And indeed there will be time
> For the yellow smoke that slides along the street,
> Rubbing its back upon the window-panes;
> There will be time, there will be time
> To prepare a face to meet the faces that you meet;
> There will be time to murder and create,
> And time for all the works and days of hands
> That lift and drop a question on your plate;
> Time for you and time for me,
> And time yet for a hundred indecisions,
> And for a hundred visions and revisions,
> Before the taking of a toast and tea.

What "murder and create" may mean we cannot tell, though it is plain what the phrase can *do;* the words have lost their connexion with the active world, lost in fact everything but their potential for neurasthenic shock. "Time for you and time for me" is as hypnotic and as meaningless as a phrase on the 'cellos. The yellow smoke rubbing its back upon window-panes is a half-realizable picture; the detail about the hands and the plate has the air of being a picture but in fact isn't, the thing that is dropped on the plate being "a question," and the hands—blurred by the phrase "works and days" which is a fusion of Hesiod and Ecclesiastes (III: 1–8)—being not quite those of God and not quite those of a butler.

> And time for all the works and days of hands
> That lift and drop a question on your plate;

these gravely irrational words evoke a nervous system snubbed by the Absolute without committing themselves as to whether that Absolute is the moral rigour of an implacable Creator or the systemized social discomfort of a Boston tea-party.

The first half of *Prufrock,* in fact, is devoted to a systematic confusion of temporal and eternal disciplines; this man's doom is an endless party-going—

> For I have known them all already, known them all:—
> Have known the evenings, mornings, afternoons,

—which he is no more at liberty to modify than one of Dante's subjects can desert his circle of Hell. As he moves wearily through the fog toward yet another entrance-hall he can toy with images of rebellion—

> And indeed there will be time
> To wonder, "Do I dare?" and, "Do I dare?"
> Time to turn back and descend the stair,
> With a bald spot in the middle of my hair—
> (They will say: "How his hair is growing thin!")

But one doesn't—the switch from social to cosmic is typical —"disturb the universe." In Hell you do what you are doing.

LAFORGUE AND OTHERS

But Jules . . .

Outside,
            De la musique avant toute chose
The thin horns gone glacial
And behind blinds, partitioning Paris
Into the rose-stained mist,
He bows to the looking-glass. Sunsets.

—Charles Tomlinson.

"The form in which I began to write, in 1908 or 1909, was directly drawn from the study of Laforgue together with the later Elizabethan drama; and I do not know anyone who started from exactly that point." This statement was deliberately phrased twenty years later, and one or two of its precisions are worth remarking. His form was drawn from the *study* of these models, not their imitation; and his English model was "the later Elizabethan drama," not the supremely dangerous Shakespeare. The models come from totally different periods, languages, and literary traditions. Intelligently studied, they correct one another's defects: Laforgue, the dramatists' rant; the drama, Laforgue's bitter-sweet dandyism. Furthermore, they provided the *form* in which he began to write, the means of disposing its entelechy, of devising ends toward which effects might be ordered; the effects themselves, the diction, the sonorous texture and the interbreeding of nuances, came in 1908 or 1909 from sources so diffuse as to be virtually anonymous, the regnant sensibility of those years. One says "Tennysonian" as one would today call much beginners' verse "Eliotic," without imputing detached study. Had he studied Tennyson and Swinburne he would have mastered the art of doing no more than they. But having without effort filled his mind with their atmosphere he studied something else instead, as Seurat studied chemistry and optics. He studied Laforgue and the dramatists.

The instinct that led him to assimilate these two forces simultaneously was Eliot's first proof of genius; ten years later he was to trace the debility of the Georgian school to its failure to do something similar:

> Verse stands in constant need of what Samuel Butler calls a cross. The serious writer of verse must be prepared to cross himself with the best verse of other languages and the best prose of all languages. In Georgian poetry there is almost no crossing visible; it is inbred. It has developed a technique and a set of emotions all of its own.

A typical Georgian poem "is unintelligible to anyone who has not substituted Georgian emotions for human ones"; in default of a "cross," verse becomes not only parochial but in the one pejorative sense of the word artificial: a special instance of the law that "bad poets are not really influenced by anything, being too obtuse."

He might have added that you cannot cross a cat with a bull pup. The two things he himself crossed with the poetic tone of the nineties were less alien to that tone than is sometimes supposed. Laforgue came Eliot's way in 1908, from a book by Arthur Symons, *The Symbolist Movement in Literature*. As for the later Elizabethan drama, from being a discovery of Lamb's it became a passion of Swinburne's. The ingredients of the Eliotic synthesis had been in the possession of the "Tragic Generation," but had not been brought together. They were, in fact, a pair of "period" interests in which no one else had the wit to be actively interested: both of them close to the emotional marrow of the decades that came to expression both in Wilde's epigrams and in his downfall. A gaslit wistfulness surrounds the bravado of the Jacobean specimens Eliot quotes in *Selected Essays:*

> Winter at last draws on the Night of Age;
> Yet still a humour of some novel fancy
> Untasted or untried, puts off the minute
> Of resolution, which should bid farewell
> To a vain world of weariness and sorrows. . . .
>
> —Ford.

And as for Laforgue, if you take a typically earnest poem of the nineties—

> The world goes by with its glory and shame,
> Crowns are bartered and blood is shed;
> I sit and broider my dreams instead. . . .

you have only to move your eye slightly from the intended angle of vision—reading, for instance, the last line quoted with an apologetic smile—to perceive, in latent principle, Laforgue's ironic perspectives.

It is true that no other poet writing in English, with or without Laforgue's assistance, did perform that slight alteration of viewpoint. But the fact that Laforgue discovered the potentialities of self-parody not in poetry at large but in the poetry of a circumscribed era, in a lyric mode closely allied with that of Dowson and Symons, one alone among the possible derivations from Baudelaire: this fact helps explain his sudden power to engulf a man who had been shaping slender lyrics at Harvard in the first decade after the nineties. Certain qualities Laforgue brought to full articulation were already accessible. We may even try the experiment of synthesizing the Laforguian quality out of three poems of Verlaine's; first, the familiar Verlaine of the translucent statement:

> Il pleure dans mon coeur
> Comme il pleut sur la ville.
> Quelle est cette langueur
> Qui pénètre mon coeur?

second, extending this simplicity by postulating a simple prota-

gonist, the mock-simplesse of *A Poor Young Shepherd,* its title
archly supplied from a foreign language:

> J'ai peur d'un baiser
> Comme d'une abeille.
> Je souffre et je veille
> Sans me reposer.
> J'ai peur d'un baiser!

third, reducing the paraphernalia of official art into formulae
at which a gentler sensibility may smile, the Laforguian diction
of *Nuit du Walpurgis classique:*

> C'est plutôt le sabbat du second Faust que l'autre,
> Un rhythmique sabbat, rhythmique, extrêmement
> Rhythmique.—Imaginez un jardin de Lenôtre,
> Correct, ridicule et charmant. . . .

This arrangement of extracts appears to bring us by three steps
from the muted *cri du coeur* to literary satire. It is actually not a
progressive sophistication but a scale of effects possible to a
single poet because his methods are everywhere sophisticated.
The correspondence between the tears in his heart and the rain
on the town was "correct et charmant" if not "extrêmement
rhythmique"; its artlessness, on examination, an illusion produced by the cunningly exploited similarity of "pleure" and
"pleut." The satiric phase doesn't insult in its literary knowing-
ness the simplicities of the lyric, because the lyric was itself
knowing, not at all of the same order as

> My heart aches, and a drowsy numbness pains
> My sense . . .

Now Laforgue's method, often misrepresented as a pretext
for fondling sentiment while despising it, is to embrace this
scale of Verlaine's within a single poem or passage. *Dimanches*
begins,

> Bref, j'allais me donner d'un "Je vous aime"
> Quand je m'avisai non sans peine
> Que d'abord je ne me possédais pas bien moi-même.
> (Mon Moi, c'est Galathée aveuglant Pygmalion!

> Impossible de modifier cette situation.)
> Ainsi donc, pauvre, pâle et piètre individu
> Qui ne croit à son Moi qu'à ses moments perdus,
> Je vis s'effacer ma fiancée
> Emportée par le cours des choses,
> Telle l'épine voit s'effeuiller,
> Sous prétexte de soir sa meilleure rose.

This isn't the method of a jejune cynic, but of a man composing a poem, and a poem with both more scope and more delicacy than were provided for by the prevalent avant-garde formulae: "De la musique avant toute chose," or "Rien de plus cher que la chanson grise où l'Indécis au Précis se joint," or even "Prends l'éloquence et tords-lui son cou!" It is a more *logical* development of Verlaine's lyric premises than these prescriptive phrases of Verlaine's, though the *Art Poétique* from which they are usually isolated contains a flawlessly rhymed fit against rhyme and is in other respects a tricky document.

Laforgue discovered that methods as deliberate as Verlaine's could be brought into touch with a wider variety of things than anyone had previously supposed. If *Dimanches* presents the Prufrock situation—

> pauvre, pâle et piètre individu
> Qui ne croit à son Moi qu'à ses moments perdus,

it presents it not by way of tranquil correspondences with unspeaking Nature—

> Il pleure dans mon coeur
> Comme il pleut sur la ville.

but with a paradoxical analytic energy that in allied poems can cope with rust on telegraph wires—

> La rouille ronge en leurs spleens kilométriques
> Les fils télégraphiques des grandes routes où nul ne passe,

or give itself over to a crafty rhetoric of sound:

> Tous les bancs sont mouillés, tant les bois sont rouillés,
> Et tant les cors ont fait ton ton, ont fait ton taine! . . .

Les cors, les cors, les cors—mélancoliques! . . .
Mélancoliques! . . .
S'en vont, changeant de ton,
Changeant de ton et de musique,
Ton ton, ton taine, ton ton! . . .
Les cors, les cors, les cors!
S'en sont allés au vent du Nord.

The North Wind's trumpet is a conventional enough figure; Laforgue builds toward it, not away from it, through an onomatopoeia of Siegfriedian imperviousness. A moment later the chill wind has brought an un-Tennysonian coughing to boarding-school dormitories,

La phtisie pulmonaire attristant le quartier,
Et toute la misère des grands centres.

Eloquence aware that it is eloquence is more useful than eloquence with its neck wrung; its self-awareness can safeguard from irrelevant sentiment anything that gets into the poem; for instance

Arms that are braceleted and white and bare
(But in the lamplight, downed with light brown hair!)

Laforgue's short pieces lend themselves admirably to pastiche; *Conversation Galante* (1909), the earliest poem in Eliot's published collection, is an exercise of that kind, based on the *Autres Complaintes de Lord Pierrot*:

And I then: "Someone frames upon the keys
That exquisite nocturne, with which we explain
The night and moonshine; music which we seize
To body forth our own vacuity."
She then: "Does this refer to me?"
"Oh no, it is I who am inane."*

There are three more in the files of the *Harvard Advocate*,

* Et si ce cri lui part: "Dieu de Dieu! que je t'aime!"
—"Dieu reconnaîtra les siens." Ou piquée au vif:
—"Mes claviers ont du coeur, tu seras mon seul thème."
Moi: "Tout est relatif."

detritus of his efforts to assimilate the Laforguian shifts of tone, the Laforguian dandyism of outlook—

> Sunday; this satisfied procession
> Of definite Sunday faces;

—and the Laforguian incorporation into art of other art become artifice:

> Blood looks effective on the moonlit ground . . .

They are none of them very effective poems; not even the deftness of *Conversation Galante,* nor its foreshadowing of the dialogue at cross-purposes which was to become an established Eliot device from *Prufrock* ("That is not what I meant at all") to *The Cocktail Party* ("And you kept on *saying* that you were in love with me—I believe you were trying to persuade yourself you were"), can dissuade us from observing that this manner, as surely as Hemingway's, tends to select its own special postures, substituting, if not Georgian, Laforguian emotions for human ones.

Laforgue's longer poems are less circumscribing. The point of crossing them with the methods of the later Elizabethan drama is to stiffen them against a virtuoso's rhythmic opportunism and an entertainer's moral evasiveness, two defects which flaw *Dimanches* and *L'Hiver qui vient* with an unsuitable headlong facility.

> Il bruine;
> Dans la forêt mouillée, les toiles d'araignées
> Ploient sous les gouttes d'eau, et c'est leur ruine.
> Soleils plénipotentiaires des travaux en blonds Pactoles
> Des spectacles agricoles,
> Où êtes-vous ensevelis?

The neat chime of "il bruine" and "c'est leur ruine" suggests, by compromising the ambient seriousness, not complexity of attitude so much as uncertainty about the scope of the disaster imaged by rain-wrecked spider-webs; and the dazzling proficiency of the last three lines hurries us over the Flaubertian

"spectacles agricoles" before we have time to assimilate the relevance of the river Pactolus.

The shallowness of Laforgue's roots in tradition, his lack of a ground-bass corresponding to Baudelaire's echo of the Alexandrines of Racine, required correction before his methods could be put to sustained uses other than his own. His very sonorities stir no depths of suggestion; they exhibit their own tricky virtuosity, exposing not a freedom from psychic involvement but the debonair panic of a man whose strategy (for all its look of elegant stasis) is to hasten across abysses he has no taste for exploring. The late Elizabethan drama, on the other hand, affords not only an arsenal of devices for dislocating the iambic pentameter but passages of grave magniloquence too self-sufficient to be really vulnerable to parody. The tradition, established by Lamb's *Specimens,* of approaching them as closet dramas, and closet dramas to be read in selection, an anthology of orations and soliloquies, made them particularly accessible for Eliot's purposes, though fifteen years later he was to reprove the fallacy of separating poetry from drama in that fashion. A soliloquy by Middleton or Tourneur arrests a mood for inspection, and by the enveloping assertions of blank verse rhythm protects its vulnerability. And these moods—this was their relevance for *Prufrock*—are affectingly self-contained, the speaker imprisoned by his own eloquence, committed to a partial view of life, beyond the reach of correction or communication, out of which arises the tragic partiality of his actions. The psychology of humours and faculties had much to do with this phenomenon; but in the late period the dramatists not only make use of these psychological principles for explicating and determining a character, but allow the character to be dominated and circumscribed by his own image of himself; "since no one goes back alive out of this gulf, without fear I expose my heart to you."

> I that am of your blood was taken from you
> For your better health; look no more upon't
> But cast it to the ground regardlessly,

Let the common sewer take it from distinction:
Beneath the stars, upon yon meteor
Ever hung my fate, 'mongst things corruptible;
I ne'er could pluck it from him; my loathing
Was prophet to the rest, but ne'er believed.
—Middleton.

"No! I am not Prince Hamlet, nor was meant to be." This eloquence of inadequacy is richly comforting, entoiling the futile man in beglamoring postulations of the impossible. If Prufrock is the sort of *persona* entailed by the viewpoints and methods of Laforgue, it is from the resources of Jacobean rhetoric that he is invested with such momentous and paradoxical magnitude, disturbing the universe and seeing his head brought in upon a platter. "The cardinal lifts up's nose like a foul porpoise before a storm": rhetoric need not be identical with dizzying magniloquence. It was not the magniloquent side of Jacobean rhetoric that interested the author of *Prufrock* at all. Eliot was attracted, as he has often indicated, to Webster, who might well have conceived a person "formulated, sprawling on a pin," indeed "pinned and wriggling on the wall," but would not have carried on about the subject in a Senecan vein. This species of rhetoric—figures of thought, not of words*—imparting as it does an air of sometimes grotesque but always impersonal invention, can supply in English the place of one untranslatable component in the French idiom, the imperturbable self-congratulating formality of which Flaubert availed himself when he concocted his honest bourgeois comment on the Great Pyramid: "Ouvrage inutile." We can see

---

* This traditional distinction had been mislaid by the time Eliot started writing. In the course of some 1919 observations on the Elizabethan "pathology of rhetoric" he finds it necessary to inform his reader that "When we come across lines like:
   There's a plumber laying pipes in my guts, it scalds.
we must not allow ourselves to forget the rhetorical basis any more than when we read:
   Come, let us march against the powers of heaven,
   And set black streamers in the firmament,
   To signify the slaughter of the gods."
It was from lines of the first sort that he chiefly learned.

Eliot applying it to motifs gleaned from French phrases: The phrase "Do I dare disturb the universe?" occurs in an 1881 letter of Laforgue's, a passing pleasantry. In the context Eliot has prepared it barely knows itself.

> And indeed there will be time
> To wonder, "Do I dare?" and, "Do I dare?"
> Time to turn back and descend the stair,
> With a bald spot in the middle of my hair—
> (They will say: "How his hair is growing thin!")
> My morning coat, my collar mounting firmly to the chin,
> My necktie rich and modest, but asserted by a simple pin—
> (They will say: "But how his arms and legs are thin!")
> Do I dare
> Disturb the universe?
> In a minute there is time
> For decisions and revisions which a minute will reverse.

He is not there yet as we hear him speaking; he will never be there, or will perpetually return there—it does not matter. But since he has known them all already, known them all, he can prefigure as he walks through half-deserted streets the further phases—past or future, it makes no difference in a cyclic eternity—of the invulnerable cycle in which he is entrapped. He toys with thoughts of defying whatever automatism propels him repeatedly through these streets, through that door, up those stairs. Could he not—an act of free will which would rock the lamplit hell to its last foundations—perform the supreme gesture of insult, turn around on the stairs after his arrival has been announced and simply make his way out? To leave would be independence, not cowardice; but cowardice ("They will say, 'How his hair is growing thin' ") will keep him, he knows, on his excruciating course. His collar at least mounts firmly, implying a will that can refrain from mounting, his necktie carries the understated touch of assertion; but the X-ray eyes of the silent women at the stair-head perceive the insufficient realities within.

It seems unnecessary to connect this terror of the stairs with Eliot's reading of *Crime and Punishment* in Paris, since it occurs in *Portrait of a Lady,* his first sustained Laforguian poem, written months earlier in 1910 at Harvard. This lady really existed, as Eliot's college friend Conrad Aiken assures us, a Cambridge hostess, "our dear deplorable friend, Miss X, the *précieuse ridicule* to end all preciosity, serving tea so exquisitely among her bric-à-brac." The skill with which her conversation is caught makes *Portrait of a Lady* unfailingly memorable: every contortion of the verse, every throbbing repetition ("so much, so much"), every delayed banality of rhyme (friends . . . ends, interlocked with find . . . blind) reproducing with uncanny exactness her anxiety for greater involvement and dependence than her guests are inclined to permit.

> "You do not know how much they mean to me, my friends,
> And how, how rare and strange it is, to find
> In a life composed so much, so much of odds and ends,
> (For indeed I do not love it . . . you knew? you are not blind!
> How keen you are!)
> To find a friend who has these qualities,
> Who has, and gives
> Those qualities upon which friendship lives.
> How much it means that I say this to you—
> Without these friendships—life, what *cauchemar!*"

Thus her eager gambit; then eight months later, perceiving him invulnerable,

> "But what have I, but what have I, my friend,
> To give you, what can you receive from me?
> Only the friendship and the sympathy
> Of one about to reach her journey's end.
>
> I shall sit here, serving tea to friends . . ."

Her morale frittered away during many years, she abandons in evident panic the resources of reticence, and plays on his inevitable sympathy. The grotesque unspoken proposal utters itself in refusing to be uttered:

> But what have I, but what have I, my friend,
> To give you, what can you receive from me?

—placing him in the intolerable position of one who expects

always to take value received; there is no possible answer except the impossible one she is fishing for.

> I take my hat: how can I make a cowardly amends
> For what she has said to me?

In October, when he has announced his determination to go abroad, she cannot forbear a thrust at what she persists in representing as his callow unresponsiveness:

> "You will find so much to learn."

A moment later she is playing the vastly regretful heroine, beclouding the parting in sweet veils of histrionic self-pity:

> "For everybody said so, all our friends,
> They all were sure our feelings would relate
> So closely! I myself can hardly understand.
> We must leave it now to fate.
> You will write, at any rate.
> Perhaps it is not too late.
> I shall sit here, serving tea to friends."

That exquisite wistful triple rhyme, and those culminating *caesurae* ("Perhaps / it is not / too late") natural in their placement but a little more than casual in their duration, display in extraordinary precocity a rare comic talent. The great successes of this one overtly dramatic Eliot poem coincide with the Lady's speeches. Her interlocutor, whose perplexed undermined self-possession must carry the moral burden of the poem, is in several passages depicted with less sureness. Not everywhere, though; his impertubable session with the morning papers stikes the right note:

> Particularly I remark
> An English countess goes upon the stage.
> A Greek was murdered at a Polish dance,
> Another bank defaulter has confessed.
> I keep my countenance,
> I remain self-possessed

In the papers other people's agonies are remote and grotesque.

If we could look into the heart of that English countess or that bank-defaulter we should find, no doubt, just such a turmoil as inhabits the breast of the lady who serves tea so anxiously; it is perhaps fortunate for our self-possession that we cannot. But despite what she has said he has an Achilles heel after all:

> I keep my countenance,
> I remain self-possessed
> Except when a street piano, mechanical and tired
> Reiterates some worn-out common song
> With the smell of hyacinths across the garden
> Recalling things that other people have desired.
> Are these ideas right or wrong?

To what extent have we a right to our necessary imperturbability? Jane Austen wrote to her sister during the Peninsular War, "How horrible it is to have so many people killed!—and what a blessing that one cares for none of them!"; a remark containing more wisdom than callousness; it is well that we can husband our psychic energies to cope with what closely concerns us. But detachment however wise will not put aside the question whether this woman crying for help—

> "I am always sure that you understand
> My feelings, always sure that you feel,
> Sure that across the gulf you reach your hand . . ."

—whether she lays claim on our practical sympathies, or only on our compassion; and whether she lays claim on compassion when she so manœuvres the conversation as to make reticent expression of compassion impossible? Is not her behaviour outrageous? She says,

> "And youth is cruel and has no remorse
> And smiles at situations which it cannot see."
> I smile, of course,
> And go on drinking tea.

The young man has prepared a face to meet the faces that he meets, and it suffices for the faces he meets in newspapers. In real life,

The October night comes down; returning as before
Except for a slight sensation of being ill at ease
I mount the stairs and turn the handle of the door
And feel as if I had mounted on my hands and knees.

He is the first of a long series of Eliot characters who will confront stairs leading to a lady; Prufrock; the departing lover in *La Figlia che Piange;* the young man carbuncular; the visitors to Dusty and Doris who come right up when they've put the car around the corner; the protagonist of *Ash-Wednesday* mounting purgatorial flights. It is a recurring image of great inherent symbolic firmness, requiring no explication, touching on such fructive situations as the self-doubt of the unwilling suitor, the squalor of a walk-up flat, the apotheosis of the attainable she, or the ladder of contemplation. In *Portrait of a Lady* the function of the stairs is simply to give the protagonist occasion for self-abasement as he approaches her door. Its symbolic extensions will come later.

But Eliot is most Eliot when not only the words but the situations stir into life restless symbolic echoes. The defects of *Portrait of a Lady* arise from its tendency to stay closer to the empirical facts than the poet's essentially portentous and generalizing technique will really permit. The contours of the situation are so specified, the lady's speech so clearly reproduced, that decorum requires a comparable definiteness in depicting the confusions into which she throws her visitor; instead of which we have an alternation of fanciful symbol and archly impenetrable behaviour:

> Among the windings of the violins
> And the ariettes
> Of cracked cornets
> Inside my brain a dull tom-tom begins
> Absurdly hammering a prelude of its own,
> Capricious monotone
> That is at least one definite "false note."

Those quotation marks are a false note; so are the epithets "absurdly" and "capricious"; so is the fact that the violins and

cornets (echoed from earlier in the poem) are as metaphorical
as the mental tom-tom. The next lines are meant to register a
welcome switch of attention:

> —Let us take the air, in a tobacco trance,
> Admire the monuments,
> Discuss the late events,
> Correct our watches by the public clocks.
> Then sit for half an hour and drink our bocks.

This passage unhappily, far from evoking a desperate anacs-
thesia temporarily sufficient to offset the lady's importunities,
is simply in its self-conscious concision ("Admire the monuments," rhyming with "Discuss the late events") a less convincing
image of human beings passing time than is the tea-table scene
it should balance.

For the Laforguian manner is not devoid of a certain snigger,
perilous at Harvard. It invites the poet to play at being a clever
person, or else to project his capacity for responsiveness on a
sensitive *jeune premier* at whom he cannot really *look*. That is
what happens in *Portrait of a Lady,* where we see the lady but
merely feel her guest. The later poem to some extent cheats its
way out of this dilemma, by creating through rhetorical
resourcefulness the illusion that J. Alfred Prufrock is accessible
to our detached scrutiny. The poet in these early works is
disguised, but we think we know how to find him. It is a
method with grave restrictions, which in fact entailed three
years of poetic silence, 1912–1915. The formula for the dis-
tinctive Eliotic *oeuvre* was not available until London had
presented him with the condition whose usefulness no study of
Laforgue could have pre-visaged: the condition of utter and
liberating anonymity.

The theme of *Portrait of a Lady*, as of most of the early poems,
is self-sufficiency threatened. It is threatened in this instance by
the obligation to be charitable; conversely, it is supposed to be
propped up by the very social rituals which provide, in the
poem, the occasion for its being undermined. Eliot's preoccupation with social ritual, from the lady's tea-parties to the

Cocktail Party of Edward and Lavinia Chamberlayne, is related to his early perception that social ritual, designed to permit human beings to associate without imposing on one another (as the ritual of art allows a man to express an emotion without exposing his wounds), may be actually the occasion of raising to nearly tragic intensity their longing to reach one another. The Eliot character feels that he needs to preserve the inviolacy of self, and simultaneously feels that he needs sympathy from others whom he cannot reach and who cannot decorously reach him. Shall we surrender decorum? Where two or more are gathered together it is the condition of life. Like the hangman on Sweeney's stairs, who is careful to knock, the very savages obey an instinct for translating even violent death and dismemberment into a ritual, with dance and song.

Behind the décor of self-sufficiency—the ready smile, the poised teacup, lies the Self; a mystery, sometimes an illusion. The Hollow Men are all mask and no inside. The upperclass characters in the late plays—*The Family Reunion, The Cocktail Party, The Confidential Clerk*—present social masks which they go to considerable trouble to keep furbished. There is normally no way of telling whether or not the mask conceals the ferment of an aroused personality—

> I am Lazarus, come from the dead,
> Come back to tell you all—

or only complacency and the potentials of panic:

> Why do we feel embarrassed, impatient, fretful, ill at ease,
> Assembled like amateur actors who have not been assigned their
> parts?
> Like amateur actors in a dream when the curtain rises, to find
> themselves dressed for a different play, or having rehearsed the
> wrong parts,
> Waiting for the rustling in the stalls, the titter in the dress circle,
> the laughter and catcalls in the gallery?

But there is no mistaking the effect when Eliot pursues his unvarying dramatic method, which is to set loose, in a drawing-room full of masks, some Lazarus.

That is the mechanism of the Eliot plot: the entry of Lazarus, the man who has crossed a frontier and come back: Harry with his Furies invading Wishwood, Sweeney the uninvited guest at the ragtime jollification, the Magi returning to a kingdom in which they are no longer at home, where an alien people clutch their gods. Prufrock is an insufficient Lazarus, the lady in the *Portrait* a pseudo-Lazarus, Tiresias in *The Waste Land* a Lazarus unseen. In "Tradition and the Individual Talent" we are invited to consider what happens "when a bit of finely filiated platinum is introduced into a chamber containing oxygen and sulphur dioxide." The mind of the poet, it turns out, is the shred of platinum; itself unchanged, it catalyzes such diverse experiences as falling in love, reading Spinoza, the noise of the typewriter, the smell of cooking, so that they form a new whole called a poem: a reaction into which, inviolate, the catalyst does not enter. This analogy will also serve for the plots of Eliot's poems: the Lazarus is introduced into a chamber containing assorted uncles and aunts, prostitutes, "American gentlemen here on business," women of Canterbury, women who talk of Michelangelo; and the effect of the juxtaposition is not merely to provide the formula for poetry, but also the scenario for a poem. Lazarus back from the far side of death may either catalyze the others—

                                    we acknowledge
That the sin of the world is upon our heads, that the blood of the
    martyrs and the agony of the saints
Is upon our heads—

or (equally dramatic) he may fail to catalyze them—

We do not like to walk out of a door, and find ourselves back in
    the same room . . .
We have suffered far more than a personal loss—
We have lost our way in the dark.

In either case, as the Unidentified Guest tells Edward Chamberlayne,

                            . . . to approach the stranger
    Is to invite the unexpected, release a new force,

Or let the genie out of the bottle.
It is to start a train of events
Beyond your control.

And whether the effects of this catalyst on the persons among
whom it arrives are cohesive or disruptive, it follows when it
leaves them the arc of its own imperturbable destiny; "the
newly formed acid contains no trace of platinum, and the
platinum itself is apparently unaffected."

We can see the elements of the Eliot catalyst-plot assembling
themselves for the first time in the development of the sequence
called *Preludes*. The first two were written at Harvard in
1909–1910, just after *Conversation Galante* and a little before
Portrait of a Lady. They present sensate fact just stirring toward
a unity chiefly pictorial:

> The winter evening settles down
> With smell of steaks in passageways.
> Six o'clock.
> The burnt-out ends of smoky days.
> And now a gusty shower wraps
> The grimy scraps
> Of withered leaves about your feet
> And newspapers from vacant lots . . .

These items are held together like the elements of a genre
painting: a subject-rhyme encouraged by the scrupulously
enervate cadence and underwritten by the presence of the
imaginary spectator.

In the third *Prelude,* however, written a year later in Paris,
a human being unites these elements in what is almost a
transfiguring vision:

> You had such a vision of the street
> As the street hardly understands;

What has come before this vision is an imperfect species of
self-knowledge

> You dozed, and watched the night revealing
> The thousand sordid images
> Of which your soul was constituted;

a revelation not comparable with that vouchsafed to the Magi or even to Sweeney, but sufficient, when attention is turned to the street, to sustain vision for at any rate a few seconds. But vision fades into empirical banality—

> Sitting along the bed's edge, where
> You curled the papers from your hair,
> Or clasped the yellow soles of feet
> In the palms of both soiled hands.

—the posture of a Degas demi-mondaine, or that of a meditating fakir. It is the fourth *Prelude* (Harvard, 1911) that is haunted, amid the

> . . . short square fingers stuffing pipes,
> And evening newspapers, and eyes
> Assured of certain certainties,

by some potential redemptive vision:

> I am moved by fancies that are curled
> About these images, and cling:
> The notion of some infinitely gentle
> Infinitely suffering thing.

No one returns from the dead on this occasion, however; and the worlds continue to "revolve like ancient women gathering fuel in vacant lots." That facts like persons have their opaque self-sufficiency, and imply the possibility of more value than they exude, is a theme that recurs in Grishkin's maisonette and the rented house of Gerontion. The *Preludes* are not "Imagist" poems written a little before Imagism, despite their technique of discrete inventory; the cardinal principle of Imagism—apart from its purely technical specifications concerning rhythm and the elision of unnecessary words—was that the natural object was always the artistically self-sufficient image; the meaning of *Preludes* is expressly that the natural object is nothing of the kind. It implies an ache, a yearning after significance, like Wallace Stevens' unpeopled landscapes.

Between the first two *Preludes* and the fourth, Eliot was working at *Prufrock*. He took with him from Harvard to Paris

in the autumn of 1910 a number of fragments including the
"Prince Hamlet" passage, and finished the poem during a visit
to Germany in the summer of 1911. Like *The Family Reunion* it
bears traces of its prolonged incubation. After the unbroken
opening arc, from the street to the ordeal on the stairs to the
implacable world of eyes and arms, brought at last to the brink
of the "overwhelming question,"

> And should I then presume?
> And how should I begin?

—on this brink Prufrock ponders a possible gambit:

> Shall I say, I have gone at dusk through narrow streets
> And watched the smoke that rises from the pipes
> Of lonely men in shirt-sleeves, leaning out of windows?

and though the poem's skeleton remains complete, a bone
suddenly slips out of place:

> I should have been a pair of ragged claws
> Scuttling across the floors of silent seas.

This would seem to be a slight aesthetic error on the poet's
part: too good a couplet to sacrifice, but not quite at home in
the context of the poem. It is prepared for, by inspired opportunism, with more skill than is always realized. The lonely
men in shirt-sleeves—Prufrock's image of lyrical self-sufficiency, his proof (supposing he mentions them to the lady)
of his having crossed some frontier beyond her experience—
the lonely men inhabit, almost enviably, like Tennyson's gods
"the lucid interspace of world and world"; and he suddenly
imagines how, from their elevation, he would look scuttling
by in the street: like a crab at the bottom of a pool.

> I should have been a pair of ragged claws
> Scuttling across the floors of silent seas.

—not even the full crab, just the claws and the scuttle. A
superb epiphany, though it appears to belong to another, unwritten, poem. This poem, subsequently, has a little trouble

regaining momentum. He returns to what he did not do, and will not do, and why:

> Should I, after tea and cakes and ices,
> Have the strength to force the moment to its crisis?

If I did, though, it would be

> But as if a magic lantern threw the nerves in patterns
>   on a screen;

and

> Would it have been worth while
> If one, settling a pillow or throwing off a shawl,
> And turning toward the window, should say:
>   "That is not it at all,
>   That is not what I meant, at all."

There follows, again somewhat inappropriately, the Prince Hamlet passage, in adapted iambic pentameter; then the trouser-bottoms, the peach, and the climactic dream-mermaids. Ezra Pound, who saw the poem before it had become famous, noted the over-finished literariness of the Hamlet passage; "but it is an early and cherished bit and T. E. won't give it up, and as it is the only portion of the poem that most readers will like at first reading, I don't see that it will do much harm."

On the rare occasions when we have the opportunity of inspecting Eliot's procedures in action, we discover a tendency of short, highly finished passages to be borne into the eddies of the poem by some rhythmic current, and to lodge there because the writer doesn't want to give them up. There is evidence that some of the components eliminated from *The Waste Land* by Pound's celebrated surgical operation found their way, transmuted, into *The Hollow Men;* others turn up, one cannot say how much altered, as *Minor Poems.* When the elements in a poem are contained by a dramatized consciousness whose associative shuttling loosely unites them, and of which in turn they indicate the tonality, it is difficult to adhere firmly to that criterion of order and selection which the advancing logic of the poem—itself subordinate, as in Debussy's music, to the display of prevalent tonalities—would imply. And what has once entrenched itself, time will hallow; protected, anyhow, by tonal coloration. Part of the poet's final satisfaction is his feeling that nothing, for the time being, is left over; no more poetry, for a while, demands writing. One suspects that Eliot is troubled by good bits left over. An inferior poem of some forty lines which he sent to *Poetry* in 1915 and later cancelled just before publication contained just five good lines, and they bothered him until seven years later he transformed them and found them a home—

> Come under the shadow of this gray rock—
> Come in under the shadow of this gray rock
> And I will show you something different from either
> Your shadow sprawling over the sand at daybreak, or
> Your shadow leaping behind the fire against the red rock. . . .

Eliot's long struggle, in the years after *Prufrock,* to arrive at a criterion of relevance and a self-sufficient logic of structure —a struggle not consummated until *Four Quartets*—suggests the penalties of doing something unforgettable, especially at an early age; the poet can never know quite how he has done it, and is subsequently as likely as his commentators to devise explanations which cover all the details. The one Eliot devised after forty-two years is in certain ways better than the famous image of the poet's mind as catalyst, catalyzing anything:

> He has something germinating within him for which he must find words . . . nothing so definite as an emotion . . . still more certainly not an idea. . . . He does not know what he has to say until he has said it, and in the effort to say it he is not concerned with making other people understand anything. . . . And when the words are finally arranged in the right way—or in what he comes to accept as the best arrangement he can find— he may experience a moment of exhaustion, of appeasement, of absolution, and of something very near annihilation, which is in itself indescribable. And then he can say to the poem: "Go away! Find a place for yourself in a book—and don't expect *me* to take any further interest in you."

By 1912 the Laforguian lode was worked out. Back at Harvard, Eliot wrote the fourth *Prelude* and *La Figlia che Piange,* a return to the situation caricatured in one of the *Harvard Advocate* poems, in which the gestures of a lovers' farewell have their value as aesthetic tableaux to a spectator who is himself, by a Prufrockian doubling of consciousness, one of the lovers:

> And I wonder how they should have been together!
> I should have lost a gesture and a pose.
> Sometimes these cogitations still amaze
> The troubled midnight and the noon's repose.

The lovers feel the pang, the spectator admires the composition. In this impasse between self-sufficiency and art we discern the Laforguian dead end. In writing *La Figlia* Eliot got off his chest the one remaining unwritten poem; he then devoted his intelligence to graduate study in metaphysics, logic, psychology, philosophy, Sanskrit and Pali, and wrote no more poems for three years.

BRADLEY

J. Alfred Prufrock is a name plus a Voice. He isn't a "character" cut out of the rest of the universe and equipped with a history and a little necessary context, like the speaker of a Browning monologue. We have no information about him whatever; even his age is ambiguous (the poet once referred casually to Prufrock in a lecture as a *young* man). Nor is he an Everyman, surrounded by poetic effects: the range of "treatment" is excessive. Everyman's mind doesn't teem with allusions to Hesiod, Hamlet, Lazarus, Falstaff, entomology, eschatology, John the Baptist, mermaids. What "Prufrock" is, is the name of a possible zone of consciousness where these materials can maintain a vague congruity; no more than that; certainly not a person. You are not, in allowing their intermodulations to echo in your mind, deepening your apprehension of an imagined character, such as Hamlet, or discerning his boundaries; Prufrock is strangely boundless; one doesn't affirm at a given point with certainty, "Here is where his knowledge would have stopped," or "These are subtleties to which he would not have aspired." Like the thing you look at when you raise your eyes from this page, he is the centre of a field of consciousness, rather yours than his: a focusing of the reader's attention, in a world made up not of cows and stones but of literary "effects" and memories prompted by the words.

Prufrock is in all these respects the generic Eliot character;

Gerontion, say, is one of his metamorphoses, another Voice with no ascertainable past and no particularized present: not even a shadowy apparatus of streets and stairs and rooms full of talking women, but a "dry month" which we take to be mataphoric and a "decayed house" whose tenants turn out to be the thoughts of his brain. The extreme case of the Eliotic pseudo-person is Tiresias in *The Waste Land:* "the most important personage in the poem," yet "a mere spectator," a congeries of effects, who is only presented personally in a footnote. "What Tiresias *sees*, in fact, is the substance of the poem"; and what Tiresias *is*—so far as he can be said to exist for the reader—is what he sees: the whole disparate poem, ravelling out boundlessly into literary echoes and mythological traditions as old as the human race. He is, once more, the name of a possible zone of consciousness where the materials with which he is credited with being aware can co-exist; and what else, we seem to hear the author ask, what else, unless a delimited shadow like "the young man carbuncular," can a developed human consciousness be said to be?

As that question implies, a quality inherent in all incantatory poetry, poetry that eschews the statement and evokes the unspoken mood, is being deliberately pressed by Eliot into the service of a corresponding view of things. Other poets have used the method, and they are comparatively innocent of the deliberate view of things the method implies. They took it as it came to them from predecessors in a literary tradition: Tennyson from Coleridge, Coleridge from Bowles and Cowper; and if the method's grip on human personality is slight, if Coleridge can project only moods of himself and Tennyson (more rashly ambitious) only a few tones, variegated by unexceptionable reflections and labelled "Arthur" or "Lancelot", that is a disability with which they put up or of which they remain unaware. It is as true of Arthur as of Prufrock that he is a name plus a Voice, surrounded by every possible vagueness, blurring into the highly literary tapestry of which he is an unemphatic feature; but what is a defect of Tennyson's intention would seem to be the thoroughly deliberated focal point of Eliot's. Eliot has achieved, for one thing, the most *generalizing* style in English literature, capable, as Marshall McLuhan has pointed out, of summing up all possible relevant case histories in an imaged "state".

> For example, the initial situation in *Prufrock* or *Gerontion* is inclusive of every mode of metamorphosis or schizophrenia from the shaman to the medium and the poet, on one hand, and of every possible combination of ultimate disappointment and rage, on the other hand. The number of possible case histories of people having such experience is the number of possible "explanations" of the state of Prufrock and Gerontion. . . . Mr. Eliot . . . is not interested in plots or case histories which trace by cause and effect the stages leading to a particular situation. He is interested in the situation which exhausts all such causes and effects and includes further levels of analogical perception.★

This capacity for generalization, latent in any "verbalist" poetic, or in any poetry descended from an efflorescent poetic drama, is brought to fruition by Mr. Eliot under the auspices of an idealist philosophy, much meditated during his student years, for which a person is continuous with τὸ πᾶν.

It is true that a poetry brewed out of the sounds and implications of words is not a medium in which to think; but as Mr. Eliot has frequently implied, he makes no pretence of thinking *in* his verse. "The poet who 'thinks'," he has written, "is merely the poet who can express the emotional equivalent of thought"; and this, he implies, is something that Tennyson and Browning could not do but that Shakespeare and Donne could do. "Tennyson and Browning are poets, and they think; but they do not feel their thought as immediately as the odour of a rose. A thought to Donne was an experience; it modified his sensibility." A thought to Donne, however, was not necessarily something he originated; it was quite likely something he picked up from his ambience. (Eliot once found it "quite impossible to come to the conclusion that Donne believed

★"Mr. Eliot's Historical Decorum," *Renascence,* Autumn 1949, pp. 13–14.

anything.") "I can see no reason for believing that either Dante or Shakespeare did any thinking on his own"; it is not the poet's job to think; his job is "to express the greatest emotional intensity of his time, based on whatever his time happened to think."

It seems not to have been asked, what thoughts modified Eliot's sensibility. He tells us, here and there, pretty clearly: the thoughts of Francis Herbert Bradley.

The intellectual world of Francis Herbert Bradley (1846–1924) apparently occupied Mr. Eliot's close attention for a longer period than that of anyone else, not a poet, in whom he has professed an interest; and began to occupy him, moreover, during his late twenties, at the time when his own intellectual stuff was most malleable. *Prufrock* was composed in 1911. The Houghton Library, Harvard, contains an unpublished doctoral dissertation, *Experience and the Objects of Knowledge in the Philosophy of F. H. Bradley,* dated 1916; "but external evidence points to the possibility that Eliot completed most, if not all of it, before that time. He was prevented by the war from returning to this country to submit his thesis at Harvard."* In 1915 he was in residence at Bradley's Oxford College, Merton. The next year he made his debut in London, not as a poet or literary critic, but as an impecunious reviewer of philosophic books; immediately we find the signature of T. Stearns Eliot appended to an eleven-page essay in the Leibniz Bicentennial issue of *The Monist:* "Leibniz's Monads and Bradley's Finite Centers" (1916). In 1922, adding notes to *The Waste Land,* he included, more in an anthologist's than an exegete's spirit, a vivid paragraph from Bradley's *Appearance and Reality* that might have been composed by a disciplined Prufrock:

> My external sensations are no less private to myself than are my thoughts or my feelings. In either case my experience falls within my own circle, a circle closed on the outside; and, with all its elements alike, every sphere is opaque to the others which surround it. . . . In brief, regarded as an existence which appears

*R. W. Church in the *Harvard Advocate,* December 1938, p. 24.

in a soul, the whole world for each is peculiar and private to that soul.

In 1927 he wrote for the *Times Literary Supplement* a tribute to Bradley's greatness disguised as a review of the reprinted *Ethical Studies;* the reference to Bradley's "polemical irony and his obvious zest in using it, his habit of discomfiting an opponent with a sudden profession of ignorance, of inability to understand, or of incapacity for abstruse thought" suggests a model for some of the polemic gestures of the critic who scored a point against Shelley by claiming not to understand some stanzas from *To a Skylark,* and has repeatedly evaded quibbles concerning his more abstrusely-based positions by claiming amateur status and incapacity for pursuing the abstruse.

By the time of that 1927 essay, Eliot's active interest in Bradley would seem to have been fading; he cites texts, but with an opportunist's interest in their usefulness for discomfiting Matthew Arnold. From his mid-twenties till his late thirties, however, he appears to have kept his knowledge of the philosopher's books in repair, and the 1916 thesis, a closely-argued and widely documented account and defence of Bradley's position concerning "immediate experience," is evidence for his unqualified ingestion of certain perspectives of Bradley's which one does not discover him ever to have repudiated. It would be surprising if this transient closeness of identification between himself and the English philosopher had not left an ineradicable stain on his mind; and it is precisely as a stain, imparting colour to all else that passes through, that Bradley is most discernible in Eliot's poetic sensibility.

He was uniquely equipped to exert that sort of tonal influence on a disciple; he is not the sort of philosopher who can be tied, rhetorically, to a cause. It is as a colouring, not as a body of doctrine, that he stays in the mind; partly because such doctrines as he professes are so little detachable from their dry and scrupulous expression by him, modified by the exact context in which he chooses to expound them. They exist, indeed, more in Bradley's prose than in the mind; paraphrase them, and they become the commonplace dancing bears from which he is at such ironic pains to distinguish them. In 1924 Eliot presented him to the reading publics of France and America* as a potential influence "upon the sensibility of one or two or more literary generations," whose philosophy, borrowing "none of the persuasiveness of science and none of the persuasiveness of literature," has none of the "meretricious captivation" of, say, Bergson's "exciting promise of immortality," and can operate, therefore, only "upon the sensibility through the intellect." It cannot even be believed in; to believe in the deliverances of a mind not your own, you must simplify them to a set of propositions that command assent without reference to the initial fragrance.

> But Bradley is wholly and solely a philosopher. . . . Philosophy may be futile or profitable, he seems to say, but if you are to pursue it at all, you must work with such and such data—which are neither literature nor science. All we can do is to accept these data and follow our argument to the end. If it ends, as it may well end, in zero, well, we have at least the satisfaction of having pursued something to the end, and of having ascertained that certain questions which occur to men to ask, are unanswerable or meaningless. Once you accept his theory of the nature of the judgement, and it is as plausible a theory as any, you are led by his arid and highly sensitive eloquence . . . to something which, according to your temperament, will be resignation or despair: the bewildered despair of wondering why you ever wanted anything and what it was that you wanted, since this philosophy seems to give you everything that you ask and yet to render it not worth wanting.

"Why should the aged eagle stretch its wings?" What Eliot's readers have frequently taken for a mood, the *Waste Land* tone, what I. A. Richards grandiloquently called "the disillusionment of a generation," is actually Bradley's deeply-thought-out *metaphysical* scepticism; and at the bottom of Eliot's frequent disavowals of capacity for abstruse thought lies ultimately not a polemical strategy but Bradley's unsettling conviction that

*In the *Nouvelle Revue Française* and *Vanity Fair,* respectively.

abstruse thought, carried on for determinate ends, is meretricious. Eliot's strategy (for strategy remains present) employs the ironic intimation that other and more ardently active people have not been brought to this realization, of how principles invoked in the press of practical disputation thereby turn into slogans, losing what little integrity they have, that of standpoints in an evasive whole of perception, and how one must therefore defend practical judgements by reference to one's impressions alone. One of the most important deposits of Bradleyism in Eliot's sensibility is visible in the disarmingly hesitant and fragmentary way in which he makes a point or expresses a conviction, doubting that he is quite the man to undertake the job in hand, or devoting an entire volume to "notes towards the definition" of a single word.

Naturally, a few odds and ends of what the plain reader of Bradley would call Bradleyan "doctrines" do turn up in Eliot's writings. This passage from *Appearance and Reality* has a very Eliotic ring:

> For whether there is progress or not, at all events there is change; and the changed minds of each generation will require a difference in what has to satisfy their intellect. Hence there seems as much need for new philosophy as there is for new poetry. In each case the fresh production is usually much inferior to something already in existence; and yet it answers a purpose if it appeals more personally to the reader. What is really worse may serve better to promote, in certain respects and in a certain generation, the exercise of our best functions.

Assaying this for traces of irony presents a characteristic difficulty; as we shall see, its most Bradleyan qualities lie less in its frontal claim than in its more elusive implications. There is no difficulty however in assigning the filiation of such Eliotisms as "Art never improves, but . . . the material of art is never quite the same"; or "Sensibility alters from generation to generation, whether we will or no; but expression is only altered by a man of genius"; or even the 1927 remark that "Christianity will continue to modify itself into something that can be believed in." It is very Bradleyan, also, to argue that "The whole of Shakespeare's work is *one* poem"; so that "what is 'the whole man' is not simply his greatest or maturest achievement, but the whole pattern formed by the sequence of plays . . . : we must know all of Shakespeare's work in order to know any of it"; or more generally, substituting the mind of Europe for that of Shakespeare, to assert that "No poet, no artist of any art, has his complete meaning alone. His significance, his appreciation, is the appreciation of his relation to the dead poets and artists"; or finally, to argue that as we change, so does the literature of the past change; we cannot read the Shakespeare Dr. Johnson read; "for order to persist after the subvention of novelty, the *whole* existing order must be, if ever so slightly, altered."

All these formulations deprive us of a simple rigid object to stare at, dangling in front of a cardboard frieze labelled "context" which we may use to make measurements from or disregard as we choose; and deprive us likewise of our assured impartial sense that we who stare are delicate but inviolable perceiving-machines, correcting our grandfathers and instructing our posterity, feeding data into our memories to be consulted when relevant. For memory is to perception as the pool to the ripples: the whole of Bradley's metaphysic emanates from his denial that the dichotomy of observer and observed is anything but a late and clumsy abstraction, of limited usefulness, crassly misrepresenting the process of knowing. The streets, the yellow fog, the drains, the coffee-spoons *are* Prufrock; the "evenings, mornings, afternoons" are Prufrock, as much so as the voice which says, "I have known them all already, known them all."

"In feeling the subject and object are one," states Eliot flatly in his 1916 thesis, paraphrasing Bradley's description of "immediate experience." "At any time," writes Bradley, "all that we suffer, do and are forms one psychical totality. It is experienced all together as a coexisting mass, not perceived as parted and joined even by relations of coexistence. It contains all relations, and distinctions, and every ideal object that at that moment exists in the soul." Hence, to reproduce the quality of immediate experience, there is exacted of verse a blending suavity, not an assured rattle of subjects and predicates, nor images standing in explicable analogy to one another.

> Among the smoke and fog of a December afternoon
> You have the scene arrange itself—as it will seem to do—
> With "I have saved this afternoon for you";
> And four wax candles in the darkened room,
> Four rings of light upon the ceiling overhead,
>   An atmosphere of Juliet's tomb
> Prepared for all the things to be said, or left unsaid.

What seems to be a salient verb, in line 2, is virtually cancelled later in the same line; for the rest, we have participles and relative clauses related to nothing, the gestures of verbs rather than their commitments, syntax not abolished but anaesthetized. Juliet's tomb, the smoke and fog, the candles, the imminent conversation form, precisely, "one psychical totality, experienced all together as a co-existing mass." What syntax will specify the infusion, into your experience of reading this book now, of the place in which you are half-aware of yourself reading it?

So *Prufrock* begins somewhere in its own epigraph, and uncoils through adverbial clauses of dubious specificity past imperatives of uncertain cogency to a "do not ask". One function of the epigraphs is to blur the beginnings of the poems; they open not with the éclat of some syntactic gesture—"Of Man's first disobedience . . ."—but with an awakened dubiety about the scope of a quotation. *The Waste Land's* initial firm show of business dissolves on inspection into a throbbing of participles attached to furtive copulae: an indeterminate breeding, mixing, stirring, covering, feeding, that invisibly smothers Chaucer's Aprille with the vibrations of the Sibyl's "I want to die."

Such writing is far from what is called in classrooms "orderly," because our criteria of orderliness were developed, late in the seventeenth century, at the behest of a smartly diagrammatic view of the world. A famous passage in Sprat's *History of the Royal Society* (1667) celebrates "the primitive purity, and shortness, when men deliver'd so many things, almost in an equal number of words." This argues an atomistic view of *things;* they lie in great numbers opaquely before the mind, awaiting arrangement and selection. The mind, on the other hand, is wholly separate from them; it is the busy finger that arranges and selects. Identities, resemblances, and differences are noted; there is nothing else to note. The archetypal statement is the equation; this fish is indistinguishable from that one; a = b. Hence "a close, naked, natural way of speaking: positive expressions; clear senses; a native easiness: bringing all things as near the Mathematical plainness, as they can."

Since that age it has been characteristically assumed that because things can be clearly and distinctly separated from our continuous experience of them, therefore clear statements about the identity and difference of things underlie whatever colours, complications, and aids to persuasion are affixed by any writer not merely confused. Thus A. E. Housman stated that metaphor and simile were "things inessential to poetry": either accessories employed "to be helpful, to make his sense clearer or his conception more vivid," or else ornaments possessing "an independent power to please." It is but a step, in this climate, to the familiar assumption that a self-evident separation between *me* and *what I experience* governs all thought, or that *what I experience* is made up of self-evident component parts, this object and that one, actions with beginnings, middles and ends mimed by sentences with subjects, verbs, and predicates, the starts and stops of sentences and paragraphs corresponding to perceived divisions in the action being chronicled. The classical rhetoricians who saw that all writing is radically artificial were discarded as inciters to artifice; and it became unfashionable to note how a simple sentence like "Jack threw the ball to Will" *imposes* a symmetrical shape and three grammatical categories upon a bit of spontaneous play. To a reader situated in that universe of schematic diagrams, naturally Eliot's prose and verse seem obscure.

For Bradley, on the other hand, "At every moment my state, whatever else it is, is a whole of which I am immediately aware. It is an experienced non-relational unity of many in one." "Non-relational" is the key phrase, here as in much of Bradley's metaphysical writing. It is Bradley's shorthand for his untiring contention that this immediate awareness in which my sentience (to call it "mine") proceeds, is not reducible to parts in a certain relation, myself confronting the exterior given, these things in this manner related to those. Nor can it be imaged by relating a subject to a predicate, both duly chamfered with modifiers.

> At any moment my actual experience, however relational its contents, is in the end non-relational. No analysis into relations and terms can ever exhaust its nature or fail in the end to belie its essence. What analysis leaves for ever outstanding is no mere residue, but is a vital condition of the analysis itself. Everything which is got out into the form of an object

—(for you are starting to simplify experience drastically the minute you say "tree")—

> implies still the felt background against which the object comes, and, further, the whole experience of both feeling and object is a non-relational immediate felt unity. . . .

It was statements like these, and their implications, that Eliot pondered for many years. Their importance, for a poet situated in the early twentieth century, is obvious; what they do, once their implications have been watchfully distilled, is ally the realities of everyday experience with the vocabulary of poetic effects out of which Tennyson and Swinburne, Verlaine and Poe, brewed a phantasmagoria of nuances. Romantic poetry had postulated a special world because the normal one had been usurped by an orderliness which was profoundly sensed to be wrong, but which in the absence of systematic grounds for that uneasy sense could only be ignored. In the prose world feeling was nascent or disorderly thought, something to be burnished away. From the poetic world, thought was exorcised as a merely calculated schematizing. And this "dissociation of sensibility, from which we have never recovered," cut poetry off from serious intellectual activity. "Jonson and Chapman," Eliot notes, "were notably erudite, and were notably men who incorporated their erudition into their sensibility: their mode of feeling was directly and freshly altered by their reading and thought." They are superseded by, say, Tennyson and Browning, who "are poets, and they think; but they do not feel their thought as immediately as the odour of a rose"; or by, say, Shelley, who incorporated his erudition into his writing, but not into his sensibility. "Sensibility" is Eliot's term for a scrupulous responsiveness to the Bradleyan "immediate experience": a responsiveness that precedes, underlies, and contains any degree of analysis. In the Shelleyan apostrophe to the West Wind—

> Thou on whose stream, 'mid the steep sky's commotion,
> Loose clouds like earth's decaying leaves are shed,
> Shook from the tangled boughs of Heaven and Ocean,

we can explain these mysterious tangled boughs as an attempted incorporation into the verse of known facts about the origin of clouds, forcibly subdued to a logic postulated by the simile of the leaves. That clouds are drawn up from the ocean by solar heat and deposited at altitudes where condensation renders them visible is a fact gleaned from books; but knowledge of these facts has not modified Shelley's apprehension of clouds, it merely complicates the image under which he regards them, the same under which he would have regarded them had no books of meteorology existed.* "The tangled boughs of Heaven and Ocean" is a construction of words, attempting under the cover of rhythmic propulsiveness to

---

*Cf. "The majority of verse writers are contented with *approximation* to meaning, an approximation which in many contemporary verse writers takes the deceptive form of a thumping scientific precision."—T. S. Eliot, 1935.

make itself adequate to known but intractable fact. Verse spends a half century ridding itself of this radical defect; Swinburne abandons himself to words entirely. Swinburne abandons, that is, "immediate experience" for a universe of language where the inclusiveness and continuity, but not the felt truth, of immediate experience can be mimed.

> When you take to pieces any verse of Swinburne, you find always that the object was not there—only the word. Compare
> > Snowdrops that plead for pardon
> > And pine for fright
> with the daffodils that come before the swallow dares. The snowdrop of Swinburne disappears, the daffodil of Shakespeare remains.

This leads Eliot to a confident affirmation of considerable scope:

> Language in a healthy state presents the object, is so close to the object that the two are identified. They are identified in the verse of Swinburne solely because the object has ceased to exist, because the meaning is merely the hallucination of meaning, because language, uprooted, has adapted itself to an independent life of atmospheric nourishment. In Swinburne, for example, we see the word "weary" flourishing in this way independent of the particular and actual weariness of flesh or spirit. The bad poet dwells partly in a world of objects and partly in a world of words, and he never can get them to fit. Only a man of genius could dwell so exclusively and consistently among words as Swinburne.

Swinburne, that is, had purchased at great cost an air of poetic inclusiveness which there could, in 1908, be no question of abandoning. "The question was, where do we go from Swinburne?" Unfortunately, Swinburne marked not only the fullest achievement of romantic inclusiveness, but the final phase of a decadence. "The answer appeared to be, nowhere."

Bradley, of course, didn't solve Eliot's initial poetic problem; there is no evidence that Eliot paid him any attention until after he had written *Prufrock* and *Portrait of a Lady*. (He did not buy his own copy of *Appearance and Reality* until mid-

1913.) The study of Bradley, however, may be said to have done three things for a poet who might otherwise not have passed beyond the phase of imitating Laforgue. It solved his *critical* problem, providing him with a point of view towards history and so with the scenario for his most comprehensive essay, "Tradition and the Individual Talent"; it freed him from the Laforguian posture of the ironist with his back to a wall, by affirming the artificiality of *all* personality including the one we intimately suppose to be our true one; not only the faces we prepare but the "we" that prepares; and it released him from any notion that the art his temperament bade him practice was an eccentric art, evading for personal and temporary reasons a more orderly, more "normal" unfolding from statement to statement. A view of the past, a view of himself and other persons, a view of the nature of what we call statement and communication; these delivered Eliot from what might well have been, after a brilliant beginning, a cul-de-sac and silence. Want of a liberating view of history had misled more than a century of poetic activity into prizing either explosive "originality" or equally sterile "traditionalism." Want of some radical insight into "personality" had led a Wordsworth to eliminate people, except as vivid apparitions or passing shadows, a Byron to dissipate energy in an endless dialectic of self-expression, mask after mask, a Dickens or a Browning to equate the personal with the arresting, and reduce persons to accumulations of flashy effects. Want of a view of poetry that could bypass the dichotomies posed by talk about "communication" had condemned the French symbolists and their English heirs of the Nineties to the status of literary experimenters, never at their most vigorous free from the imputation of creating or delimiting a "special" world with which alone poetry can concern itself. Baudelaire, it is true, elevated imagery of the sordid life of a great metropolis "to the *first intensity*"—

> On voit un chiffonnier qui vient, hochant la tête,
> Buttant, et se cognant aux murs comme un poète—

but the old ragpicker remains subordinated to an "on voit," a piquant item in the landscape of "poetic" perception. No one, however, who had allowed the Bradleyan phenomenology to invade his mind would (except in makeshift prose) compel a presentation to dangle from "one sees," unless to throw ironic light on the perceiver ("I should have lost a gesture and a pose"). Contrast Eliot's metropolitan landscape:

> Under the brown fog of a winter dawn,
> A crowd flowed over London Bridge, so many,
> I had not thought death had undone so many.
> Sighs, short and infrequent, were exhaled. . . .

The unobtrusive "I" neither dominates nor creates this scene, being itself subordinated to a barely grammatical subordination, and in any case embedded in a quotation from Dante; the very exhalation is impersonal; and a definite article deprives "the brown fog" of unique reported status, consigning it to that co-operatively constructed world (made up of London, Dante, crowds, sighs, you, and I) in which brown fogs pass without undue remark.

If Eliot's sense of poetry, of personality, and of history are all congruent with Bradley's philosophy, that is largely because the man who developed those views also found Bradley congenial. For that matter, Laforgue no doubt drew his attention to Schopenhauer, who was interested in Buddhism and wished men to recognize their true condition, each one alone in an illusory world. Laforgue, too, presumably sponsored Eliot's famous two-year sojourn in Oriental mazes. But in helping him develop his sense of the past, Bradley's was the active role. "Tradition and the Individual Talent" (1919) concludes a train of thought which can be traced through earlier *Egoist* articles to its origins in the Bradley thesis three years earlier. It follows from Bradley's denial of any separation "of feeling from the felt, or of the desired from desire, or of what is thought from thinking," that our attempt to separate the past from our knowledge of it, what really happened from the way we imagine things to have been, is ultimately meaningless.

Early in his thesis Eliot notes that for a geologist to conceive of the development of the world, he must present it as it would have looked had he, with his body and his nervous system, been there to see it. It follows that we cannot conceive of a past indifferent to us; obversely, that all that we know of the past is part of our experience now. And it follows that "the conscious present is an awareness of the past in a way and to an extent which the past's awareness of itself cannot show."

Eliot's poems, we have already noted, differ from reader to reader to an unusual degree, posed between meaning nothing and meaning everything, associating themselves with what the reader thinks of, and inclines to wonder whether Eliot was thinking of. So he despatches, perhaps, a genetic query to London—does the end of *Prufrock* contain an allusion to Donne's "Teach me to hear mermaids sing?" and is no doubt informed that if Donne did indeed enter into the composition of those lines, his presence must have been quite unconscious. He is present, of course, if you find it helpful to think of him; the nature of this poetry is to appropriate anything that comes near. In Chapter II of *The Great Gatsby* we read of "a valley of ashes," a "gray land" above which brood "the eyes of Doctor T. J. Eckleburg," blue and gigantic, their retinas one yard high. There is no point in asking Mr. Eliot whether this is a source for *The Hollow Men,* because *The Hollow Men* was finished just before *The Great Gatsby* existed for Eliot to read. Nevertheless *The Hollow Men* appropriates the valley of ashes and the eyes of Doctor Eckleburg once the two works have entered the same consciousness, and become members of our present, which is an awareness of things that were never aware of each other.

A book is a set of words; it is we who give them life; and it is our life that we give them. So every author we read becomes as we read him a more or less alien contemporary; but a contemporary whose own sense of the past is imperfect compared to ours. The author of *Hamlet* is by definition a poet who has never heard of Pope or Byron, who has read nothing

published subsequent to 1601. This consideration leads Eliot
to one of his most pregnant epigrams:

> Some one said: "The dead writers are remote from us because
> we *know* so much more than they did." Precisely, and they are
> that which we know.

Every age, furthermore, is an age of transition; we are not to
be misled by the look of Augustan stability, or by the convenient parentheses within which literary historians enclose
several decades of serial activity. Nor is even, say "Shakespeare"
—let alone "the Elizabethan drama"—a fixed point, for the
Shakespeare who wrote *Romeo and Juliet* was not the Shakespeare we think of, but a Shakespeare who had not written
Hamlet. If Shakespeare at any moment thought that he had at
length achieved a plateau and an identity, Shakespeare was
deceived;

> The knowledge imposes a pattern and falsifies,
> For the pattern is new in every moment
> And every moment is a new and shocking
> Valuation of all we have been.

This brings us to the "person", of whom Bradley notes
that "the usual self of one period is not the usual self of another."

> It is impossible to unite in one mass these conflicting psychical
> contents. Either then we accept the man's mere history as his
> self, and if so why call it one? Or we confine ourselves to periods,
> and there is no longer any single self.

And if the present self is evasive, the past one is illusory:

> My past self is arrived at only by a process of inference. . . .
> We are so accustomed each to consider his past self as his own,
> that it is worth while to reflect how very largely it may be
> foreign. My own past is, in the first place, incompatible with
> my own present, quite as much as my present can be with another
> man's. . . . I may regard it even with a feeling of hostility and
> hatred. It may be mine merely in the sense of a persisting incum-
> brance, a compulsory appendage, joined in continuity and
> fastened by an inference. . . .

C   · 51 ·

"Who are you now?" the Unidentified Guest asks Edward Chamberlayne.

> You don't know any more than I do,
> But rather less. You are nothing but a set
> Of obsolete responses. The one thing to do
> Is to do nothing. Wait.

The next day Edward learns that his wife is to come back "from the dead."

EDWARD: That figure of speech is somewhat . . . dramatic,
   As it was only yesterday that my wife left me.
UNIDENTIFIED GUEST: Ah, but we die to each other daily.
   What we know of other people
   Is only our memory of the moments
   During which we knew them. And they have changed
    since then.
   To pretend that they and we are the same
   Is a useful and convenient social convention
   Which must sometimes be broken. We must also re-
    member
   That at every meeting we are meeting a stranger.

The roots of this exchange are in a comment Eliot wrote on Bradley more than thirty years before. Someone else, he notes, may call my view of the world "subjective," a merely personal appendage of "me"; I, however, cannot call it subjective, because to call it subjective would be to separate me from it; and my experience is inseparable from the conviction that the three things my interlocutor would separate—I, the objective world, and my feelings about it, are an indissoluble whole. It is only in social behaviour, Eliot concludes, in the conflict and readjustment of what Bradley calls "finite centers," that feelings and things are torn apart: "we die to each other daily."

The meaning of the term "finite center" is less important than the process by which Bradley arrives at it. Let us try the experiment of asking him who Prufrock is (his own gambit was to pose the question, What is the real Julius Caesar?). If you ask him what is Mr. Prufrock's essential self, he will first discard "essential" as implying that of which Prufrock himself is self-consciously and therefore distortedly aware; and reply at some length that the real Prufrockian focus of consciousness (he will not say the real Prufrock, any more than he will say the real you) is a finite centre. ("The finite Centre," writes Eliot, "so far as I can pretend to understand it, *is* immediate experience.") Further than that Bradley is evasive. If you look at a finite centre the gaze of your mind's eye corrupts it, or you start thinking things into it. So Bradley shrinks from discussing it directly, though he will invoke it with his own peculiar tentative confidence while discussing something else. His ultimate answer to the question about Julius Caesar was that, Caesar's experience of himself being as inaccessible, and as irrelevant, as a geranium's experience of itself, the "real Julius Caesar" cannot be less than—for us—every impression, every sentiment, that attracts itself to that name, and every effect that can be attributed to it. In the same way J. Alfred Prufrock exists only while someone is reading or remembering the poem, and exists only *as* each particular reader experiences him.

Julius Caesar, being dead, is of course like Prufrock a tradition and a literary character. Who or what is my real dinner companion? is a more difficult question; since the cheese and the jugged hare presumably figure in his immediate experience as they do in mine. I figure in it also. "A self," Eliot noted, describing Bradley's epistemology in *The Monist,*

> is an ideal and largely practical construction, one's own self as much as others. My self remains "intimately one thing with that finite centre within which my universe appears. Other selves on the contrary are for me ideal objects." The self is a construction in space and time. It is an object among others, a self among others, and could not exist save in a common world.

As for an object,

> For Bradley, I take it, an object is a common intention of several souls, cut out (as in a sense are the souls themselves) from immediate experience. The genesis of the common world can only be described by admitted fictions . . . on the one hand our

experiences are similar because they are of the same objects, and on the other hand the objects are only "intellectual constructions" out of various and quite independent experiences. So, on the one hand, my experience is in principle essentially public. My emotions may be better understood by others than by myself; as my oculist knows my eyes. And on the other hand everything, the whole world, is private to myself. Internal and external are thus not adjectives applied to different contents within the same world; they are different points of view.

A reader in quest of formulae for mediating between the mental landscapes of Prufrock, Gerontion, or Tiresias and the thoughts and feelings of their author would be wise to approach his problem through that paragraph, where according to his temperament he will either find what he wants or be discouraged from seeking it.

Bradley has an attractive mind, though he has perhaps nothing to tell us. He is an experience, like the taste of nectarines or the style of Henry James; to rethink him is to recall with labour a landscape once seen in a dream; he is like a vivid dream in that, as Eliot said, he modifies the sensibility. Since the physical world, he writes, is a state of my brain, and my brain is part of the physical world, "the physical world is an appearance; it is phenomenal throughout. It is the relation of two unknowns, which, because they are unknown, we cannot have any right to regard as really two, as related at all. It is an imperfect way of apprehension, which gives us qualities and relations, each the condition of and yet presupposing the other."

We have in such remarks not elements of a vision, but statements about the impossibility of framing a vision in which the imagination may repose. They underwrite, however, poetry Eliot had already written when he began to pay them attention, and dissolve any temptation not to continue writing in a similar mode. Whoever ponders such statements will see how a poet who deeply pondered them could not regard "things" as subject-matter, or "images" in a poem as references to substantiality. Images, consequently, are absorbed into literary tradition, as the bones in Part II of *Ash-Wednesday* occupy simultaneously Ezekiel's vision, a tale of the Grimms, and the area of association implied by the *Ash-Wednesday* context of three leopards, a juniper-tree, and a Lady. Subject-matter, similarly, is absorbed into states of feeling, as in the third part of *Ash-Wednesday* it is equally meaningless to say that the ascent of the stairs is or is not an actual imagined happening, dissolving as it does, under a kind of inspection irrelevant to the experiencing of the poetry, into Dante's purgatorial stairs, the Eliotic stairs of *Prufrock* and *La Figlia,* and some still more nebulous suggestion of a tradition of psychic ascent. The poem is a continuum in which the perceiving mind, intent on the quality of its own feelings, constantly adjusts the scope and emphasis of its perceptions.

Such a description fits *Appearance and Reality* as well; and fits *Four Quartets*, with their drily intense opening abstractions

> . . . If all time is eternally present
> All time is unredeemable . . .

modulated, without desertion of the abstract plane, into the injunction to

> be still and still moving
> Into another intensity
> For a further union, a deeper communion. . . .

The method of the *Quartets* bears a close resemblance to that of the book which begins with the apparently suicidal remark that "Metaphysics is the finding of bad reasons for what we believe upon instinct, but to find these reasons is no less an instinct," but which later, without alteration of its essential tone or modus, can speak of "that absolute self-fruition that comes only when the self bursts its limits, and blends with another finite self." There are even resemblances of detail, as when Bradley speaks of an Absolute which

. . . is timeless, but it possesses time as an isolated aspect, an aspect which, in ceasing to be isolated, loses its special character. It is there, but blended into a whole which we cannot realize;

and Eliot of an unmoving Love,

> Timeless, and undesiring
> Except in the aspect of time
> Caught in the form of limitation
> Between un-being and being.

Bradley, again, states that Science

> . . . quite ignores the existence of time. For it habitually treats past and future as one thing with the present . . . The character of an existence is determined by what it has been and by what it is (potentially) about to be. But if these attributes, on the other hand, are not present, how can they be real? . . .

Which is perhaps the germ of the *Burnt Norton* opening:

> Time present and time past
> Are both perhaps present in time future,
> And time future contained in time past.
> If all time is eternally present
> All time is unredeemable.
> What might have been is an abstraction
> Remaining a perpetual possibility
> Only in a world of speculation.
> What might have been and what has been
> Point to one end, which is always present.

When we have done contrasting the spareness dominated by Eliot's taut verse rhythms with the loosening effect of Bradley's constant scrupulousness of qualification, we may note one quality this prose and this verse have in common: an eschewal of eloquence. It is the absence of ornament, of blur and ready satisfaction, of otiose diction—

> Life, like a dome of many-coloured glass,
> Stains the white radiance of Eternity,
> Until Death tramples it to fragments . . .

that confers on Eliot's maturest verse that tension which, until Eliot had achieved it, no one would have thought to include among the possible modes of poetry; and it is a comparable quality of Bradley's argument, neither dissolving into whimsical sub-predications like a philosophical Henry James, nor like Plato choosing the short cut of myth and peroration, that permits him to include feeling without engendering it, and rise, in his predications of an Absolute where all contradictions are reconciled, into an exciting tautness of implication. *Appearance and Reality* is a great triumph of style, style that never deserts its proper business of completing and clarifying the deliverances of the intellect. Though he has no message to deliver, he fills the mind, yet each time we want to see with what he fills it, we must reread the book. No aftertaste lingers with which we may solace ourselves, only the satisfaction of having pursued the sinuosities of a memorably adequate performance. With perhaps the sole exception of the paragraph quoted in the notes to *The Waste Land,* no quotations survive the whole. This chaconne for unaccompanied violin has no extra-philosophical attractions; Eliot has noted how by contrast "Bergson's exciting promise of immortality" has "a somewhat meretricious captivation," and how a Rousseau "has proved an eternal source of mischief and inspiration," whereas Bradley, with "the melancholy grace, the languid mastery, of the late product" has "expounded one type of philosophy with such consummate ability that it will probably not survive him." This man who lacked "the permanence of the pre-Socratics, of all imperfect things," exerted his permanent fascination for Eliot's temperament precisely through his ability to touch every aspect of thought and feeling that concerned his endeavour while remaining within the proper limits of prose; the purple patch is a confession of insufficiency. If he remains on the thin ice of phenomenology, he is phenomenology's most accomplished skater, producing a book conformed, in everything but its mode of organization, to the most austere canons of art: like Brancusi's bird which is made out of polished bronze and contains no hint of a compromise with feathers.

It was not unnatural, in a world which contained so

satisfying a book, to resolve that it was not the poet's business to think; not only because Bradley had nullified all trenchant thought as abrupt and partial, but because he had disqualified "responsible" thought for poetry by demonstrating that like poetry it is a full-time occupation, leading not to apothegms but to a decantation of verbal substances that will satisfactorily fill up the voids in mental existence, though with a different filler than the poet's. The philosopher does not start, Bradley insists, with certain axioms from which he reasons downward toward the familiar; he starts, like the poet in Eliot's account, with a want to be satisfied, for him a theoretical want, a desire "to find a way of thinking about facts in general which is free from contradiction."

> It is assumed that, if my thought is satisfied with itself, I have, with this, truth and reality. But as to what will satisfy I have, of course, no knowledge in advance. My object is to get before me what will content a certain felt need, but the way and the means are to be discovered only by trial and rejection.

Bradley's way is the way of satisfying *those* needs; the needs a poet sets out to satisfy are different needs, needs that will be satisfied by the existence of the unique particular poem toward which he is obscurely impelled. For either one to borrow from the other's methods is to avail himself of an illegitimate short cut: illegitimate because he will take satisfaction in the result only by a perpetuated self-deceit. The radical criticism of *Adonais* is that it fails to exercise that kind of intelligence "of which an important function is the discernment of exactly what, and how much, we feel in any given situation."

We can learn from Bradley's drily impassioned style that he took the model of clarity to be not mathematical process but an impersonal human being talking. One may profitably contrast *Appearance and Reality* with the Whitehead and Russell *Principia Mathematica,* a book to be worked through rather than read. (Eliot worked far enough through it to find the pronouncement with which he once startled a hasty correspondent in *The Athenaeum.*)* Nor on the other hand does his method at all resemble that of Santayana, whose extra-philosophic impulses not only begat a novel, but suffused his essays with personality. Bradley disciplined philosophy until it gave his powers full satisfaction. He arrives at no conclusions, at no incitements to action. As late as 1924 Eliot supposed that his influence would grow and spread, with that of Henry James and Sir James Frazer, in a future whose characteristic sensibility might be "infinitely more disillusioned" than that of Shaw, or Thomas Hardy, or Anatole France, perhaps "harder and more orderly: but throbbing at a higher rate of vibration with the agony of spiritual life." Alas, he was insufficiently disillusioned to guess that the "one or two or more literary generations" on whose behalf he prophesied would find Freud and Marx more to their taste.

---

*This man deserves notice as a pioneer in the dangerous game of supposing that Eliot's informality of critical organization bespeaks a genteel indifference to logic. He objected that an Eliotic generalization was belied by Eliot's own practice, and was picked off his limb by a nicely aimed citation of Whitehead and Russell on the paradox of the Cretan liar. The moral is clearly that the next man who wishes to make that particular protest will have to outflank the entire *Principia Mathematica* first, but this moral has not been heeded.

II. IN THE VORTEX

Chronology
  Merton College, Oxford, 1915.
    Read Aristotle with Professor Joachim.
    Aunt Helen
    Morning at the Window
    The Boston Evening Transcript
    Cousin Nancy
    Mr. Apollinax
    Hysteria
    Married Vivien Haigh-Wood, July, 1915.
    Prufrock published June, 1915. Commencement of frequent publication.
  London, 1915–1916.
    Teaching, book reviewing.
    Bradley thesis completed.
  London, 1917–1920.
    Work in Lloyd's Bank.
    French poems written.
    Quatrain poems written.
    Prufrock and Other Observations published June, 1917.
    Associated with *The Egoist,* 1917–1919.
    Reviewing for *New Statesman, Athenaeum.*
    "Tradition and the Individual Talent," 1919.
    Gerontion, 1919.
    Poems published 1920.

SATIRES

i

Ezra Pound to Harriet Monroe, 1914–1915.

London, 22 September.
An American called Eliot called this P.M. I think he has some sense tho he has not yet sent me any verse. . . .

★　　★　　★

London, 30 September.
. . . I was jolly well right about Eliot. He has sent in the best poem I have yet had or seen from an American. PRAY GOD IT BE NOT A SINGLE AND UNIQUE SUCCESS. He has taken it back to get it ready for the press and you shall have it in a few days.

He is the only American I know of who has made what I can call adequate preparation for writing. He has actually trained himself *and* modernized himself *on his own*. The rest of the *promising young* have done one or the other but never both (most of the swine have done neither). It is such a comfort to meet a man and not have to tell him to wash his face, wipe his feet, and remember the date (1914) on the calendar.

★　　★　　★

London, October.
Here is the Eliot poem. The most interesting contribution I've had from an American.
P.S. Hope you'll get it *in* soon.

★　　★　　★

London, 9 November.

Your objection to Eliot is the climax. . . .

No, most emphatically I will not ask Eliot to write down to any audience whatsoever. I dare say my instinct was sound enough when I volunteered to quit the magazine quietly about a year ago. Neither will I send you Eliot's address in order that he may be insulted. . . .

★ ★ ★

Coleman's Hatch, 31 January (1915).
. . . "Mr. Prufrock" does not "go off at the end." It is a portrait of failure, or of a character which fails, and it would be false art to make it end on a note of triumph. . . . A portrait satire on futility can't end by turning that quint-essence of futility, Mr. P., into a reformed character breathing out fire and ozone. . . . I assure you it is better, "more unique," than the other poems of Eliot which I have seen. Also that he is quite *intelligent* (an adjective which is seldom in my mouth). . . .

★ ★ ★

London, 10 April.

. . . *Do* get on with that Eliot. . . .

———————

The four-year-old *Love Song of J. Alfred Prufrock,* by "Mr. T. S. Eliot, a young American poet resident in England," was at length published in *Poetry* for June, 1915, as end-piece to an issue led off by one Ajan Syrian, a poet with considerably more biography to his credit (". . . born twenty-eight years ago on the Syrian desert, has studied at Columbia University, and is now the adopted son and employee of Mr. Gajor M. Berugjian of Brooklyn.") The following month Wyndham Lewis published *Preludes* and *Rhapsody on a Windy Night* in *Blast,* where the company was more austere. By September Pound had placed *Portrait of a Lady* in Alfred Kreymborg's *Others;* in October *Poetry* used three more poems; in November five appeared in Pound's *Catholic Anthology.* By June, 1917,

The Egoist Ltd. had published *Prufrock and Other Observations,* forty pages in stiff buff paper wrappers; the same month Eliot was installed as assistant editor of Harriet Weaver's *The Egoist,* the paper which had serialized *Tarr* and *Portrait of the Artist as a Young Man.* Glacial masses appeared to be shifting. It did not become evident until about 1920 that the Great London Vortex had been early dissipated by war, and that what had been going on for several years—more a work of publishing than of creating—had been kept moving chiefly by Pound's manic energy.

Eliot, equipped, in Pound's phrase, with "all the disadvantages of a symmetrical education," tumbled into the Vortex by chance. Since the autumn of 1911 he had been pursuing graduate study at Harvard, employed as part-time instructor and devoting his attention not to poetry but to metaphysics, logic, psychology, philosophy, Sanskrit and Pali. After three years he went abroad as a Frederick Sheldon Travelling Fellow, and established residence at Marburg University in Germany, there to observe the conviction with which Professor Eucken pounded the table, exclaiming *Was ist Geist? Geist ist. . . .* In undertaking graduate study in Germany Eliot was pursuing the traditional course for distinguished Harvard scholars; the supremacy of German scholarship was one of the West's unwaning verities, like the Five-foot Shelf and the Austro-Hungarian Empire. The years ahead held their normal prospect of return to Harvard and the slow accumulation of academic distinction: the monograph, the definitive treatise. Early in the summer of Eliot's arrival at Marburg the Archduke Franz Ferdinand was assassinated at Sarajevo.

Three weeks after the outbreak of the war Eliot had made his way to England, where he proposed to redeem some of the wreckage of the academic year. The first visit to Ezra Pound's triangular flat, on September 22nd, was merely an incident in a year devoted to reading the Posterior Analytics with Professor Joachim at Merton College, Oxford. The following July he was married to an Englishwoman, Miss Vivien Haigh-Wood, and looking about for employment. Apparently the idea of an academic career was only slowly abandoned. The Bradley thesis was finished, sent back to Harvard, and accepted in partial fulfilment of the requirements for the doctorate. But that, in 1916, was his last academic gesture. Cut off from return to Harvard by the war, he never completed the formalities nor received the degree.

For the next ten years this at first involuntary expatriate was condemned to labour at no profession in particular under constant financial strain. We hear of him teaching French, mathematics, history, geography, drawing and swimming at High Wycombe Grammar School for a stipend of £140 and one meal a day; undertaking for a year comparable labours at Highgate Junior School, for £160 plus dinner and tea; collecting book reviewer's crumbs from the *International Journal of Ethics* and the *New Statesman* (titles like *Theism and Humanism, Social Adaptation, The Ultimate Belief, Philosophy and War*); preparing and delivering during two years some sixty-five extension lectures on French and English literature; finally entering the foreign exchange department of Lloyd's Bank (£120 per annum to start, no meals). When the United States Navy tendered him a medical rejection in 1918 he had for some years been working fifteen hours a day. It is not surprising that the poetic output of his first five years in England is represented in the collected volume by no more than eighteen pages, and those not among his most vital.

ii

His first poems since *La Figlia che Piange* were a group of six written at Oxford in 1915, the sequence that runs from *Morning at the Window* to *Hysteria*. They are smart and brief, and they do without seductive incantation. Each gets under way with an air of syntactic orthodoxy—

They are rattling breakfast plates in basement kitchens—

whose matter-of-factness both protects and offsets the fantastic dream-imagery into which the first sentence invariably dissolves:

> I am aware of the damp souls of housemaids
> Sprouting despondently at area gates.

The method is quite unlike that of the *Preludes,* in which the mode of perception is elusive from the outset:

> The winter evening settles down
> With smell of steak in passageways. . . .

Here, in the tradition of Eliot's characteristically sidelong openings, an abstraction governs a metaphoric verb, qualified by a "with" the exact sense of which is unspecifiable, and assisted by a muted, confident rhythm which almost conceals the audacity of diminishing so bland a generalization into so specialized and isolated an instance. The next line—"Six o'clock"—has more the air of reflection than of notation; the next, "The burnt-out ends of smoky days," traffics, with poised opportunism, in "that surprise which has been one of the most important means of poetic effect since Homer." When we come to notation at last—

> And at the corner of the street
> A lonely cab-horse steams and stamps—

the effect of "lonely" is to suffuse the cab-horse with feelings which "single" would not evoke; he looms, portentous and pathetic, incorporated into a whole of emotion, reflection and perception, simultaneously giving and receiving significance ("In immediate experience the subject and object are one.").

In *Morning at the Window,* on the other hand, the damp souls of housemaids are created by the wit of the observer out of elements not all of which are present before him; it is impossible to be sure just what he sees. Nor is his mood evoked directly; it is deducible from the manner in which he feels it relevant to apply his faintly exacerbated cleverness. The Oxford poems abandon empathy for a virtuosity from which speaker and reader are alike detached. In a detail like

When evening quickens faintly in the street,
Wakening the appetites of life in some
And to others bringing the *Boston Evening Transcript,**

we are waved back by that patronizing "faintly," and watch
from a vantage-point outside the poem this notion of a faint
quickening spread down like a stain through the languid
puppet-world of "some" and "others," "the appetites of life,"
we are convinced, as sadly mechanical as the embalmed detachment of those who unfolding the evening paper partake of
appetites at second-hand.

This point is clearly made at the climax of the poem about
Aunt Helen, out of deference to whose death

The shutters were drawn and the undertaker wiped his feet—
He was aware that this sort of thing had occurred before.

After she has gone, certain other entelechies likewise manifest
transience:

But shortly afterwards the parrot died too;

certain things endure:

The Dresden clock continued ticking on the mantelpiece;

and certain novelties of behaviour are asserted:

And the footman sat upon the dining-table
Holding the second housemaid on his knees—
Who had always been so careful while her mistress lived.

This Bostonian orgy (for Boston fulfils itself in many ways)
brings to epiphany such a conception of the appetites of life as
Boston permits itself. Aunt Helen in life, it is plain, inhibited
no Dionysius. Her cardboard propriety held at bay a cardboard tiger; like Miss Nancy Ellicot's aunts who

were not quite sure how they felt about it
But they knew that it was modern.

*For years the American edition of *Murder in the Cathedral* carried on its
jacket a severe testimonial from the *Boston Evening Transcript:* "Mr. Eliot
makes himself much clearer in this work than he has in the past."

The Oxford poems are experiments with a revised satiric mechanism; the French poems which followed them carry the deliberate desiccation of language further, by confining themselves to a vocabulary and idiom which, at least in a foreigner's hands, are unlikely to trouble precision with unexpected resonances. Thus the honeymooners

> . . . restent sur le dos écartant les genoux
> De quatre jambes molles tout gonflées de morsures.
> On relève le drap pour mieux égratigner.

The arid, Eliot noted in 1917, is a less dangerous path for poetry than the vague. *Lune de Miel* doesn't vibrate with contempt for the tourists from Terre Haute; it sets forth with spare detachment the elements of a complex confrontation. It constates with witty passion; it is devoid of facility. The modified Alexandrines measure out the elements of the poem with a severe dignity for which there is no English metrical equivalent; and the scientific dryness of the French declarative sentence—"Ils restent sur le dos," where in English one would have to write "they lie on their backs"—helps strip our perception of empathic quiverings, either of sympathy or revulsion.*

> Ils vont prendre le train de huit heures
> Prolonger leurs misères de Padoue à Milan
> Où se trouvent la Cène, et un restaurant pas cher.

"The Last Supper," and an inexpensive restaurant; the collocation, governed by an impersonal "ou se trouvent," was discoverable in Baedeker before it became the formula for the tourists' dissipation of attention. If they are mocked by anything, it is by their incapacity for Baedeker's dispassionate compendiousness, like a metaphysical poet's. With fine impartiality, Baedeker dispenses his financial advice; as for the honeymooner,

---

*This experiment with the French declarative sentence no doubt underwrote at least one remarkable detail in *The Waste Land*:
> At the violet hour, when the eyes and back
> Turn upward from the desk. . . .

Lui pense aux pourboires, et rédige son bilan.*

The word "pense" betrays him; "pourboires" do not coexist in his attention with "The Last Supper," in a condition of benevolent neutrality.

> Et Saint Apollinaire, raide et ascétique,
> Vieille usine désaffectée de Dieu, tient encore
> Dans ses pierres écroulantes la forme précise de Byzance.

Though the stones crumble, the form persists; the delicate shift of focus from the Saint himself to his church near Ravenna ("raide et ascétique, vieille usine désaffectée de Dieu" would apply to either) helps circumscribe and enrich a laconic terminal image: that which continues to be true although the tourists who left by the eight o'clock train did not perceive it. And the means by which Saint Apollinaire en Classe enounces cultural history rhymes with the method of the poem itself, the implication never escaping from its visible embodiment. Like the Baedeker paraphrases in the poem, at Saint Apollinaire "la forme précise de Byzance" is not labelled, it is simply present.

Lune de Miel, though far from being one of Eliot's considerable poems, is the first to discover an appropriate method and employ it without irrelevance, deviation, incidental felicity, or local impenetrability. This is a more important critical point than the fact that its personages are treated with no special compassion. They are bodies circulating within the sufficient system of the poem itself, which does not appropriate them for ridicule but contains them as elements in its own economy. Its objectivity is more efficacious than the studied insensibility of

> The worlds revolve like ancient women
> Gathering fuel in vacant lots

*"I hope I shall not be destroying some sentimental illusion if I record that to my surprise I remarked that my companion entered most scrupulously in a small notebook the day's expenses. This he would do in the evening at a café table when we had our night-cap. There was not much more he could spend before he got to bed."

—Wyndham Lewis, on travelling with Eliot.

(the prologue to which is "Wipe your hand across your mouth, and laugh"). Its formality, compatible with the opening play on "les Pays-Bas" and Terre Haute, or the grave specification of "deux centaines de punaises"—two hundred fleas, not an insupportable thousand—is in touch with a more fecund universe of suggestion than

> Miss Helen Slingsby was my maiden aunt,
> And lived in a small house near a fashionable square
> Cared for by servants to the number of four.

Yet its suggestiveness inheres in the materials liberated by the aridity of expression, not in the auras and resonances of words. Even the poem's one metaphor, "Vieille usine désaffectée de Dieu," is of a very different order from the quip about the damp souls of housemaids sprouting.

Not long after the publication of *Lune de Miel* we find Eliot commenting on the poetic of Jean de Bosschère, whose methods are untainted by "charming flirtation with obscure, semiphilosophic sentiments." Unlike a poet whose "utensils are provided with adjectives which connect them with human emotions—'the gentle bed,' 'you my well-trampled boots,'" de Bosschère can write

> Il est l'époux de feu
> L'aimé des flammes,

without permitting either "époux" or "aimé" any sentimental associations.

> M. de Bosschère is in fact almost a pure intellectual; leaving, as it were disdainfully, our emotions to form as they will round the situation which his brain has selected. The important thing is not how we are to feel about it, but how it is. De Bosschère's austerity is terrifying.

Prufrock's "yellow smoke that rubs its muzzle on the windowpanes" has by now been left far behind; the whimsical *trouvaille*, elaborated by incantation, is being superseded by a more taxing, more orderly, more philosophic procedure for registering simultaneously feeling and perception. Eliot praises de Bosschère's

> . . . obstinate refusal to adulterate his poetic emotions with ordinary human emotions. Instead of refining ordinary human emotions (and I do not mean tepid human emotions, but human however intense—in the crude living state) he aims direct at emotions of art.★ He thereby limits the number of his readers, and leaves the majority groping for a clue which does not exist. The effect is sometimes an intense frigidity which I find altogether admirable.

The man who wrote that had the principles of *The Waste Land* in his grasp.

When a poet has reached a certain degree of deliberateness, what interests him about a newly interesting "model" is not what it feels like but how it works. Eliot was not possessed by Gautier in 1917 as he had been by Laforgue in 1910; Gautier was a maker of clocks, the insides of which merited examining. Eliot touches on Gautier's quatrains in the course of explaining what is meant by perfecting a method; he is rebuking a *Times Literary Supplement* dismissal of Professionalism as "a device for making things easy."

> The writer in *The Times,* belittling technique, appears to identify technique with what may be learned from a manual of prosody. This is making technique easy. If mathematics consisted in learning the multiplication table up to 1,000,000 that would be making mathematics easy. Technique is more volatile; it can only be learned, the more difficult part of it, by absorption. Try to put into a sequence of simple quatrains the syntactic variety of Gautier or Blake, or compare these two with A. E. Housman. Surely professionalism in art is hard work on style with singleness of purpose.

Following the tip and comparing these two with A. E. Housman, we discover that Housman has no curiosity concerning the resources of the quatrain, that he is content to use it over

★Cf. "The effect of a work of art upon the person who enjoys it is an experience different in kind from any experience not of art."—"Tradition and the Individual Talent," written two years after the article about de Bosschère.

and over—not without a certain Stoical smugness—as a four-sided hollow box in which youthful aspiration can be shut away:

> By brooks too broad for leaping
>   The lightfoot boys are laid;
> The rose-lipt girls are sleeping
>   In fields where roses fade.

Sentences terminate as predictably as lives, always on the rhyme-word; antitheses are resolved with unfailing symmetry; the guillotine rises and descends, chronometrically, in oiled grooves. Eliot, on the other hand, concerns himself with a "continuous variety," syntactic and otherwise, such as the English quatrain has seldom been called upon to support. In *The Hippopotamus* there is a surprise around every corner.

> The broad-backed hippopotamus
> Rests on his belly in the mud;

The ludicrous is beginning to stir; "broad-backed" sounded for a moment like a Homeric epithet. But this hero "rests" (as a boulder in a cow-pasture, perhaps, or in repose after labours?); and on his belly; and in the mud (not a Housman rhyme-word).

> Although he seems so firm to us

(of all the words expressive of substantiality, "firm," with its Victorian moral overtones, is the most precarious that could have been selected.)

> He is merely flesh and blood.

(So it was not metrical exigency that threw "to us" into a rhyming position; this behemoth is *one of us*. Yet we are not sure whether or not to be unsettled by that "merely.")

> Flesh and blood is weak and frail

(This *sorites* appears to be leading us away from the hippo; "frail" would bracket him with Whistler's "Mother.")

> Susceptible to nervous shock

(Only six lines ago he squatted in broad-backed repose like—
well, like a hippopotamus.)

> While the True Church can never fail
> For it is based upon a rock.

(Any theologian worth his salt would argue, under pressure,
that the True Church is more substantial than a hippopotamus,
though he might not choose the assignment, or lead up to the
proof in quite this way.)

> The hippo's feeble steps may err

(His legs do seem insufficient; as for "err," it means "wander";
so the brute is condemned not merely to move with difficulty,
but to waste much of his motion—)

> In compassing material ends

(an unexpectedly philosophic way of putting it; but then it is
to be granted that all sentient motion has an object in view,
even that of a hippopotamus. It is at least clear that the ends of
the unerring Church are immaterial; we await with confidence
some expression of eternal sapience)—

> While the True Church need never stir
> To gather in its dividends.

In subsequent stanzas we see the Hippopotamus Frustrated, the
Hippopotamus as Troubadour, the Hippopotamus About His
Business; he is an engaging creature, nearly as ridiculous as a
human being; the Church, meanwhile, transcends, as it ought,
human limitations, at one with God, sleeping and feeding at
once. Finally the Hippopotamus ascends like a complacent
blimp, to take his place, "by all the martyr'd virgins kist," in
an economy that permits "performing on a harp of gold";
and we discover with surprise a new gravity of cadence that
sets the three final stanzas to the tune of "Old Hundredth"—

> While the True Church remains below
> Wrapt in the old miasmal mist.

The elegance of the quatrains, we discern, has been superimposed on the theology of Billy Sunday; and if the poem is perhaps the objective correlative of the smirk on the face of young Possum, it is, detail by detail, a triumph of the inventive intelligence over the metric of the *Bay State Hymn Book*.

Mr. Eliot's Sunday Morning Service carries to a further extreme similar principles of construction, juxtaposing and intercutting four perspectives on Christian experience: the Christ of Greek theologians and the patristic controversialists ("In the beginning was the Word"); the Christ of Pre-Raphaelite iconography, painted in the act of receiving John's baptism by water

> (The wilderness is cracked and browned
> But through the water pale and thin
> Still shine the unoffending feet);

the nonconformist Christians of "invisible and dim" devoutness, their most solemn ritual the taking up of the collection; and ape-neck Sweeney, indifferent to these bewildering matters, paddling in his bath of a Sunday morning. Each has one point in common with its neighbour. The painted Christ stands in baptismal water, Sweeney sits in his secular font, shifting from ham to ham. As Sweeney stirs water, so do "the masters of the subtle schools" agitate terminological questions. As these masters—notably the castrated Origen—are made eunuchs for the kingdom of heaven's sake, so the bees along the garden-wall do the "blest office of the epicene," distributing pollen from flower to flower. Thus from the opening "polyphiloprogenitive" run several lines of generation: the conception by a virgin *secundum carnem* which brought into being the embodied God with the "unoffending feet"; the neo-Platonic superfetation of essences descending from the Word; the filiation of concepts sponsored by the "sapient sutlers" of patristic controversy; the reproduction of flowers assisted by the bees' "hairy bellies"; and the generation, also *secundum carnem,* of an increasingly carnal humanity: Origen, the painter, the sable presbyters and their "red and pustular" offspring, Sweeney who laves his own hide. In the concluding stanza Sweeney at one end of the scale is juxtaposed with the intellectual anchor-men at the other:

> The masters of the subtle schools
> Are controversial, polymath.

It isn't a contrast that particularly discredits either party.

Plainly, the quatrain, like Pope's couplets, is in Eliot's usage primarily a vehicle for sudden juxtapositions, an aristocratic form devoid alike of *The Ecstasie's* ceremonious passion and the ballads' ritual simplicities. These poems constitute an attempt to create a satiric medium for twentieth-century usage, nurtured by the perception that satire in verse works by assembling a crazy-quilt of detail, each detail an unchallengeable fact (everything in *Mr. Eliot's Sunday Morning Service,* from the sable presbyters to the bees' hairy bellies, exists on the plane of fact). The satiric decasyllabic couplet, of course, implies a mock-heroic convention. Eliot, reversing the telescope, manufactures in octosyllabic quatrains a convention of mock-casualness. The method of *Whispers of Immortality,* the most celebrated of the quatrain poems, is to shift at mid-point from one historic limit of the quatrain to the other; from the grave meditative idiom of Donne or Lord Herbert of Cherbury—

> Webster was much possessed by death
> And saw the skull beneath the skin

—to a brave *fin-de-siècle* smartness:

> Grishkin is nice; her Russian eye
> In underlined for emphasis.

The "Whispers" in the title effects a sinister inflection of Wordsworth's bucolic "Intimations"; located midway in time between Webster and Grishkin, between a world dead and one powerless to be born, Wordsworth contrived cosmic exhilarations ("Everything that is is blest") out of the undeniable fact that he didn't, in middle life, feel as blest as he believed he once had. If he refused to consider "the skull beneath the skin," neither would he have known what to make of Grishkin. In the ages of metaphysical intuition, however,

> Webster was much possessed by death:

—possessed as by a lover, or by a devil?—

> And breastless creatures under ground
> Leaned backward with a lipless grin,

adopting postures of compliant sexuality in

> a fine and private place,
> But none, I think, do there embrace.

His morbid delectation—thought clinging round dead limbs —was but a perversion of a fact, that the vehicle of thought is the corrupting body; lusts and luxuries, however cerebral, are "tightened" with a sensation of physical tension. Webster was the contemporary of Donne, who preached in his shroud and imagined his own skeleton exhumed with "a bracelet of bright hair about the bone"; but the living body, however puzzling its role, is never for Donne an occasion of morbidity or an impediment to spiritual joys. ("They are ours, though they're not wee, Wee are / the intelligences, they the spheare.")

> Donne, I suppose, was such another
> Who found no substitute for sense,
> To seize and clutch and penetrate;

The three sequential verbs create their predicate; but the predicate, not being specified, may as well be metaphorical as personal; Donne's understanding came through his sense, though it ached to transcend the senses; he was not "controversial, polymath," a "religious caterpillar" beclouding himself with a cocoon of deductions or (though a preacher) an "enervate Origen" doing the "blest office of the epicene."

> He knew the anguish of the marrow
> The ague of the skeleton;
> No contact possible to flesh
> Allayed the fever of the bone.

The bone's fever is to know; as the finite centres cry out from their blood heat for union and communion. Donne dared more than Prufrock, but (except as an artist) accomplished no more; his words

> suggest unmistakably the awful separation between potential passion and any actualization possible in life. They indicate also the indestructible barriers between one human being and another.

Eliot wrote those sentences about Stendhal and Flaubert; but his preamble makes it clear that he means them to be of general application to any artist honest enough to "dispense with atmosphere" and "strip the world," any man of "more than the common intensity of feeling, of passion."

> It is this intensity, precisely, and consequent discontent with the inevitable inadequacy of actual living to the passionate capacity, which drove them to art and to analysis. The surface of existence coagulates into lumps, which look like important simple feelings, which are identified by names as feelings, which the patient analyst disintegrates into more complex and trifling, but ultimately, if he goes far enough, into various canalizations of something again simple, terrible and unknown.

The second half of the poem, consequently, brings us to Grishkin, a world that awaits stripping;

> Uncorseted, her friendly bust
> Gives promise of pneumatic bliss.

"Pneumatic," of course, evokes by its etymology the things of the spirit, though it is unlikely that Grishkin is one of the "martyr'd virgins." And her presence reduces those "important simple feelings" which coagulated on the surface of existence to baffle Prufrock, into something "simple, terrible and unknown":

> The couched Brazilian jaguar. . . .

She is an opportunity for a Donne; her charms defy indifference; they abound, tightening lusts and luxuries into a concreteness to which Abstract Entities are merely external, circumambulant; "one might almost say her body thought," if any thought is indeed to be predicated. But her superior corporeality polarizes the superior delicacy of such people as we are, of a legation of Prufrocks (inheritors of Wordsworth's poetic chastity), which

> crawls between dry ribs*

as between dry sheets, or as a spider in a rib-cage, the bone feverless,

> To keep our metaphysics warm.

For Grishkin abolishes that which is beyond the physical, and "our lot" prizes nothing else. A passage from Bradley's "Principles of Logic" which Eliot quoted in a *New Statesman* review the year before this poem was published may be invoked as its unofficial epigraph:

> That the glory of this world is appearance leaves the world more glorious if we feel it is a show of some fuller splendour; but the sensuous curtain is a deception and a cheat—if it hides some colourless movement of atoms, some spectral woof of impalpable abstractions, or unearthly ballet of bloodless categories.

These three poems, the best of the seven poems in quatrains (since *Sweeney Among the Nightingales,* their peer in local accomplishment, is deliberately involved in Eliot's besetting vice, a never wholly penetrable ambiguity about what is supposed to be happening): these three poems concentrate in miniature Eliot's methodological activity of the early London years. They advance on the Harvard poems in this way: they are constructed out of facts, out of epigrams which are tempered facts, and out of words which attest to the substantiality of fact. Not every fact, however; as Pound noted in the *Pisan Cantos,* what Mr. Eliot "missed, after all, in composing his vignette" was the personal identity of Grishkin, as conveyed by a photograph of her face. The achievement remains. At the core of the Harvard poems—of *Prufrock* or the *Preludes*—is reverie; the

---

*Le squelette était invisible
Au temps heureux de l'Art païen.

flow of a participant's musings. The Oxford poems turn on an observer's opinions and valuations; what is observed defines the angle of view of an observer. The best of the quatrain poems are self-sufficient in a new way, poetic mechanisms whose parts circulate about one another, while the poet rests invisible.

CRITICISM

i

These poems are slighter work, however, than his critical achievement of the same period. In the five years, 1917–1921, Eliot, in some seventy pieces of critical prose, some of them hasty, some peripheral, many of them incidental to a long struggle to live by his pen, carried out what must be the most arduous, the most concentrated critical labour of which detailed record exists: nothing less than a rethinking, in the specific terms exacted by conscientious book reviewing, of the traditional heritage of English letters. Coleridge accumulated his millions of words more easily; he had ideas to lighten them. Arnold in his lifetime did not come to grips with so many minutiae. Johnson said well what he thought on principle. Eliot looked with novel intensity at everything that came his way. "Who, for instance," he asked in 1918, "has a first-hand opinion of Shakespeare? Yet I have no doubt that much could be learned by a serious study of that semi-mythical figure " Typically, Eliot wrote no systematic study of that semi-mythical figure; chance brought him for review a second-rate book on *Hamlet,* which precipitated some six pages of greater concentrated relevance than would be six pages or sixty of a conceivable systematic survey. It is the same with essay after essay, month after month, sometimes week after week, for five years, an incredible fecundity of insight marshalled into gnomic paragraphs that have precipitated, in the slim selection called *The Sacred Wood* (1920) and the even slimmer culling incorporated into the much fatter *Selected Essays*, that view of the literature of the past which the twentieth century recognizes as peculiarly its own. There is not often reason to be grateful that a man of genius was so much distracted from his chief vocation by "early necessity of earning small sums quickly."

The elimination of book-reviewing paraphernalia from the familiar selected volumes has led readers to suppose that the author chose his angles of approach, and that the essays were conceived as chapters in a comprehensive critical message delivered by Mr. Eliot to posterity. To this impression the gnomic gravity of deliverance has also contributed. The rays of light are so exactly defined that we are tempted to calculate the position of the sun. It is worth emphasizing that, with numerically insignificant exceptions of which "Tradition and the Individual Talent" is the most important, Eliot's essays, both the few that have been collected and the hundreds that have not, were commissioned by editors who sent along something for review; that the compression of style arose largely from the necessity for fitting the perspectives opened up by the job in hand into the few paragraphs a periodical like *The Athenaeum* could spare; that the frequently complex tone is related with ironic sensitivity to what the *Athenaeum* or *Egoist* reader expected reviewing to sound like; and that the author, far from enjoying acclaim as the most distinguished man of letters in England, was in the years of his most vital critical activity a virtually anonymous foreigner aged about thirty.

Book-reviewing, for a brittle and fussy public leafing through weekly papers, is an essentially absurd activity. Wyndham Lewis blasted the British "life of looker-on," and cursed those who would "hang over this manifesto with silly canines exposed." The manifesto, of course, was so phrased as to invoke that glaciating grin: not a lapse of strategy, since one can't enlighten the grinner anyhow, but an occasion for that tableau grimace of defiance which was Lewis' way of bringing home to his dozen or so sympathetic readers one of the essential facts in any modern cultural situation: their own isolation in a world of performing dolls. It requires a unique personality to sustain Pound's infinite variations on (his own paraphrase): "Joyce is a writer, GODDAMN your eyes. Joyce is a writer, I tell you Joyce etc. etc. Lewis can paint, Gaudier knows a stone from milk-pudding. WIPE your feet!!!!!" The Pound method remains a tempting one, requiring as it does a minimum of guile and inhibition. Mr. Pound has recalled an occasion, perhaps around 1916, when Eliot was "about to commit a rash act." He had written several pages of untrammelled shillelagh-swinging, and brought them round to 5 Holland Place Chambers for scrutiny. The response was prophetic: "That's not your style at all. You let *me* throw the bricks through the front window. You go in at the back door and take out the swag."

The method Eliot discovered—how consciously there is no telling—was to capitalize on his anonymity and play a role. The role depended on the magazine; once assumed, it permitted him the freedom of a whimsical but purposeful *Poltergeist*. For *The Egoist,* as Assistant Editor at £1 a week, he adopted, on behalf of a very small body of readers who were not deterred by novelty but uncertain in what it consisted, a tone of deft buffoonery

> . . . but there is a simple sincerity which strikes out a good line here and there ("when I am old and quite worn out") and which would stand the author in good stead if he would read the right things and work hard.

There is no evidence that Eliot wrote this sentence from the May, 1918, "Shorter Notices." Its knowing mimicry of British weekly reviewing belongs to the corporate personality of the magazine. This description of the 1916–1917 Georgian anthology is unquestionably by Eliot:

> . . . Mr. Squire slips in, referring to a house as a "mean edifice."

. . . Mr. Graves has a hale and hearty daintiness. Mr. Gibson asks, "we, how shall we . . ." etc. Messrs. Baring and Asquith, in war poems, both employ the word "oriflamme." Mr. Drinkwater says, "Hist!" . . .

The Egoist also anthologized the wisdom of its contemporaries:

At a moment like this we should try to think clearly.
—The Times.
The chief pillars of Shakespeare's fame are not his English historical plays.
—The Times.

John Milton was a great poet.
—The Times

On one occasion Eliot concocted five outrageous Letters to the Editor, to fill up space:

. . . There was a serious and instructive article on Constantinople by a Mr. Symons which I greatly enjoyed. It is good for us to keep our minds open and liberal by contemplation of foreign ways, and though the *danse du ventre* is repellent to the British imagination, we ought to know that these things exist. I cannot speak so pleasantly of Mr. Lewis's . . .
CHARLES JAMES GRIMBLE
The Vicarage, Leays.

Neither the Rev. Mr. Grimble, nor "J. A. D. Spence, Thridlington Grammar School" (who wrote to deplore Pound's attempted rehabilitation of Ovid) nor "Charles Augustus Coneybeare, The Carlton Club, Liverpool" ("I am accustomed to more documentation; I like to know where authors get their ideas from"), nor even "Muriel A. Schwarz, 60 Alexandra Gardens, Hampstead, N.W.," would have been recognized by *Egoist* readers as one of themselves; the little family of *Egoist* readers included *inter alia* the followers of the Contributing Editor, Miss Dora Marsden, who occupied the first pages of every issue with a new instalment of her dogged philosophical cliff-hanger, *Lingual Psychology*; also, whatever suffragette sympathizers, or less definable holders of advanced political views, had followed the paper from its earlier phase as

The New Freewoman; and, of course, the friends and acquaint-
ances of the regular contributors. It was not for a cross-section
of *The Times*-reading British public that Eliot with a little
quotation assisted Amy Lowell to display her Chautauqua
sensibility:

> . . . But Miss Lowell's words are well trained: and fly obediently
> from trope to trope at her bidding. Thus *Poetry* was to be "a
> forum in which youth could thrash out its ideas, and succeed or
> fail according to its deserts, unhampered by the damp blanket of
> obscurity."

(He also quotes: "The whole farming industry of New England
had been knocked on the head by the opening up of the West,"
and the sublimely fatuous "Carl Sandburg's father was a
Swedish immigrant whose real name was August Johnson."
To force the subject to expose himself, was his summary, three
years later, of the ideal critical procedure.) The pages of *The
Egoist* have a familial intimacy; and in his steady polemic
against the *faux-moderne*, Eliot with incomparable deftness of
phrase manœuvres into the light cliché after cliché which he is
confident thirty or forty readers will find amusing. We even
discover him begging leave to state in the correspondence
columns, ". . . (in response to numerous inquiries) that to the
best of my knowledge and belief Captain Arthur Eliot, joint
author of 'The Better 'Ole,' is not, roughly speaking, a member
of my family."

The Egoist reviews were often satiric in method. In a long
sequence of reviews written for Middleton Murry's *Athenaeum*,
Eliot extended and generalized his *Egoist* manner into what was
to be, until fame overtook him, his fundamental critical strategy: a close and knowing mimicry of the respectable. So
thoroughly did he master this technique that he was able to
compose two of his most important and blandly subversive
essays, "Andrew Marvell" and "The Metaphysical Poets,"
within the confines of reviewing commissions from *The Times
Literary Supplement* itself. The rhetorical layout of essay after
essay can best be described as a parody of official British literary

discussion: its asperities, its pontification, its distinctions that do not distinguish, its vacuous ritual of familiar quotations and bathetic solemnities. The texture of an Eliot review is almost indistinguishable from that of its neighbours; only the argument, and the tone derived from an extreme economy of phrase, are steadily subversive.

The well-known "Euripides and Professor Murray"* is a *tour de force* in this manner:

> Professor Murray has simply interposed between ourselves and Euripides a barrier more impenetrable than the Greek language. We do not reproach him for preferring, apparently, Euripides to Aeschylus. But if he does, he should at least appreciate Euripides. . . .

These sentences catch exactly the frigid appeal to classical snobbery which used to be a part of *The Times'* stock in trade. To a conventional review reader they make their point with a soothing obviousness. To a reader who had progressed to the stage of dissatisfaction with the *TLS* they would yield a complex comic satisfaction.

This subversive cooperation with what the reader expects was not only a means of walking in the back door the better to take away the swag; it also very greatly contributed to defining Eliot's role both as poet and critic, and hence his unique dual eminence in our time. Never again is the poet embarrassed to the slightest degree by his relationship with some reader whom he cannot help puzzling. Hereafter he moves with confidence in what the reader, still puzzled but less disoriented, can be counted on to half-recognize as the Great Tradition. It is unnecessary for the writer to play any overt role whatever, even the role, as in the quatrains, of one pretending not to be there. From *Gerontion* to *Little Gidding,* the authority of poem after poem prevails: an authority derived from the impersonal gravity of its commerce with an acknowledged past. We do

*It appeared in *Art & Letters,* not *The Athenaeum.* No matter.

not think of Thomas Eliot, M.A. English poetry is continuing to write itself, as it always has.

As for Eliot the critic, he was freed, once he had mastered the devices, from the conscientious reviewer's besetting problem, the problem of being cast in the role of pedagogue at a hearthside where all that is expected is a little "cultural" solemnity or a little entertainment. Thrown among a people who prided themselves upon taking seriously—to the extent of letters to *The Times*—"standards" they had no intention of examining: thrown among them, furthermore, as that most vulnerable of impostors, an American,* Eliot cultivated a blandness that freed him from elaborate tactical considerations so that he could give his whole energy to pursuing the implications of the subject.

For the subject, the thing thrust beneath the reviewer's scrutiny, is everything. Deliverances of principle occur only as some nexus in the anatomizing of the subject requires them, and, like the famous sentence about the objective correlative, they come with great pregnancy precisely because they are not major premises to an argument but generalizations forced upward into visibility by the pressures of some particular instance. He tells us, for instance, that an "objective correlative" is the only way a dramatist can express a character's emotion; it is a formula that occurs to him in connexion with the puzzling contrast between Macbeth's "Tomorrow and tomorrow and tomorrow . . ." which emerges out of the action of the play, and Hamlet's soliloquies, which are anthology pieces dealing with the cosmos in general, so little rooted in the particular action that an actor-manager feels free to shuffle them into coincidence with his notions of pace. It follows that Shakespeare is attempting to express Hamlet's emotions to us discursively; it follows that he has failed to fix, in drafting this play, just that concatenation of incidents and images which would make Hamlet's emotion comprehensible and inevitable, and so

*"A bore, and what is more, an American bore"—Eminent British Academic, of Ezra Pound.

release the soliloquies just where they occur; it follows (with a little reflection) that such a concatenation is the condition of artistic "inevitability," and hence that

> the only way of expressing emotion in the form of art is by finding an "objective correlative"; in other words, a set of objects, a situation, a chain of events which shall be the formula of that *particular* emotion; such that when the external facts, which must terminate in sensory experience, are given, the emotion is immediately evoked.

This makes perhaps a more general claim than Eliot intended; he could hardly have foreseen its misapplication to the job of the lyric poet, preoccupied as he was with simply explaining why *Hamlet* is "the Mona Lisa of literature." Like Matthew Arnold, he has a dangerous gift of phrase.

For he was not devising a dangling interdependent system of abstractions, like Alexander Calder, but writing *ad hoc*. He will call Kyd "that extraordinary dramatic (if not poetic) genius" when he is making a point about Kyd, and with equal legitimacy deplore the habit of distinguishing between drama and poetry, when he is making a point about poetic drama. What Eliot did with his freedom was not so much plot an elaborate campaign in the cellars of entrenched Respectability, as seize a succession of opportunities for enlightening himself. Each review is an occasion to think something out as he goes along, and while the last paragraph remembers the first, the first does not often foresee the last. He ends when his space has run out, and grows very adroit at prevising this contingency while there is still half a page left in which to turn round.

Thus on one occasion (*Athenaeum*, May 9, 1919) a new volume of Kipling's verse comes up for review. Eliot begins by reflecting that if Kipling is "a laureate without laurels, a neglected celebrity," if the intelligentsia take no notice whatever of a new book of his, it is not because he is anathema but because he is not discussed. "Most of our discerning critics have no more an opinion on Mr. Kipling than they have on the poetry of Mr. John Oxenham. The mind is not sufficiently curious, sufficiently brave, to examine Mr. Kipling." He is persuading himself to undertake a more than superficial notice. Comparison and analysis,* then: the tools of criticism. And the comparison—at first sight unlikely—is with Swinburne. They are alike in their use of sound, which they use for oratorical purposes, to persuade. "Swinburne and Mr. Kipling have, like the public speaker, an idea to impose; and they impose it in the public speaker's way, by turning the idea into sound, and iterating the sound." So far, a routine piece of review-making; but at this juncture a cogent generalization suggests itself:

> And like the orator they are personal: not by revelation, but by throwing themselves in and gesturing the emotion of the moment. The emotion is not "there" simply, coldly independent of the author, of the audience, there and for ever like Shake-speare's and Aeschylus' emotions: it is present so long only as the author is on the platform and compels you to feel it.
> > I look down at his feet: but that's a fable.
> > If that thou be'st a devil, I cannot kill thee,
> is "there," cold and indifferent.
> > Nothing is better, I well think,
> > Than love; the hidden well-water
> > Is not so delicate a drink.
> > This was well seen of me and her
> (to take from one of Swinburne's poems which most resembles a statement); or
> > The end of it's sitting and thinking
> > And dreaming of hell-fires to see—
> these are not statements of emotion, but ways of stimulating a particular response in the reader.

This distinction is something gained; without the exercise of reviewing Kipling it might never have been concretely achieved. Four months later it irrupts into another review, and we have the paragraph on the "objective correlative," which, one may conjecture, might never have been written if the

*This phrase, placed in general circulation by the 1923 "Function of Criticism" in *Selected Essays,* occurs in several essays written five years earlier. Eliot originally directed its slightly austere dogmatism at the readers of *The Egoist.*

problem of defining Kipling's use of sound had not arisen four months earlier. Five weeks later another of this review's incidental remarks, that cohesion is imposed not by logic but by a point of view,* recurs in a discussion of the normal inadequacy of English periodical reviewing; another five months, and it is one of the seminal notions of another classic essay, the one on Ben Jonson. As for the Kipling review, there being some five hundred words to spare after the comparison with Swinburne is exhausted, it touches on one new topic—Kipling's amalgamation, denied to the eighteenth century, of cynicism and sentiment—and then, with five lines to go, manages a last cogent flourish on this topic which began by promising so little:

> It is wrong, of course, for Mr. Kipling to address a large audience; but it is a better thing than to address a small one. The only better thing is to address the one hypothetical Intelligent Man who does not exist and who is the audience of the Artist.

"Kipling Redivivus," which has never been reprinted and does not need to be, was one of four essays of comparable length published by Eliot that month, and one of two dozen that year. Five are still in print in *Selected Essays*, records of occasions when the appropriate assignment chanced to precipitate in durable form some phase of the author's continual critical activity.

After 1925 or so the critical activity ceases to be continual: partly because Eliot had arrived at that working understanding of the past which his own poetry required; partly because he was editing the *Criterion*, which exacted from his pen many thousands of words but few paragraphs of permanent interest; partly because he was no longer anonymous but, for a determining number of readers, including the editors who commissioned

---

*A Bradleyan notion which Eliot originally formulated in writing about Bradley for *The Monist*: the "subjective" is one point of view, the "objective" is another; they are equally valid, and on Bradley's premises there is no way to reconcile them, though like the personages in *The Waste Land* they "melt into each other by a process which we cannot grasp."

prefaces and reviews, a man whose seminal opinions and perceptions were matter of record, and who could be called upon to adorn some occasion. He still sought freedom in camouflage, but the available roles—the Reverend Eliot, the Pope of Russell Square, the Elder Statesman of Poetic Revolution—were more constricting. By the 1940's we discover the extreme of his emergence from the role of anonymous reviewer: he is subject to recurrent conscription as the academy orator or the platform Goethe, delivering the W. P. Ker Memorial Lecture, the Presidential Address to the Virgil Society, the eleventh Annual Lecture of the National Book League, the first annual Yeats Lecture to the Friends of the Irish Academy at the Abbey Theatre, Dublin. It seems hardly a coincidence that we also discover the newly visible poet writing little poetry. *The Cultivation of Christmas Trees* (1954) gets under way with some difficulty, like a commissioned Pronouncement:

> There are several attitudes towards Christmas,
> Some of which we may disregard.

"One seems to become a myth," he told an interviewer, "a fabulous creature that doesn't exist." His 1952 bibliography includes an Address at the National Book League Celebration of the Centenary of the Death of Louis Braille, and an Address to Members of the London Library, by T. S. Eliot, O.M., on the occasion of his assuming the office of President of the Library, delivered at the annual general meeting of members in the reading room, 22 July, 1952; while in 1954 he was called on to supply a cookbook, published for the benefit of the St. Louis Symphony, with a recipe for Mrs. Runcie's Pudding. In a noiseless and dignified orbit around the world of Literature, predictably on course, he observes with genial scrupulousness what can be seen from a great unchanging distance, no longer combining the novel insight with the definitive statement, but adjusting the proportions of such majestic generalities as the Social Function of Poetry, What is a Classic?, and Virgil and the Christian World.

ii

The critical preoccupation of Eliot the poet may be summed up in this way: of the possible unwritten poems, to write the right ones. It is conceivable that a man working at random might put together a passage which could afford rich satisfaction to a sensibility not yet developed, not to be developed for another two centuries. And this passage might not satisfy its creator; might seem to him a failure, or more likely (we are partial to what we have done) an attractive novelty. And such a success—anticipating the canons of a posterity which has not arrived—is of no *use* to the poet who achieves it now; because, answering to no criteria he can grasp, it contains no indications accessible to him respecting what he next proposes to write. He cannot develop, he can only experiment. To develop is to understand enough of your own past achievement to go on with it: to see what has so far been done by yourself and by others, your predecessors and contemporaries; and a young poet in 1917 can only see what the most alert 1917 eyes are sensitized to.

Hence Eliot's preoccupation with tradition; tradition is simply what has been done, so far as we can understand it. And the more deeply we understand it, the more subtle our apprehension of what already exists, the more thoroughly shall our minds be prepared to understand what we ourselves do. We do it we know not how; and unless we understand it when we have done it: understand, that is, not what brought our own words into being (impossible), but how, once in being, they relate to what already exists, we have no means of going on, of doing anything but wait for another piece of luck which we may not recognize when it has happened. If the man who wrote *Prufrock* at twenty-three had not kept his head, he would either have written more Prufrocks, which is pointless; or dabbled at random; or written no more. Like the Pope of the *Essay on Criticism*, Eliot was in the most dangerous possible situation for a supremely gifted magician of words; he had brought off while not yet mature a greater success than he was in a position to develop.

The past unexamined perpetuates itself. "If our predecessors cannot teach us to write better than themselves," Eliot wrote in 1918, "they will surely teach us to write worse: because we have never learned to criticize Keats, Shelley, and Wordsworth (poets of assured though modest merit), Keats, Shelley and Wordsworth punish us from their graves with the annual scourge of the Georgian Anthology." For this reason "every generation, every turn of time when the work of four or five men who count has reached middle age, is a *crisis*"; and a crisis to be met not by insurrection but by tireless inspection of all that exists with fresh eyes.

> We must insist upon the importance of intelligent criticism. I do not mean Sainte-Beuve, for the work of that great restless curious brain is rather a part of history than of literature, the history of manners, memoirs, boudoir whispers; or the political-ethical-religious writing of Brunetière or the highly superior Extension Lectures of M. Faguet: I mean the ceaseless employment of criticism by men who are engaged in creative work. It is essential that each generation should reappraise everything for itself. Who for instance has a first-hand opinion of Shakespeare? . . .

He ends this article by telling the readers of *The Egoist* something many of them were no doubt unprepared to hear, being infatuated with dissidence, novelty, new styles (by Paquin), political emancipation, and the like: that the critic's chief business is "bringing the art of the past to bear upon the present, making it relevant to the actual generation through his own temperament, which must itself interest us."

If Eliot keeps reminding the readers of *The Egoist*, enamoured of the new, that to justify his high spirits the revolutionist needs to know more than he supposes, and that *all* the new is not on our side ("the forces of deterioration are a large crawling mass, and the forces of development half a dozen men"), he keeps reminding the readers of *The Athenaeum,* comfortable with the old, that we do not possess what we have never examined; "tradition cannot be inherited." This is the strategic purpose beneath his bland announcement that *Hamlet* is "almost certainly an artistic failure," or that Kipling's antecedents are to be discovered in Swinburne, or that a cogent refutation of Thomas Rymer's objections to *Othello* remains to be produced. It is for the benefit of these readers, meanwhile, that he examines Rostand, Donne's sermons, Jonson's comedy, Yeats, Pound, *The Education of Henry Adams,* Saintsbury on Beyle and Balzac, the second volume of a *History of American Literature,* Swinburne's criticism, and other topics concerning which received opinion is stable, and informed opinion nonexistent.

The topics, at this distance, matter less than Eliot's increasingly discernible pattern of interests and perceptions. Thus, contemplating the lameness of Robert Lynd's *Old and New Masters,* he observes how that critic "never quite dares to treat a book austerely by criteria of art and of art alone; . . . the public would not stand that." Nor does he "dissect a personality to its ultimate constituents; the public does not want to know so much." That

> human kind
> Cannot bear very much reality

is a constant assumption of Eliot's; as when he ends his famous rebuttal of the public notion that the artist expresses personality and releases emotion by asserting drily, "but of course, only those who have personality and emotions know what it is to want to escape from these things"; or when he brings the Furies into an English country-house, or presents the observer of the waste land under the figure of Tiresias, who is prohibited by the sharpest injunctions from divulging the reason why the curse has fallen on Thebes. Bradley, we remember, without difficulty collapsed all comforting hypotheses into the domain of Appearance, and left the reader wondering what it was he wanted and whether it was worth the trouble of getting it;

beneath Eliot's bland surface glows the unwavering conviction that the poet, in the morning coat or drinking tea, possesses chiefly a more honest mind than most minds, yielding him at the end of rigorous ardours the intuition of some hidden reality of which one aspect, as it was for Conrad's Kurtz, is horror. And the poet walks through the streets of London or Boston bearing this intermittent knowledge. That is why it is intolerable that he shall be confounded with the Georgians. In the Lynd review what the public will not stand isn't "the atmosphere of unknown terror and mystery in which our life is passed," but real knowledge of any kind:

> Analysis and comparison methodically, with sensitiveness, intelligence, curiosity, intensity of passion and infinite knowledge: all these are necessary to the great critic. Comparison the periodical public does not want much of: it does not like to be made to feel that it ought to have read much more than it has read before it can follow the critic's thought; analysis it is afraid of.

Analysis and comparison methodically, with sensitiveness, intelligence, curiosity, intensity of passion and infinite knowledge, are equally necessary to the great writer. Two weeks earlier Eliot had noted that "Dostoyevsky's point of departure is always a human brain in a human environment, and the 'aura' is simply the continuation of the quotidian experience of the brain into seldom explored extremities of torture. Because most people are too unconscious of their own suffering to suffer much, this continuation appears fantastic. But Dostoyevsky begins with the real world, as Beyle does; he only pursues reality farther in a certain direction." That is why "in the great artist imagination . . . becomes a fine and delicate tool for an operation on the sensible world," and why "Stendhal's scenes, some of them, and some of his phrases read like cutting one's own throat; they are a terrible humiliation to read, in the understanding of human feelings and human illusions of feeling that they force upon the reader."

This conviction, that the great artist does an essentially analytic job with intense but undramatic honesty, is central to

Eliot's criticism in these years. It is not, as he maintains it, a lurid Baudelairean

> Je ne vois qu'infini par toutes les fenêtres;

leading to

> Lis-moi, pour apprendre à m'aimer;

the man who performs a delicate operation upon reality is more like a biologist than a dramatist. The man who has, like Pascal, "son gouffre, avec lui se mouvant" is not *thereby* equipped for writing poetry; he may merely be tormented.

The creative mind, according to an intuition toward which Eliot was working in the early essays, isn't a personal force but a kind of uterine permissiveness. It makes use of the personality to which it is attached, and that is only one of the things of which it makes use. But there are certain typical arrangements of the personality with which the creative mind seems unable to co-exist; two of these, national types with which Eliot felt temperamental affinities, one American, one English, one Puritan, one Romantic, he subjected to illuminating scrutiny. His occasions were books by Henry Adams and George Wyndham.

Eliot in London in 1919, five years out of America, draws in his review of *The Education of Henry Adams* a startling picture of what an American in Europe may become. The Adams of his account is a wealthy Prufrock, driven—Eliot uses this verb —by the Erinnys. He belongs to a class of sensitive people with both the means and the desire to do something great; but on account of a poison Boston is uniquely capable of implanting, "dogged by the shadow of self-conscious incompetence, they are predestined failures."

> Conscience made him aware that he had been imperfectly educated at Harvard and Berlin, and that there was a vague variety of things he ought to know about. He was also aware, as most Bostonians are, of the narrowness of the Boston horizon. But working with and against conscience was the Boston doubt . . . a product, or a cause, or a concomitant, of Unitarianism; it is not destructive, but it is dissolvent.

In no overwhelming question could Adams believe; he wrote an article demolishing the myths that surround Pocahontas, "and the pleasure of demolition turned to ashes in his mouth. . . . Wherever this man stepped, the ground did not simply give way, it flew into particles"; he might have been an impressionable student of Bradley. "The Erinnys which drove him madly through seventy years of search for education—the search for what, upon a lower plane, is called culture—left him much as he was born: well-bred, intelligent, and uneducated."

What kept this Prufrock perpetually immature ("he remains little Paul Dombey asking questions") was, Eliot surmises, an incapacity for sensuous experience. "It is probable that men ripen best through experiences which are at once sensuous and intellectual; certainly many men will admit that their keenest ideas have come to them with the quality of sense-perception; and that their keenest sensuous experience has been 'as if the body thought.'" Adams simply wrote a book about the middle ages.

The Henry Adams of this review is Eliot's Hugh Selwyn Mauberley, almost but not quite a *persona;* and the experience of meditating on his career (May, 1919) no doubt entered obscurely into the composition of *Gerontion* (first printed in December of that year).

If the austere American affords no model for the creative mind, neither does the romantic Englishman. The romantic, as in Wyndham Lewis' analysis of the flamboyant non-artist in *Tarr*, allows some catalyst to fuse in his life the ingredients only art should be allowed to bring together. Eliot writes of George Wyndham, "His literature and his politics and his country life are one and the same thing. They are not in separate compartments, they are one career. Together they made up his world: literature, politics, riding to hounds. In the real world these things have nothing to do with each other." (1919) With which compare:

The ordinary man's experience is chaotic, irregular, fragmentary. The latter falls in love, or reads Spinoza, and these two experiences have nothing to do with each other, or with the noise of the typewriter or the smell of cooking; in the mind of the poet these experiences are always forming new wholes.

(1921)

George Wyndham's is the case of romanticism in life; and "there may be a good deal to be said for Romanticism in life, there is no place for it in letters." The Romantic poet is he who allows the all-important fusion to occur in the world in which he lives, who does not defer that process until it comes time for the poem he is to write. Eliot contrasts Wyndham with Leonardo, who also did many things and appears to have made one life of them. But that "one life," like an Eliot poem, preserved the inviolacy of its parts. "Leonardo turned to art or science, and each was what it was and not another thing. . . . He lived in no fairyland, but his mind went out and became a part of things." This was so because Leonardo conducted his life impersonally (like a self-possessed alien in London): "he had no father to speak of, he was hardly a citizen, and he had no stake in the community. . . . George Wyndham was Gentry. He was chivalrous, the world was an adventure of himself." This leads to an important formulation:

> What is permanent and valuable in Romanticism is curiosity . . . a curiosity which recognizes that any life, if accurately penetrated, is interesting and always strange. Romanticism is a shortcut to the strangeness without the reality, and it leads its disciples only back upon themselves.

And "the only cure for Romanticism is to analyze it."

Analyzed, its diverse impulses may be separated and redirected separately upon fact. Only then is it possible for the poet to think, and to feel his thought "as immediately as the odour of a rose." For the poet who has not performed this dissociation of his own impulses, the rose is an adventure of his sensibility, and thought is a means of relating it to other adventures. The "unified sensibility" of which Eliot speaks in "The Metaphysical Poets," like the "wit" he is at pains to analyze in "Andrew Marvell," depends on the poet's ability to maintain distinctly numerous levels of passionate involvement with "immediate experience." "It involves, probably, a recognition, implicit in the expression of every experience, of other kinds of experience which are possible," a recognition which cannot occur when there are no "other kinds" because all experience alike is an adjective of the self. Thus as the poet of his hypothetical example fused Spinoza, the noise of the typewriter, and the smell of cooking, Eliot, in the year in which he wrote for *The Times Literary Supplement* these two last of his great essays, drew together a line out of Dante, the way the bell of St. Mary Woolnoth delivered its ninth stroke ("a phenomenon which I have often noticed"), the phrase "dead sound" out of North's Plutarch (noted in the course of a book-reviewing job), the sensation of going to his post in Lloyd's Bank of a morning, and a typical hour for executions in British prisons; and because these varieties of experience were simultaneously accessible to him, produced nine lines of *The Waste Land*. By contrast the quatrain poems are synthetic, the Oxford poems facile extensions of a point of view, the Harvard poems insufficiently consious. And having raised to deliberateness at last what had been at best an intuitive poetic method, he wrote little more prose of concentrated urgency.

iii

Two of Eliot's most important essays, "Tradition and the Individual Talent," and "Rhetoric and Poetic Drama," are more or less definitive summations of these and allied meditations. The first has been investigated with too much solemnity, as though it were Eliot's "theory of poetry." It is not that; it is a meditation on how the old is related to the new, the extensive summation of many *obiter dicta*. It appeared in *The Egoist*, where he had from time to time urged the janissaries of revolution to consider the past more systematically; its understatement of the role of the creative imagination reflects the fact that the readers of *The Egoist* needed no incitement on that score. It is one of Eliot's very few pieces of prose not hitched to a specific book under inspection; a lecture-room décor is consequently implied, and finely parodied with the superbly Holmesian "I invite you to consider" near the end of the first instalment.

> There remains to define this process of depersonalization and its relation to the sense of tradition. It is in this depersonalization that art may be said to approach the condition of science. I, therefore, invite you to consider, as a suggestive analogy, the action which takes place when a bit of finely filiated platinum is introduced into a chamber containing oxygen and sulphur dioxide.

At this moment, as it were, the bell rang; and the readers of *The Egoist* were left to gnaw their knuckles for two months.

The first part of the essay sets out to correct that misapprehension of the scope of "tradition" which Eliot had drily characterized in *The Egoist* two years earlier:

> All the ideas, beliefs, modes of feeling and behaviour which we have no time or inclination to investigate for ourselves we take second-hand and sometimes call tradition.

To this he appended a learned footnote: "For an authoritative condemnation of theories attaching extreme importance to tradition as a criterion of truth, see Pope Gregory XVI's encyclical *Singulari nos* (July 15, 1834), and the Vatican Council canon of 1870, *Si quis dixerit . . . anathema sit.*" When the Pope can be quoted against Tradition, Tradition is obviously misunderstood. What Eliot now sets out to show is that Tradition is not a bin into which you relegate what you cannot be bothered to examine, but precisely that portion of the past, and only that, which you have examined scrupulously. You cannot admire, you cannot learn from, you cannot even rebel against what you do not know. "Tradition . . . cannot be inherited, and if you want it you must obtain it by great labour." To obtain it both requires and nourishes (Eliot's portmanteau-word is "involves") "the historical sense," which "compels a man to write not merely with his own generation in his bones, but with a feeling that the whole of the literature of Europe from Homer and within it the whole of the literature of his own country has a simultaneous existence and composes a simultaneous order." Bradley's mind lies behind that sentence; what does not exist now, does not exist. As for how Shakespeare's plays existed in 1616, any reconstructions we can form remain twentieth-century fictions, built out of our experience now with the aid of our present sensibilities: sensibilities which, unlike those of Shakespeare's contemporaries, have encountered, say, Shelley. Hence "the past is altered by the present as much as the present is directed by the past"; the new work is not simply the latest term in a series, it alters (like a new chair in the living room) the value of every other item. "What happens when a new work of art is created is something that happens simultaneously to all the works of art which preceded it"; and this is because works of literary art have, except as paper and ink, no unequivocal objective existence; they exist as they are experienced, and the sensibility that has experienced novelty becomes an altered sensibility.

"The past and future," wrote Bradley in a remarkable essay, "What is the Real Julius Caesar?" (*Essays on Truth and Reality*), "the past and future vary, and they have to vary, with the changes of the present, and, to any man whose eyes are open, such variation is no mere theory but is plain fact."

Partly, one supposes, to evade a digression on the mode of literary existence, partly also to maintain the curator's tone with which we detect him amusing himself throughout the essay, Eliot employed the metaphor of "monuments." "The existing monuments form an ideal order among themselves, which is modified by the introduction of the new (the really new) work of art among them." It is a charmingly comic sentence, its terminology exactly mimicking that of *The Times*, evoking the busts of the poets, and the complacence with which "England puts her Great Writers away securely in a Safe Deposit Vault, and curls to sleep like Fafnir."

That is Tradition. As for the Individual Talent, to the extent that it is aware of its capacities for modifying the past, it will also "be aware of great difficulties and responsibilities." The poet has a responsibility to himself, which is the responsibility of digesting whatever nutriment the past affords him; for "not only the best, but the most individual parts of his work may be those in which the dead poets, his ancestors, assert their immortality most vigorously." And he has a responsibility to the dead poets his ancestors, and to the readers in cooperation with whom he is engaged in keeping viable traditions alive. "What happens is a continual surrender of himself as he is at the moment to something which is more valuable. The progress of an artist is a continual self-sacrifice, a continual extinction of personality."For the poet's or anyone else's personality (here Bradley asserts himself vigorously) is a working fiction, that provisional management of desires, perceptions, and memories, the prepared face with which he confronts the faces that he meets. It is, to borrow a phrase from *Little Gidding*, "of little importance though never indifferent." It is not to be confused with what Eliot elsewhere calls his temperament, that volitional identity which alone confers intensity, confers interest. George Wyndham had an arresting personality; his energies were invested in his personality, and the world was an adventure of himself. But he was not, and indeed for that reason was not, "a finely perfected medium in which special, or very varied, feelings are at liberty to enter into new combinations"; precisely because his feelings were not at liberty; they were turned all one way by the magnetism of the personality to which they adhered. Wyndham's gestures of enthusiasm were, however generous, predictable.

That is why it is not necessary that the poet shall prepare himself for writing a great poem by feeling greatly. The death of Edward King was the occasion for a great deal that Milton had in him, in suspension, to combine and enter articulation; but the intensity of *Lycidas* is not the intensity of Milton's mourning for King. And among the elements that entered into the precipitate called *Lycidas* was Milton's indignation concerning "our corrupted clergy, then at their height"; but this indignation, when later propelled by Milton's personality, issued not a second time as poetry, but as the baroque rant of the ecclesiastical pamphlets. "The more perfect the artist"—and the Milton of *Lycidas* is an artist of considerable stature—"the more completely separate in him will be the man who suffers and the mind which creates; the more perfectly will the mind digest and transmute the passions which are its material." In fact, as he later notes in a Valéry preface, "One is prepared for art when one has ceased to be interested in one's own emotions and experiences except as material." And these are (he remarks apropos of Joyce) "material which he must accept—not virtues to be enlarged or vices to be diminished."

This whole account has been censured as attributing to the poet an inhuman repose; which censure misses the crucial point, that the repose—precisely, inhuman—exists not in the poet but in the poem. In the poem the emotion "is 'there,' cold and indifferent." Whatever turmoil the poet may be in, his job is not to infect us with his turmoil.

His job is to explicate turmoil: which leads us directly to "Rhetoric and Poetic Drama," the gambit of which is simply that the large, moving speeches in poetic plays are not aimed at the audience. They are components in a dramatic machine; they express not what the author wants to say to the audience, but what the character wants to say to other characters. This is obvious enough, but it is not all. Eliot's originality consists in his having noticed that many of the most famous speeches in Shakespeare contain a higher rhetorical charge than is called for by the mere exigencies of communication between person and person:

> TIMON: Come not to me again; but say to Athens,
>   Timon hath built his everlasting mansion
>   Upon the beached verge of the salt flood . . .

What Timon is doing in that speech is not conveying information but *exhibiting* the intensity of his own nihilism, which suddenly impresses him. "The really fine rhetoric in Shakespeare occurs in situations where a character in the play *sees himself* in a dramatic light." Exactly; Timon is expressing his personality, his prepared face, which he has created out of "the damage of a lifetime." In a later essay Eliot quotes Othello's final speech, and extends his formula of self-dramatization:

> "What Othello seems to me to be doing in making this speech is *cheering himself up*. He is endeavouring to escape reality, he has ceased to think about Desdemona, and is thinking about himself. . . . Othello succeeds in turning himself into a pathetic figure, by adopting an *aesthetic* rather than a moral attitude, dramatising himself against his environment. He takes in the spectator, but the human motive is primarily to take in himself."

These words explicate a good deal of *Prufrock*. They also achieve a formulation necessary for carrying moral analysis beyond *Prufrock*. It is this: the more rhetorical the language, the more resonant the line, and the more surely the words send down tentacular roots among the deepest feelings and desires, then to exactly that extent the more morally corrupt will be that imagined personage—whether a character in a play, or the solo speaker of a lyric monologue—whom we imagine to be speaking. The bad poet tries to express his personality; the mature poet shows us the gestures by which a personality expresses itself. This is not an account that will cover all poetry, but it covers the poetry Eliot had it in him to write in 1920, a poetry proposing to play with fire, with the resounding word and the stirrings of the mighty line. Eliot's poetic sensibility inhabited a world made out of radioactive words, not a world of moral discriminations (though he invokes those), not a world of impassioned self-possession

> Go, lovely rose!
> Tell her, that wastes her time and me. . . .

but the world where words, numinous and substantial, strain to make human speakers sound more significant than they are. The Oxford poems, the French poems, the quatrains, all seek some formula of control over the self-aggrandizement inherent in the deeply satisfying phrase:

Time for you and time for me,
And time yet for a hundred indecisions,
And for a hundred visions and revisions . . .

I have heard the mermaids singing each to each . . .

We have lingered in the chambers of the sea . . .

The method of control employed in *Prufrock* (where without it the protagonist would be a freak like Marlowe's Barabas) was to allow the protagonist himself to confess inability to sustain the heroic note:

I do not think that they will sing to me.

The method of control employed in the poems of 1915-1917 is either to eschew the resonant line altogether

They are rattling breakfast plates in basement kitchens . . .

or else to confine the energies of the poem within a verse form taut enough to diminish the comic potentialities of modulating from "Webster was much possessed by death" to "Grishkin is nice." The method employed in *Gerontion* (1919) follows directly on Eliot's analysis of Jacobean rhetoric. There are neither collapses into fatuity nor formal constraints. The old man with neither past nor present, reduced to a Voice, employs that Voice, fills up the time of the poem with the echoes and intermodulations of that Voice, draws sustenance from the Voice and existence itself from the Voice for as long as he can animate the silence. And in the poem, quite deliberately, the dead poets who perfected the irregular iambic pentameter monologue assert their immortality with vigour, as a rhythm drops or a line-ending turns back in a haunted echo-chamber where each sound falls with the ring of impersonal authority. For the protagonist has no voice but a collective past which he has never made his own by great labour, which consequently uses him, blows him with restless violence through phrase after phrase without substance or satisfaction. It is a great grotesque conception, greatly achieved, everywhere evading the deadness of pastiche, everywhere embodying the deadness of retrospect, the hollowness of personality which can express itself so admirably, and still express nothing but the bits of purely verbal intensity with which it has filled itself out of books.

GERONTION

. . . the effortless journey, to the empty land . . .

i

"Here I am"—like the Henry Adams whose senses "neither flowered nor fruited," whom the Erinnys drove madly through seventy years of search;

> Here I am, an old man in a dry month,
> Being read to by a boy, waiting for rain.

Adams' *Education* provided the poem with one line, "dogwood and chestnut, flowering Judas"; a Life of Edward Fitzgerald provided another: "in a dry month, old and blind, being read to by a country boy, longing for rain"; and Fitzgerald had confined himself while he had his prime within one form of resonant Stoicism:

> Come, fill the cup, and in the fire of spring
> Your winter-garment of repentance fling;
> The bird of time hath but a little way
> To flutter—and the bird is on the wing.

"Gull against the wind, in the windy straits. . . ." There is no need to trace such sources, though since we happen to know them there is no harm in allowing them to indicate the sort of human career Eliot was contemplating when the poem formed itself.

> My house is a decayed house

—the Voice searches out all the recesses of "house": the habitation, the family stock (not doomed like the House of Atreus but simply withered), the European family, the Mind of Europe, the body, finally the brain. This is for the first time since *Prufrock* the Eliot of the unique generalizing style, the words like Seurat's points of colour blending not on the page but in the reader's mind to delimit a protagonist who is more substantial than a type, more general than a man: an auditory illusion within the confines of which the components of the poem circulate and co-exist. Rhythmic authority marshals these particulars, confers the illusion of personal coherence; the sense of personal presence can at any moment be resolved into a purely technical management of stresses and *caesurae*—

> Nor knee deep
> in the salt marsh,
>   héaving a / cútláss
>   bítten by / flíes fóught.

Though he is read to by a boy, he is not Samson Agonistes, nor was he meant to be; nor was he at Thermopylae, "the hot gates"; nor presumably at the more recent war which incorporated the word "estaminet" into colloquial English. He decays, however, like Europe; which in a hall of mirrors four old men in 1919 rearranged, contriving a corridor, for instance, between Poland and the sea.

> After such knowledge, what forgiveness? Think now
> History has many cunning passages, contrived corridors
> And issues, deceives with whispering ambitions,
> Guides us by vanities.

In this echo-chamber, word dissolves into word. There are cunning passages in history-books, as well as passages-at-arms; and if "corridors" evokes other sorts of passages, then History turns, like Gerontion's brain, into a ramshackle house. Issues let us out of a maze; historians talk of issues; the past, sometimes unluckily, never dies without issue. "Deceives with whispering ambitions": the echo of "passages," twice since reinforced, still lingers to evoke at this point the whispering galleries where a voice originating in a hidden place speaks into one's ear; temptation whispers; and the feel of palace intrigue ("a word in your ear") haunts the phrase. Corridors and passages are places to wander, places where a lone man may move toward a prepared doom or toward an illicit bed, guided by vanity or (since vanity is emptiness) admonished by a shade. In the next sentence the corridors grow vaginal, the sexual overtones of "issues" and "vanities" deepen, and History is metamorphosed into an immemorial harlot:

> Think now
> She gives when our attention is distracted
> And what she gives, gives with such supple confusions
> That the giving famishes the craving.

Like Cleopatra of the treacherous "infinite variety," she makes hungry when most she satisfies. "For vilest things become themselves in her, that the holy priests bless her when she is riggish." Two sentences later something she gives too soon into weak hands is refused, and in consequence of the refusal there is a propagation: in this phantom world contraceptives and rejected opportunities usurp one another's negative functions. But it was a "fear" that was propagated; physical union has perhaps engendered only a terror, or is it that the refusal to join bodies has by some twist of retrospect induced fear with the paradoxical force of a propagation? These are of course unanswerable questions; the uniquely specifying rhythms, the richly explicit verbs, the syntactic muscularity of a sequence of declarative sentences, all these specificities of gesture expend themselves in weaving the wind, their intimate narrative energy handling only ambiguities, phantoms, footless metaphors. We are not in a world where statements handle facts.

The generative metaphors persist; in the next sentence

"Unnatural vices are *fathered* by our heroism"; again the specified act, the evasive issue.

Virtues

Are forced upon us by our impudent crimes.
These tears are shaken from the wrath-bearing tree.

Down through the passage an issueless "think . . . think . . . think . . ." asserts itself in onanistic frenzy; impotence at length enforces virtue; and as for the wrath-bearing tree (wrath borne as a fruit, or as a burden?), its enigma encompasses the Cross, Blake's Poison Tree which was "watered with tears," the blighted figtree (Matthew : XXI : 19), but chiefly perhaps the Tree of the Knowledge of Good and Evil:

After such knowledge, what forgiveness?

This passage of fifteen lines fairly represents the method of *Gerontion*, in which terrors and vacuities of great scope are suggested but nothing is identified or separated from the indefinite web of possibilities: and this precisely because no unbroken thread of volition can be traced through the speaker's life. This historical nightmare, in which no act has a clear nature and clear consequences, is neither a summary of his experiences, nor of his observation that has caused him to refrain from experience; it is something bearing little reference to either experience or observation, for the speaker has neither experienced nor observed, having insufficient moral presence. He is simply a zone where more or less energetic notions are incorporated, to agitate themselves tirelessly; where, as to the backward look every family tree contains hanged men, so to the foreseeing eye every action is choked by the potentiality of monstrous consequences; where it is not possible to muster the will to say, as in *The Dry Salvages,*

And do not think of the fruit of action . . .
Not fare well,

But fare forward, voyagers.

No other Eliot poem exploits an ambiguity of dissolving keywords to this degree. There is no up nor down, no ground on which declaration may stand. The merest show of a containing *mise-en-scène* for plainly metaphoric discourse proves to be itself metaphoric ("Tenants of the house, thoughts of a dry brain"). Nor is this a method to be used twice; the poem is "about" the unique justification of its own method, the unique case of the law it implies: the law uniting acedia of spirit with the narcotic exploitation of a phantom past.

It is not only, of course, the presentation of a timeless moral state, as precise and as general as a Newtonian equation; it is also an image of Europe, 1919. "The present is no more than the present existence, the present significance, of the entire past"; conversely, the entire past comes to bear on it: day by day, an increasing burden, and no present fact can evade this weight, just as no written word moving without local context can shrug off the allusive weight of its own history. "Hot gates," when there are no specifiable hot gates, cannot avoid evoking Thermopylae; "a dry month" connotes more than this year's meteorological freak, it evokes the despairs, symbolisms, and ceremonies that have attended immemorial seasons of drought. Thus the Jew who was spawned in some estaminet of Antwerp cannot but prolong into the present the reputation of another who was born in a different inn; and the sequence Antwerp, Brussels, London, financial capitals, the third in a different country, remotely echoes Bethlehem, Jerusalem, Rome. If the Jew is the owner of the house, then to the extent that the house is Gerontion's consciousness the Jew is Christ waiting to take back what has been lent. But he is also a 1919 slum landlord; and correspondingly the eating, dividing, and drinking (under the shadow of the phrase "flowering judas") is carried on in 1919 "among whispers" which are not necessarily any longer whispers of religious awe, but the whispers of conspirators, or just of tourists.

> . . . by Mr. Silvero
> With caressing hands, at Limoges
> Who walked all night in the next room;

"walked," so this is a memory; and we are not told what Mr.
Silvero's hands caressed, or whether they were merely hands of
a caressing kind. His name, tainted with silver, sounds like a
no-name with a grandee's flourish. As for his walking all night;
had he partaken of the sacrament without absolution, or consummated a deal or an assault, or simply been unable to sleep?
The roll of his companions suggests other possibilities—

> By Hakagawa, bowing among the Titians;
> By Madame de Tornquist, in the dark room
> Shifting the candles; Fräulein von Kulp
> Who turned in the hall, one hand on the door.
>   Vacant shuttles
> Weave the wind. . . .

The robed figure bows; candles are shifted; someone entering
or leaving a room that no doubt gives off one of those "cunning
passages" is anxious not to be observed; and in a summarizing
image the motions of weaving a fabric are performed in
vacancy. Some rite, not innocent, unites these persons; and we
observe that like J. Alfred Prufrock they are persons only at the
prompting of their own names, that the names are eerily
suggestive, that the candles shifted in the dark room recall those
of the altar, and that Fräulein von Kulp, "Who turned in the
hall, one hand on the door," climaxes the series with an epiphany of guilty terror that throws over the preceding eight
lines the lurid malaise of some cosmopolitan Black Mass: the
recurrent plaything of societies too bored to abandon belief.
The words "Vacant shuttles weave the wind" lead us to
Stephen Dedalus' meditation, in the first chapter of *Ulysses*, on
Mulligan the parody-priest:

> Words Mulligan had spoken a moment since in mockery to the
> stranger. Idle mockery. The void awaits surely all them that
> weave the wind: a menace, a disarming and a worsting from
> those embattled angels of the church.

The void awaits them:

> De Bailhache, Fresca, Mrs. Cammel, whirled

Beyond the circuit of the shuddering Bear
In fractured atoms.

The Bear came from *Bussy D'Ambois*:

> fly where men feel
> The cunning axle-tree, or those that suffer
> Under the chariot of the snowy Bear.

Chapman's Bear is snowy, Eliot's shuddering: perhaps not only
with cold; there is a quaint tradition that the Bear's orgasm
lasts nine days.

It is by a fearsome access of self-consciousness that the Communion of the Faithful has turned into a Black Mass: not even,
with that roll-call of cosmopolitan names, honest mediaeval
deviltry, but something late, knowing, and depraved. But there
are hierarchies of illicit knowledge. Madame de Tornquist and
Mrs. Cammel (the latter, one feels sure, a cousin of the "dear
Mrs. Equitone" who ordered a horoscope) are relatively in-
advertent cases of moral suicide: the one a Modigliani subject,
the other a silly woman seeking amusement. Gerontion has
known more than they; he has known *them*. "After such
knowledge, what forgiveness?" It is his degree of consciousness
that damns him, or so he thinks. The others are scarcely distinguishable from such an ambience as Ezra Pound was to recall
decades later:

> Her Ladyship arose in the night
> and moved all the furniture
> (that is her Ladyship YX)
> her Ladyship Z disliked dining alone and
> The proud shall not lie by the proud
> amid dim green lighted with candles

"The proud may lie by the proud," says the First Musician
near the close of Yeats' *Deirdre*: these lines recall perhaps a
private perfomance. It was a close, indoor world, and Pound
frequented the best of it:

> Mabel Beardsley's red hair for a glory
> Mr Masefield murmuring: Death

> and old Neptune meaning something unseizable
> in a discussion of Flaubert
> Miss Tomczyk, the medium
> baffling the society for metaphysical research . . .

Madame de Tornquist and Fräulein von Kulp merely partake, at several removes, of this world's tone.

Gerontion is not only aware, like them, of the presence of guilt, but also of the extent of that which presses, of his own acedia, and of the process, partly moral, partly historical, by which, as his own life and the Great Year of twenty centuries approach simultaneous close, the redeemer, once

> The word within a word, unable to speak a word

looms as avenger:

> The tiger springs in the new year. Us he devours. Think at last
> We have not reached conclusion, when I
> Stiffen in a rented house.

"Conclusion" has more than one significance. He remonstrates with Christ the Tiger; or perhaps, in this poem of systematized ambivalences, with a missed love remembered from his Prufrockian days:

> I would meet you upon this honestly.
> I that was near your heart was removed therefrom
> To lose beauty in terror, terror in inquisition.
> I have lost my passion: why should I need to keep it
> Since what is kept must be adulterated?

"Inquisition" and "passion" are in simultaneous touch with religious history and amatory misadventure; "kept" and "adulterated" taint the idiom of the penny papers and the divorce courts with a metaphor from spoilt meat.

> These with a thousand small deliberations
> Protract the profit of their chilled delirium,
> Excite the membrane, when the sense has cooled
> With pungent sauces, multiply variety
> In a wilderness of mirrors.

There were deliberations about History in the Hall of Mirrors at Versailles, and Sir Epicure Mammon proposed aphrodisiac glasses

> Cut in more subtle angles to disperse
> And multiply my image as I walk
> Naked between my succubae;

there was also a celebrated Parisian brothel which adopted this device. But these lines image also the method of the poem itself, an affair of "pungent sauces" and allusions thrice redoubled, proper to the decadence of a poetic tradition which at one time could do all that was needed with open exactness—

> And smale fowles maken melodye

—but must now manipulate "small deliberations" in a culture whose sense of such unpretentious precisions has cooled.

Lechery unindulged, in the last fifteen lines of the poem, gives way to usury unattempted: usury, a controlling passion that expresses itself in small deliberations rather than subtle confusions, and that can protract, after "the sense has cooled," the lifelong abstract appetite for exploiting nature. "Profit," "multiply," the weevil and the spider, the bear of falling markets, the gull, the Trades; these are among the key terms of the closing section. Correspondingly, sensation grows more abstract, the rhetoric less vibrant; images of interstellar spaces and of winds over stormy capes replace the house, the dark room, and the corridors. The poem closes as it opened on images of adventure; but by comparison with the muscular immediacy of the conquistador "heaving a cutlass, bitten by flies," the windy straits of Belle Isle or the Horn are evoked with a cartographer's abstractness. Nor do the trade ships beating around the Horn occupy attention: merely a single gull whose fate ("white feathers in the snow") is comparable in nature but not at all in scope with that of the folk who were blown

> Beyond the circuit of the shuddering Bear
> In fractured atoms.

"Horn" does not vibrate, as it would have earlier in the poem, with sexual connotations; a dreamy obviousness is overtaking Gerontion's reflections,

> an old man driven by the Trades
> To a sleepy corner.

The poem ends with a plausible bridge into the world where images have a Lockean patness and applicability:

> Tenants of the house,
> Thoughts of a dry brain in a dry season.

This has a look of exegetic universality, clearing up everything, resolving all, and restoring us to daylight. Actually it is an index of the speaker's failed imagination, at the furthest extreme from his earlier polysemous intensity. He begins to talk what we are accustomed to regard as sense only at the instant when he is too fatigued to hang onto the rich vision any longer.

ii

One poem like this is enough; it purges the language. *Gerontion* exploits systematically what a decade later Mr. William Empson was to denominate as the norm of English poetic effect, describing as "alien to the habits of the English language" a Dryden's lack of interest in "the echoes and recesses of words." The author of *Gerontion* is enquiring into the past of that world made out of words which the author of *Prufrock* had received from Swinburne and Tennyson: a world in which poetic effects are inclined to glide succulently down among words, looking like sleep, proffering the reader a strong toil of grace; in which the poet more or less consciously capitalizes on the abundance, in English, of words which, like "toil" and "grace," incorporate barely differentiated the force of verb, noun, and adjective simultaneously, and so discourage a sentence from going unambiguously about its business.

These effects, these potentialities, began to be exploited in that region of the English poetic past from which *Gerontion* draws most of its sap: the verse drama of the sixteenth and seventeenth centuries. They were exploited by dramatists confronted with a special problem, the necessity for taking the spectator's mind off what he could be shown. A Marlowe's or a Shakespeare's descriptive passages dream richly away from the visible; this, on the stage before us, is *not* the face that launched a thousand ships, so it is incumbent on the speaking voice to dizzy our faculties with "topless towers" and "wanton Arethusa's azur'd arms." The air on the Elsinore battlements is "nipping and eager"—an odd half-realizable metaphor—because the real air is merely that of a theatre on a London afternoon. The "temple-haunting martlet" builds her "tender bed and procreant cradle" because for the actor to gesture less enchantingly toward imagined birds' nests would simply rivet the spectators' attention on the pillars of the stage, where no birds' nests are in sight. Cleopatra

> looks like sleep,
> As she would catch another Antony
> In her strong toil of grace

because—and this principle is operative whenever we are apparently invited to look at the heroine—only language blending the "echoes and recesses" of several levels of meaning can prevent us at such a moment from focusing our attention, disastrously, on how the boy-actor actually looks.

This capacity for transfiguring the visible was developed at the expense of many other potentialities of English. Certain Chaucerian virtues were permanently abandoned; and by 1600 or so the main current of English pentameter verse had lost all touch with the sort of lucidity in which Marlowe dealt when the exigencies of the stage did not confront him:

> The air is cold, and sleep is sweetest now. . . .

And after the Civil War put the Jacobean drama into eclipse, the dramatists' rhetoric was succeeded not by Chaucerian immediacy but, unluckily, by verbalism of another kind: by

Dryden's "magniloquence," by Milton's self-sufficient syntactic constructions; while, except for the song-writers sustained by the example of Jonson or by a living tradition of
music, minor verse, equally remote from the presented fact
but devoid of a Dryden's or a Milton's propulsiveness, simply
went decadent.

Gerontion was written by an American, who, acquiring this
corrupt tradition by great labour—notably, by detailed study
of the later Jacobean dramatists—resembles no other American
writer so much as he does Poe. Poe was the one earlier instance
of a notable American who, impressed from the outside by a
poetry of majestic imprecision and incantation, adopted its
detachable procedures, though what he made with them, confining himself as he did to procedures rather than seeking to
install himself in a tradition, is self-sufficient as no native English
verse could be, a sport rather than a development.

> . . . the scoriac rivers that roll . . .
> Their sulphurous currents down Yaanek
> In the ultimate climes of the Pole—

—as Eliot said, not only the *reductio ad absurdum* but the completion. Though we can trace *Ulalume's* derivation from English
romanticism, it has the air of a complete poetic method invented out of nothing and then exhausted, leaving no more for
a successor to do. On the other hand

> Oxus, forgetting the bright speed he had
> In his high mountain cradle in Pamir

or

> Of meadows drowsy with Trinacrian bees . . .

—such fragments written in England, however unimportant,
imply a tradition, pointing back to effects that have been
achieved earlier and suggesting others still to be achieved.

Eliot's dealings with such methods were more knowing and
subtle than Poe's, founded on close analysis, a quickened historical sense (Poe's past is a collective yesterday, not a process),

and considerable careful apprenticeship. Yet they do not, since Eliot remains an American, at all resemble the methods of even so eccentric a native to the tradition as "Beddoes, prince of morticians."★ Eliot's ventriloquial pastiche incorporates with great deliberateness the possible historical range of every word, each word adjusted to its neighbours in order to generate a maximum of controlled ambiguity which does not constitute a poetic aura surrounding the statement, but is itself the "meaning," subsuming statement. In Coleridge's line,

> Through caverns measureless to man

"measureless," which vibrates with more than the paraphrasable meaning "not measurable by," is a membrane stretched over a hollow space, to make the sense of the line drum and echo. In Poe's line,

> It was down by the dank tarn of Auber,

a "dank tarn" is something existing neither in the past nor in the normal present, but only in the unique world of Poe's imagination. But in Eliot's line

> After such knowledge, what forgiveness?

each word is a crevasse opening down into infinite temporal recesses: not merely all the senses of all the words as listed on historical principles by the Oxford dictionary ("knowledge," for instance, a word with sexual and Biblical as well as epistemological contexts) but inarticulate terrors and desires on which the dictionary is incapable of touching. One is not

---

★Curious, is it not, that Mr. Eliot
Has not given more time to Mr Beddoes
   (T.L.) prince of morticians
  where none can speak his language
centuries hoarded
to pull up a mass of algae
          (and pearls)
or the odour of eucalyptus or sea-wrack. . . .
                 —Pound, Canto 80.

tempted to suppose that the line was put together in cold blood, but long detached contemplation of each of these words in many possible contexts lay behind the moment when the line was achieved. The language of *Gerontion* is not in any identifiable American poetic idiom, indeed it counteracts the characteristic twentieth-century development of American poetry; but it is an exploitation of certain English traditions carried out with an exhaustive, deliberate thoroughness only possible to an American sufficiently detached from the traditions to see from the outside what they were. It exploits and exhausts one of the historical implications of the idiom of Jacobean drama. Its brilliance is that of the conflagration attending the burning of dead moss off building stones. It need not be done twice, and Eliot does not do it again. The words of *The Waste Land* have an echoing gravity of quite another order.

iii

A poet so intensively concerned as is Eliot with moral states did not fail to investigate the moral implications of Jacobean rhetoric: concretely in *Gerontion*, discursively eight years later in the long essay, "Seneca in Elizabethan Translation." There he notes that the Senecan play is meant to be delivered as a monologue, its characters and events all subsisting in the texture of a continuous flow of words inflected by a single speaking voice; and comparing this unacted drama with the Greek, he observes of the Greek that behind its dialogue

> we are always conscious of a concrete visual actuality, and behind that of a specific emotional actuality. Behind the drama of words is the drama of action, the timbre of voice and voice, the uplifted hand or tense muscle, and the particular emotion.

The spoken or printed play is thus "shorthand" for "the actual and felt play, which is always the real thing." In the plays of Seneca, on the other hand,

> the drama is all in the word, and the word has no further reality behind it:

a fair description of *Gerontion*, and in tendency true of the Elizabethan plays as well.

Eliot's interest in the sixteenth-century cult of Seneca, which occupied his attention at about the time when he was writing the *Sweeney Agonistes* fragments, focuses on some hidden connexion between a theatre of declamation and a morality of postures. "The 'beliefs' of Stoicism," he observes, "are a consequence of scepticism; and the ethic of Seneca's plays is that of an age which supplied the lack of moral habits by a system of moral attitudes and poses. . . . The ethic of Seneca is a matter of postures. The posture which gives the greatest opportunity for effect . . . is the posture of dying: death gives his characters the opportunity for their most sententious aphorisms—a hint which Elizabethan dramatists were only too ready to follow."

These statements supply some scholarly underpinning to the view outlined in "Rhetoric and Poetic Drama," that the artistically valid rhetoric in Shakespeare's plays occurs when the character sees himself in a dramatic light. He sees himself in a dramatic light because in a crisis a dramatic image of himself gives him a comfort the mere facts of the situation will not give him, imprisoning him or crumbling away beneath his feet. "Stoicism . . . is the permanent substratum of a number of versions of cheering oneself up. The Stoical attitude is the reverse of Christian humility."

And the attitude of Gerontion, drawing accesses of lurid comfort from the notion that the Christ who will judge him is a devouring tiger, is also the reverse of Christian humility.

> The tiger springs in the new year. Us he devours. Think at last
> We have not reached conclusion, when I
> Stiffen in a rented house. Think at last
> I have not made this show purposelessly
> And it is not by any concitation
> Of the backward devils.
> I would meet you upon this honestly.

We note the emphatic placement of "I" before "stiffen," the

implication that "this show," purposeful or not, is at least of his own making, the ascription to himself of conspicuous honesty at the moment (he rather likes to suppose) of damnation. This theatre of words, where the word has no firm reality behind it, is as much as the theatre of Seneca or Chapman a theatre of moral postures, of the Stoicism which is the permanent substratum of a number of versions of cheering oneself up. Eliot's next *persona*, Tiresias (1921), is not concerned with cheering himself up; he is concerned, as Gerontion in his phantasmagoric cycle of images is not, with the identity of that which he discerns, with the moral nature of others who are caught on the wheel. A later *persona*, Simeon (1928), suppresses even the self-dramatization inherent in claiming to "foresuffer all"; he says simply,

There went never any rejected from my door.

And *A Song for Simeon* is as we shall see a carefully arranged antithesis to *Gerontion*.

III. THE DEATH OF EUROPE

Chronology
London 1921–1925.
"London Letters" in *The Dial*, 1921–1922.
"Lettres d'Angleterre" in *La Nouvelle Revue Française*,
1922–1923.
Editorship of *The Criterion* commenced October, 1922.
The Waste Land published October, 1922.
Portions of *The Hollow Men* published 1924–1925.
Poems 1909–1925 published November, 1925, including
The Waste Land and the complete *The Hollow Men*.

THE WASTE LAND

This dust will not settle in our time.
                    —Samuel Beckett.

i

The Waste Land was drafted during a rest cure at Margate
("I can connect Nothing with nothing") and Lausanne ("In
this decayed hole among the mountains") during the autumn
of 1921 by a convalescent preoccupied partly with the ruin of
post-war Europe, partly with his own health and the conditions
of his servitude to a bank in London, partly with a hardly exor-
able apprehension that two thousand years of European continuity had for the first time run dry. It had for epigraph a
phrase from Conrad's *Heart of Darkness* ("The horror! The
horror!"); embedded in the text were a glimpse, borrowed
from Conrad's opening page, of the red sails of barges drifting
in the Thames Estuary, and a contrasting reference to "the
heart of light." "Nothing is easier," Conrad had written,
". . . than to evoke the great spirit of the past upon the lower
reaches of the Thames."

In Paris that winter, Ezra Pound has recalled, "*The Waste
Land* was placed before me as a series of poems. I advised him
what to leave out." Eliot, from about the same distance of
time, recalls showing Pound "a sprawling chaotic poem . . .
which left his hands, reduced to about half its size, in the form

in which it appears in print." Since "the form in which it appears in print," with its many sudden transitions and its implication, inhering in tone and cross-references and reinforced by notes, of a centre of gravity nowhere explicitly located, remained for many years the most sensational aspect of *The Waste Land*, this transaction requires looking into. The manuscript with the Conrad epigraph and Pound's blue-pencilling has been lost sight of; John Quinn appears to have made a private bestowal of it before his collection was dispersed in 1924. From surviving clues—chiefly three letters that passed between Pound and Eliot in the winter of 1921–1922—one may hazard guesses concerning the nature of the original series.

The letters, though they were exchanged after the major operation on the poem had been performed, disclose Eliot still in the act of agonizing not only about residual verbal details but about the desirability of adding or suppressing whole sections. "There were long passages in different metres, with short lyrics sandwiched in between," he has since recalled. The long passages included "a rather poor pastiche of Pope," which was presumably the occasion of Pound's dictum, elsewhere recorded, that pastiche is only justified if it is better than the original; "another passage about a fashionable lady having breakfast in bed, and another long passage about a shipwreck, which was obviously inspired by the Ulysses episode in the *Inferno*." This would have led up to the "death by water" of the "drowned Phoenician sailor"; Victor Bérard's speculations concerning the possible origin of the *Odyssey* in Phoenician *periploi* had been in print for twenty years and had occupied the attention of James Joyce. The deletion of these passages was apparently accepted without protest. The lyrics, on the other hand, contained elements Eliot struggled to preserve. After they have been removed from the body of *The Waste Land* he proposes putting them at the end, and is again dissuaded: "The thing now runs from 'April . . .' to 'shantih' without a break. That is 19 pages, and let us say the longest poem in the English langwidge. Don't try to bust all records by prolonging it three pages further." One of the lyrics contained a "sweats with tears" passage which Eliot, after deletion from its original context, proposed working into the "nerves monologue: only place where it can go." Pound vetoed it again: "I dare say the sweats with tears will wait." It didn't wait long; we find it in a poem contributed pseudonymously to Wyndham Lewis' *Tyro* a little before the publication of *The Waste Land*, and later revised for publication in a triad of *Dream Songs*, all three of which may have descended from the *ur-Waste Land*.★ Pound also dissuaded Eliot from installing *Gerontion* as a prelude to the sequence, forebade him to delete "Phlebas the Phoenician," and nagged about the Conrad epigraph until a better one was discovered in Petronius.

These events are worth reconstructing because they clarify a number of things about the scope and intention of the poem. It was conceived as a somewhat loose medley, as the relief of more diffuse impulses than those to which its present compacted form corresponds. The separate preservation of the *Dream Songs* and the incorporation of some of their motifs, after much trial and error, into what is now *The Hollow Men*, testifies to Eliot's stubborn conviction that there was virtue in some of the omitted elements, whether or not their presence could be justified within the wholeness, not at first foreseen by the author, which the greater part of *The Waste Land* at length assumed. That wholeness, since it never did incorporate everything the author wanted it to, was to some extent a compromise, got by permuting with another's assistance materials he no longer had it in him to rethink; and finally, after Pound, by simply eliminating everything not of the first intensity, had revealed an unexpected corporate substantiality in what sur-

---

★Two of them, *The wind sprang up* and *Eyes that last I saw in tears,* are preserved in the collected volume as *Minor Poems*. The third is now part iii of *The Hollow Men*. The poem in *The Tyro* is called *Song to the Opherian* and signed "Gus Krutzsch," a portmanteau-name of which Kurtz seems to be one of the components. There are many small signs that *The Hollow Men* grew from rejected pieces of *The Waste Land*.

vived, Eliot's impulse was to "explain" the poem as "thoughts of a dry brain in a dry season" by prefixing *Gerontion*.

That is to say, the first quality of *The Waste Land* to catch a newcomer's attention, its self-sufficient juxtaposition without copulae of themes and passages in a dense mosaic, had at first a novelty which troubled even the author. It was a quality arrived at by Pound's cutting; it didn't trouble Pound, who had already begun work on *The Cantos*. But Eliot, preoccupied as always with the seventeenth-century drama and no doubt tacitly encouraged by the example of Browning, naturally conceived a long poem as somebody's spoken or unspoken monologue, its shifts of direction and transition from theme to theme psychologically justified by the workings of the speakers' brain. *Prufrock* and *Gerontion* elucidate not only a phase of civilization but a perceiving—for the purpose of the poem, a presiding—consciousness. For anyone who has undergone immersion in the delicate phenomenology of Francis Herbert Bradley, in fact, it is meaningless to conceive of a presentation that cannot be resolved into an experienced content and a "finite centre" which experiences. The perceiver is describable only as the zone of consciousness where that which he perceives can coexist; but the perceived, conversely, can't be accorded independent status; it is, precisely, all that can coexist in this particular zone of consciousness. In a loose sequence of poems these considerations need give no trouble; the pervading zone of consciousness is that of the author: as we intuit Herrick in *Hesperides*, or Herbert in *The Temple*. But a five-parted work of 434 lines entitled *The Waste Land*, with sudden wrenching juxtapositions, thematic links between section and section, fragments quoted from several languages with no one present to whose mind they can occur: this dense textural unity, as queer as *Le Sacre du Printemps*, must have seemed to Eliot a little factitious until he had got used to the poem in its final form; which, as everyone who has encountered it knows, must take some time. So we discover him endeavouring to square the artistic fact with his pervasive intuition of fitness by the note on Tiresias, which offers to supply the poem with a nameable point of view:

> Tiresias, although a mere spectator and not indeed a "charac-
> ter", is yet the most important personage in the poem, uniting
> all the rest. Just as the one-eyed merchant, seller of currants, melts
> into the Phoenician Sailor, and the latter is not wholly distinct
> from Ferdinand Prince of Naples, so all the women are one
> woman, and the two sexes meet in Tiresias. What Tiresias *sees*,
> in fact, is the substance of the poem.

If we take this note as an afterthought, a token placation, say, of the ghost of Bradley, rather than as elucidative of the assumption under which the writing was originally done, our approach to *The Waste Land* will be facilitated. In fact we shall do well to discard the notes as much as possible; they have bedevilled discussion for decades.

The writing of the notes was a last complication in the fractious history of the poem's composition; it is doubtful whether any other acknowledged masterpiece has been so heavily marked, with the author's consent, by forces outside his control. The notes got added to *The Waste Land* as a con-sequence of the technological fact that books are printed in multiples of thirty-two pages.

The poem, which had appeared without any annotation whatever in *The Criterion* and in the *Dial* (October and Novem-ber, 1922, respectively), was in book form too long for thirty-two pages of decent-sized print and a good deal too short for sixty-four. So Eliot (at length disinclined, fortunately, to insert *Gerontion* as a preface or to append the cancelled lyrics) set to work to expand a few notes in which he had identified the quotations, "with a view to spiking the guns of critics of my earlier poems who had accused me of plagiarism."* He dilated on the Tarot Pack, copied out nineteen lines from Ovid and thirty-three words from Chapman's *Handbook of Birds of*

---

*This incredibly illiterate literary society seems to have been wholly unaware of the methods of Pope, or else to have supposed that a period allegedly devoted to "profuse strains of unpremeditated art" had rendered such methods obsolete.

Eastern North America, recorded his evaluation of the interior of the Church of St. Magnus Martyr, saluted the late Henry Clarke Warren as one of the great pioneers of Buddhist studies in the Occident, directed the reader's attention to a hallucination recorded on one of the Antarctic expeditions ("I forget which, but I think one of Shackleton's"), and eventually, with the aid of quotations from Froude, Bradley, and Hermann Hesse's *Blick ins Chaos*, succeeded in padding the thing out to a suitable length. The keying of these items to specific passages by the academic device of numbering lines—hence Eliot's pleasantry, twenty-four years later, about "bogus scholarship" —may be surmised to have been done in haste: early in *What the Thunder Said* a line was missed in the counting. "I have sometimes thought," Eliot has said, "of getting rid of these notes; but now they can never be unstuck. They have had almost greater popularity than the poem itself. . . . It was just, no doubt, that I should pay my tribute to the work of Miss Jessie Weston; but I regret having sent so many enquirers off on a wild goose chase after Tarot cards and the Holy Grail." We have license therefore to ignore them, and instead "endeavour to grasp what the poetry is aiming to be . . . to grasp its entelechy."

That the entelechy is graspable without source-hunting, and without even appeal to any but the most elementary knowledge of one or two myths and a few Shakespearean tags, is a statement requiring temerity to sustain in the face of all the scholarship that has been expended during a third of a century on these 434 lines. It inheres, however, in Dr. Leavis' admirably tactful account of the poem in *New Bearings*, and in Pound's still earlier testimony. In 1924 Pound rebutted a piece of reviewers' acrimony with the flat statement that the poem's obscurities were reducible to four Sanskrit words, three of which are

> so implied in the surrounding text that one can pass them by
> . . . without losing the general tone or the main emotion of the
> passage. They are so obviously the words of some ritual or other.

[One does need to be told that "shantih" means "peace."]

> For the rest, I saw the poem in typescript, and I did not see the notes till 6 or 8 months afterward; and they have not increased my enjoyment of the poem one atom. The poem seems to me an emotional unit . . .
>
> I have not read Miss Weston's *Ritual to Romance,* and do not at present intend to. As to the citations, I do not think it matters a damn which is from Day, which from Milton, Middleton, Webster, or Augustine. I mean so far as the functioning of the poem in concerned. One's incult pleasure in reading *The Waste Land* would be the same if Webster had written "Women Before Woman" and Marvell the *Metamorphoses.*

His parting shot deserves preservation:

> This demand for clarity in every particular of a work, whether essential or not, reminds me of the Pre-Raphaelite painter who was doing a twilight scene but rowed across the river in day time to see the shape of the leaves on the further bank, which he then drew in with full detail.

ii

A Game of Chess is a convenient place to start our investigations. Chess is played with Queens and Pawns: the set of pieces mimics a social hierarchy, running from "The Chair she sat in, like a burnished throne," to "Goonight Bill. Goonight Lou. Goonight May. Goonight." It is a silent unnerving warfare

> ("Speak to me. Why do you never speak. Speak.
> "What are you thinking of? What thinking? What?
> "I never know what you are thinking. Think.")

in which everything hinges on the welfare of the King, the weakest piece on the board, and in this section of the poem invisible (though a "barbarous king" once forced Philomel.) Our attention is focused on the Queen.

> The Chair she sat in, like a burnished throne,
> Glowed on the marble, where the glass
> Held up by standards wrought with fruited vines
> From which a golden Cupidon peeped out

(Another hid his eyes behind his wing)
Doubled the flames of sevenbranched candelabra
Reflecting light upon the table as
The glitter of her jewels rose to meet it,
From satin cases poured in rich profusion. . . .

This isn't a Miltonic sentence, brilliantly contorted; it lacks
nerve, forgetting after ten words its confident opening ("The
Chair she sat in") to dissipate itself among glowing and smoul-
dering sensations, like a progression of Wagner's. Cleopatra
"o'erpicturing that Venus where we see / The fancy outwork
nature") sat outdoors; this Venusberg interior partakes of "an
atmosphere of Juliet's tomb," and the human inhabitant appears
once, in a perfunctory subordinate clause. Pope's Belinda conducted "the sacred rites of pride"—

> This casket India's glowing gems unlocks,
> And all Arabia breathes from yonder box.

The woman at the dressing-table in *The Waste Land*, implied
but never named or attended to, is not like Belinda the moral
centre of an innocent dislocation of values, but simply the
implied sensibility in which these multifarious effects dissolve
and find congruence. All things deny nature; the fruited vines
are carved, the Cupidons golden, the light not of the sun, the
perfumes synthetic, the candelabra (seven-branched, as for an
altar) devoted to no rite, the very colour of the fire-light
perverted by sodium and copper salts. The dolphin is carved,
and swims in a "sad light," not, like Antony's delights, "showing his back above the element he lives in."

No will to exploit new sensations is present; the will has
long ago died; this opulent ambience is neither chosen nor
questioned. The "sylvan scene" is not Eden nor a window but
a painting, and a painting of an unnatural event:

> The change of Philomel, by the barbarous king
> So rudely forced; yet there the nightingale
> Filled all the desert with inviolable voice
> And still she cried, and still the world pursues,
> "Jug Jug" to dirty ears.

Her voice alone, like the voice that modulates the thick fluid of this sentence, is "inviolable"; like Tiresias in Thebes, she is prevented from identifying the criminal whom only she can name. John Lyly wrote down her song more than two centuries before Keats (who wasn't interested in what she was saying):

> What bird so sings yet so dos wayle?
> O 'Tis the ravishd Nightingale.
> Jug, Jug, Jug, tereu, shee cryes,
> And still her woes at Midnight rise.
> Brave prick song! . . .

Lyly, not being committed to the idea that the bird was pouring forth its soul abroad, noted that it stuck to its script ("prick song") and himself attempted a transcription. Lyly of course is perfectly aware of what she is trying to say: "tereu" comes very close to "Tereus." It remained for the nineteenth century to dissolve her plight into a symbol of diffuse *Angst,* indeed to impute "ecstasy" amid human desolation, "here, where men sit and hear each other groan"; and for the twentieth century to hang up a painting of the event on a dressing-room wall, as pungent sauce to appetites jaded with the narrative clarity of mythologies, but responsive to the visceral thrill and the pressures of "significant form." The picture, a "withered stump of time," hangs there, one item in a collection that manages to be not edifying but sinister:

> staring forms
> Leaned out, leaning, hushing the room enclosed.

Then the visitor, as always in Eliot, mounts a stairway—

> Footsteps shuffled on the stair.

—and we get human conversation at last:

> "What is that noise?"
>   The wind under the door.
> "What is that noise now? What is the wind doing?"
>   Nothing again nothing.

"Do
"You know nothing? Do you see nothing? Do you remember
"Nothing?"
    I remember
Those are pearls that were his eyes.

"My experience falls within my own circle, a circle closed
on the outside; and, with all its elements alike, every sphere
is opaque to the other which surround it." What is there to
say but "nothing"? He remembers a quotation, faintly appo-
site; in this room the European past, effects and *objets d'art*
gathered from many centuries, has suffered a sea-change, into
something rich and strange, and stifling. Sensibility here is the
very inhibition of life; and activity is reduced to the manic
capering of "that Shakespeherian Rag," the past imposing no
austerity, existing simply to be used.

        "What shall we do tomorrow?
"What shall we ever do?"
        The hot water at ten.
And if it rains, a closed car at four.
And we shall play a game of chess,
Pressing lidless eyes and waiting for a knock upon the door.

If we move from the queens to the pawns, we find low life
no more free or natural, equally obsessed with the denial of
nature, artificial teeth, chemically procured abortions, the
speaker and her interlocutor battening fascinated at second-
hand on the life of Lil and her Albert, Lil and Albert interested
only in spurious ideal images of one another

(He'll want to know what you done with that money he gave you
To get yourself some teeth. . . .
He said, I swear, I can't bear to look at you.)

And this point—nature everywhere denied, its ceremonies
simplified to the brutal abstractions of a chess-game

(He's been in the army four years, he wants a good time,
And if you don't give it him, there's others will, I said.
Oh is there, she said. Something o' that, I said.
Then I'll know who to thank, she said, and give me a straight look.)

—this point is made implicitly by a device carried over from *Whispers of Immortality,* the juxtaposition without comment or copula of two levels of sensibility: the world of one who reads Webster with the world of one who knows Grishkin, the world of the inquiring wind and the sense drowned in odours with the world of ivory teeth and hot gammon. In Lil and Albert's milieu there is fertility, in the milieu where golden Cupidons peep out there is not; but Lil and Albert's breeding betokens not a harmony of wills but only Albert's improvident refusal to leave Lil alone. The chemist with commercial impartiality supplies one woman with "strange synthetic perfumes" and the other with "them pills I took, to bring it off," aphrodisiacs and abortifacients; he is the tutelary deity, uniting the offices of Cupid and Hymen, of a world which is under a universal curse.

From this vantage-point we can survey the methods of the first section, which opens with a denial of Chaucer:

> Whan that Aprille with his shoures soote
> The droughte of March hath perced to the roote
> And bathed every veyne in swich licour
> Of which vertu engendred is the flour. . . .
> Thanne longen folk to goon on pilgrimages. . . .

In the twentieth-century version we have a prayer-book heading, *The Burial of the Dead,* with its implied ceremonial of dust thrown and of souls reborn; and the poem begins,

> April is the cruellest month, breeding
> Lilacs out of the dead land, mixing
> Memory and desire, stirring
> Dull roots with spring rain.

No "vertu" is engendered amid this apprehensive reaching forward of participles, and instead of pilgrimages we have European tours:

> we stopped in the colonnade,
> And went on in sunlight, into the Hofgarten,
> And drank coffee, and talked for an hour.

Up out of the incantation breaks a woman's voice, giving tongue to the ethnological confusions of the new Europe, the subservience of *patria* to whim of statesmen, the interplay of immutable fact and national pride:

Bin gar keine Russin, stamm' aus Litauen, echt deutsch.

—a mixing of memory and desire. Another voice evokes the vanished Austro-Hungarian Empire, the inbred malaise of Mayerling, regressive thrills, objectless travels:

And when we were children, staying at the archduke's,
My cousin's, he took me out on a sled,
And I was frightened. He said, Marie,
Marie, hold on tight. And down we went.
In the mountains, there you feel free.
I read, much of the night, and go south in the winter.

"In the mountains, there you feel free." We have only to delete "there" to observe the collapse of more than a rhythm: to observe how the line's exact mimicry of a fatigue which supposes it has reached some ultimate perception can telescope spiritual bankruptcy, deracinated ardour, and an illusion of liberty which is no more than impatience with human society and relief at a temporary change. It was a restless, pointless world that collapsed during the war, agitated out of habit but tired beyond coherence, on the move to avoid itself. The memories in lines 8 to 18 seem spacious and precious now; then, the events punctuated a terrible continuum of boredom.

The plight of the Sibyl in the epigraph rhymes with that of Marie; the terrible thing is to be compelled to stay alive. "For I with these my own eyes have seen the Cumaean Sibyl hanging in a jar; and when the boys said, 'What do you want, Sibyl?' she answered, 'I want to die.'" The sentence is in a macaronic Latin, posterior to the best age, pungently sauced with Greek; Cato would have contemplated with unblinking severity Petronius' readers' jazz-age craving for the cosmopolitan. The Sibyl in her better days answered questions by flinging from her cave handfuls of leaves bearing letters which the postulant was required to arrange in a suitable order; the wind commonly blew half of them away. Like Tiresias, like Philomel, like the modern poet, she divulged forbidden knowledge only in riddles, fitfully. (Tiresias wouldn't answer Oedipus at all; and he put off Odysseus with a puzzle about an oar mistaken for a winnowing-fan.) *The Waste Land* is suffused with a functional obscurity, sibylline fragments so disposed as to yield the utmost in connotative power, embracing the fragmented present and reaching back to "that vanished mind of which our mind is a continuation." As for the Sibyl's present exhaustion, she had foolishly asked Apollo for as many years as the grains of sand in her hand; which is one layer in the multi-layered line, "I will show you fear in a handful of dust." She is the prophetic power, no longer consulted by heroes but tormented by curious boys, still answering because she must; she is Madame Sosostris, consulted by dear Mrs. Equitone and harried by police ("One must be so careful these days"); she is the image of the late phase of Roman civilization, now vanished; she is also "the mind of Europe," a mind more important than one's own private mind, a mind which changes but abandons nothing en route, not superannuating either Shakespeare, or Homer, or the rock drawing of the Magdalenian draughtsmen; but now very nearly exhausted by the effort to stay interested in its own contents.

Which brings us to the "heap of broken images": not only desert ruins of some past from which life was withdrawn with the failure of the water supply, like the Roman cities in North Africa, or Augustine's Carthage, but also the manner in which Shakespeare, Homer, and the drawings of Michelangelo, Raphael, and the Magdalenian draughtsmen coexist in the contemporary cultivated consciousness: fragments, familiar quotations: *poluphloisboio thalasse,* to be or not to be, undo this button, one touch of nature, etc., God creating the Sun and Moon, those are pearls that were his eyes. For one man who knows *The Tempest* intimately there are a thousand who can identify the lines about the cloud-capp'd towers; painting is a miscellany of reproductions, literature a potpourri of quotations, history a chaos of theories and postures (Nelson's telescope, Washington crossing the Delaware, government of, for and by the people, the Colosseum, the guillotine). A desert wind has blown half the leaves away; disuse and vandals have broken the monuments—

> What are the roots that clutch, what branches grow
> Out of this stony rubbish? Son of man,
> You cannot say, or guess, for you know only
> A heap of broken images, where the sun beats,
> And the dead tree gives no shelter, the cricket no relief,
> And the dry stone no sound of water. . . .

Cities are built out of the ruins of previous cities, as *The Waste Land* is built out of the remains of older poems. But at this stage no building is yet in question; the "Son of man" (a portentously generalizing phrase) is moving tirelessly eastward, when the speaker accosts him with a sinister "Come in under the shadow of this red rock," and offers to show him not merely horror and desolation but something older and deeper: fear.

Hence the hyacinth girl, who speaks with urgent hurt simplicity, like the mad Ophelia:

> "You gave me hyacinths first a year ago;
> They called me the hyacinth girl."

They are childlike words, self-pitying, spoken perhaps in memory, perhaps by a ghost, perhaps by a wistful woman now out of her mind. The response exposes many contradictory layers of feeling:

> —Yet when we came back, late, from the Hyacinth garden,
> Your arms full, and your hair wet, I could not
> Speak, and my eyes failed, I was neither
> Living nor dead, and I knew nothing,
> Looking into the heart of light, the silence.

The context is erotic, the language that of mystical experience: plainly a tainted mysticism. "The Hyacinth garden" sounds queerly like a lost cult's sacred grove, and her arms were no doubt full of flowers; what rite was there enacted or evaded we can have no means of knowing.

But another level of meaning is less ambiguous: perhaps in fantasy, the girl has been drowned. Five pages later *A Game of Chess* ends with Ophelia's words before her death; Ophelia gathered flowers before she tumbled into the stream, then lay and chanted snatches of old tunes—

> Frisch weht der Wind
> Der Heimat zu . . .

while her clothes and hair spread out on the waters. *The Burial of the Dead* ends with a sinister dialogue about a corpse in the garden—

> Has it begun to sprout? Will it bloom this year?
> Or has the sudden frost disturbed its bed?

—two Englishmen discussing their tulips, with a note of the terrible intimacy with which murderers imagine themselves being taunted. The traditional British murderer—unlike his American counterpart, who in a vast land instinctively puts distance between himself and the corpse—prefers to keep it near at hand; in the garden, or behind the wainscoting, or

> bones cast in a little low dry garret,
> Rattled by the rat's foot only, year to year.

The Fire Sermon opens with despairing fingers clutching and sinking into a wet bank; it closes with Thames-daughters singing from beneath the oily waves. The drowned Phlebas in Section IV varies this theme; and at the close of the poem the response to the last challenge of the thunder alludes to something that happened in a boat:

> your heart would have responded
> Gaily, when invited, beating obedient
> To controlling hands

—but what in fact did happen we are not told; perhaps nothing, or perhaps the hands assumed another sort of control.

In *The Waste Land* as in *The Family Reunion*, the guilt of the protagonist seems coupled with his perhaps imagined responsibility for the fate of a perhaps ideally drowned woman.

> One thinks to escape
> By violence, but one is still alone
> In an over-crowded desert, jostled by ghosts.

(Ghosts that beckon us under the shadow of some red rock)

> It was only reversing the senseless direction
> For a momentary rest on the burning wheel
> That cloudless night in the mid-Atlantic
> When I pushed her over

It must give this man an unusual turn when Madame Sosostris spreads her pack and selects a card as close to his secret as the Tarot symbolism can come:

> Here, said she,
> Is your card, the drowned Phoenician Sailor,
> (Those are pearls that were his eyes. Look!)—

and again:

> this card,
> Which is blank, is something he carries on his back
> Which I am forbidden to see.

(In what posture did they come back, late, from the Hyacinth Garden, her hair wet, before the planting of the corpse?) It is not clear whether he is comforted to learn that the clairvoyante does not find the Hanged Man.

Hence, then, his inability to speak, his failed eyes, his stunned movement, neither living nor dead and knowing nothing: as Sweeney later puts it,

> He didn't know if he was alive
> and the girl was dead
> He didn't know if the girl was alive
> and he was dead
> He didn't know if they both were alive
> or both were dead. . . .

The heart of light, the silence, seems to be identified with a waste and empty sea, *Oed' und leer das Meer;* so Harry, Lord

Monchensey gazed, or thought he remembered gazing, over the rail of the liner:

You would never imagine anyone could sink so quickly. . . .
That night I slept heavily, alone. . . .
I lay two days in contented drowsiness;
Then I recovered.

He recovered into an awareness of the Eumenides.

At the end of *The Burial of the Dead* it is the speaker's acquaintance Stetson who has planted a corpse in his garden and awaits its fantastic blooming "out of the dead land": whether a hyacinth bulb or a dead mistress there is, in this phantasmagoric cosmos, no knowing. Any man, as Sweeney is to put it,

has to, needs to, wants to
Once in a lifetime, do a girl in.

Baudelaire agrees:

Si le viol, le poison, le poignard, l'incendie,
N'ont pas encore brodé de leurs plaisants dessins
Le canevas banal de nos piteux destins,
C'est que notre âme, hélas! n'est pas assez hardie.

This is from the poem which ends with the line Eliot has appropriated to climax the first section of *The Waste Land:*

You! hypocrite lecteur!—mon semblable,—mon frère!

Part Two, *A Game of Chess* revolves around perverted nature, denied or murdered offspring; Part Three, *The Fire Sermon*, the most explicit of the five sections, surveys with grave denunciatory candour a world of automatic lust, in which those barriers between person and person which so troubled Prufrock are dissolved by the suppression of the person and the transposition of all human needs and desires to a plane of genital gratification.

The river's tent is broken: the last fingers of leaf
Clutch and sink into the wet bank. The wind
Crosses the brown land, unheard. The nymphs are departed.
Sweet Thames, run softly, till I end my song.

The "tent," now broken would have been composed of the overarching trees that transformed a reach of the river into a tunnel of love; the phrase beckons to mind the broken maidenhead; and a line later the gone harmonious order, by a half-realizable metamorphosis, struggles exhausted an instant against drowning. "The nymphs are departed" both because summer is past, and because the world of Spenser's *Prothalamion* (when nymphs scattered flowers on the water) is gone, if it ever existed except as an ideal fancy of Spenser's.

The river bears no empty boxes, sandwich papers,
Silk handkerchiefs, cardboard boxes, cigarette ends
Or other testimony of summer nights. The nymphs are departed.

From the "brown land," amorists have fled indoors, but the river is not restored to a sixteenth-century purity because the debris of which it is now freed was not a sixteenth-century strewing of petals but a discarding of twentieth-century impedimenta. The nymphs who have this year departed are not the same nymphs who departed in autumns known to Spenser; their friends are "the loitering heirs of city directors," who, unwilling to assume responsibility for any untoward pregnancies,

Departed, have left no addresses.

Spring will return and bring Sweeney to Mrs. Porter; Mrs. Porter, introduced by the sound of horns and caressed by the moonlight while she laves her feet, is a latter-day Diana bathing; her daughter perhaps, or any of the vanished nymphs, a latter-day Philomel

(So rudely forc'd.
Tereu.)

Next Mr. Eugenides proposes what appears to be a pederastic assignation; and next the typist expects a visitor to her flat.

The typist passage is the great *tour de force* of the poem; its gentle lyric melancholy, its repeatedly disrupted rhythms, the automatism of its cadences, in alternate lines aspiring and falling nervelessly—

> The time is now propitious, as he guesses,
> The meal is ended, she is bored and tired,
> Endeavours to engage her in caresses
> Which still are unreproved, if undesired.

—constitute Eliot's most perfect liaison between the self-sustaining gesture of the verse and the presented fact. Some twenty-five lines in flawlessly traditional iambic pentameter, alternately rhymed, sustain with their cadenced gravity a moral context in which the dreary business is played out; the texture is lyric rather than dramatic because there is neither doing nor suffering here but rather the mutual compliance of a ritual scene. The section initiates its flow with a sure and perfect line composed according to the best eighteenth-century models:

At the violet hour, when the eyes and back

which, if the last word were, for instance, "heart," we might suppose to be by a precursor of Wordsworth's. But the harsh sound and incongruous specification of "back" shift us instead to a plane of prosodic disintegration:

> when the eyes and back
> Turn upward from the desk, when the human engine waits
> Like a taxi throbbing waiting,

The upturned eyes and back—nothing else, no face, no torso—recall a Picasso distortion; the "human engine" throws pathos down into mechanism. In the next line the speaker for the first time in the poem identifies himself as Tiresias:

> I Tiresias, though blind, throbbing between two lives,
> Old man with wrinkled female breasts, can see . . .

There are three principal stories about Tiresias, all of them relevant. In *Oedipus Rex,* sitting "by Thebes below the wall" he knew why, and as a consequence of what violent death and what illicit amour, the pestilence had fallen on the unreal city, but declined to tell. In the *Odyssey* he "walked among the lowest of the dead" and evaded predicting Odysseus' death by water; the encounter was somehow necessary to Odysseus' homecoming, and Odysseus was somehow satisfied with it, and did get home, for a while. In the *Metamorphoses* he underwent a change of sex for watching the coupling of snakes: presumably the occasion on which he "foresuffered" what is tonight "enacted on this same divan or bed." He is often the prophet who knows but withholds his knowledge, just as Hieronymo, who is mentioned at the close of the poem, knew how the tree he had planted in his garden came to bear his dead son, but was compelled to withhold that knowledge until he could write a play which, like *The Waste Land*, employs several languages and a framework of allusions impenetrable to anyone but the "hypocrite lecteur." It is an inescapable shared guilt that makes us so intimate with the contents of this strange deathly poem; it is also, in an age that has eaten of the tree of the knowledge of psychology and anthropology ("After such knowledge, what forgiveness?"), an inescapable morbid sympathy with everyone else, very destructive to the coherent personality, that (like Tiresias' years as a woman) enables us to join with him in "foresuffering all." These sciences afford us an *illusion* of understanding other people, on which we build sympathies that in an ideal era would have gone out with a less pathological generosity, and that are as likely as not projections of our self-pity and self-absorption, vices for which Freud and Frazer afford dangerous nourishment. Tiresias is he who has lost the sense of other people as inviolably other, and who is capable neither of pity nor terror but only of a fascination spuriously related to compassion, which is merely the twentieth century's special mutation of indifference. Tiresias can see

> At the violet hour, the evening hour that strives
> Homeward, and brings the sailor home from sea,
> The typist home at teatime, clears her breakfast, lights
> Her stove, and lays out food in tins.

Syntax, like his sensibility and her routine, undergoes total collapse. A fine throbbing line intervenes:

> Out of the window perilously spread

and bathos does not wholly overtopple the completing Alexandrine:

> Her drying combinations touched by the sun's last rays.

"Combinations" sounds a little finer than the thing it denotes; so does "divan":

> On the divan are piled (at night her bed)
> Stockings, slippers, camisoles and stays.

Some transfiguring word touches with glory line after line:

> He, the young man carbuncular, arrives,

If he existed, and if he read those words, how must he have marvelled at the alchemical power of language over his inflamed skin! As their weary ritual commences, the diction alters; it moves to a plane of Johnsonian dignity without losing touch with them; they are never "formulated, sprawling on a pin."

"Endeavours to engage her in caresses" is out of touch with the small house-agent's clerk's speech, but it is such a sentence as he might *write;* Eliot has noted elsewhere how "an artisan who can talk the English language beautifully while about his work or in a public bar, may compose a letter painfully written in a dead language bearing some resemblance to a newspaper leader and decorated with words like 'maelstrom' and 'pandemonium.'" So it is with the diction of this passage: it reflects the words with which the participants might clothe, during recollection in tranquillity, their own notion of what they have been about, presuming them capable of such self-analysis; and it maintains simultaneously Tiresias' fastidious impersonality. The rhymes come with a weary inevitability that parodies the formal elegance of Gray; and the episode modulates at its close into a key to which Goldsmith can be transposed:

When lovely woman stoops to folly and
Paces about her room again, alone,
She smoothes her hair with automatic hand,
And puts a record on the gramophone.

With her music and her lures "perilously spread" she is a
London siren; the next line, "This music crept by me upon
the water," if it is lifted from the *Tempest*, might as well be
adapted from the twelfth book of the *Odyssey*.

After the Siren, the violated Thames-daughters, borrowed
from Wagner, the "universal artist" whom the French Symbolists delighted to honour. The opulent Wagnerian pathos,
with its harmonic rather than linear development and its trick
of entrancing the attention with *leitmotifs*, is never unrelated to
the methods of *The Waste Land*. One of the characters in "A
Dialogue on Dramatic Poetry," though he has railed at
Wagner as "pernicious," yet would not willingly resign his
experience of Wagner; for Wagner had more than a bag of
orchestral tricks and a corrupt taste for mythologies, he had
also an indispensable sense of his own age, something that
partly sustains and justifies his methods. "A sense of his own
age"—the ability to "recognize its pattern while the pattern
was yet incomplete"—was a quality Eliot in 1930 was to ascribe
to Baudelaire.* One who has possessed it cannot simply be
ignored, though he is exposed to the follies of his age as well
as sensitive to its inventions. At the very least he comes to
symbolize a phase in "the mind of Europe" otherwise difficult
to locate or name; at best, his methods, whether or not they
merited his own fanaticism, are of permanent value to later
artists for elucidating those phases of human sensibility to the
existence of which they originally contributed. This principle
is quite different from the academic or counter-academic notion
that art must be deliberately adulterated because its preoccupations are.

Wagner, more than Frazer or Miss Weston, presides over

---

*The quoted phrases are from a book by Peter Quennell, which Eliot
cites in his essay on Baudelaire.

the introduction into *The Waste Land* of the Grail motif. In Wagner's opera, the Sangreal quest is embedded in an opulent and depraved religiosity, as in Tennyson's *Holy Grail* the cup, "rose-red, with beatings in it, as if alive, till all the white walls of my cell were dyed with rosy colours leaping on the wall," never succeeds in being more than the reward of a refined and sublimated erotic impulse. Again Eliot notes of Baudelaire that "in much romantic poetry the sadness is due to the exploitation of the fact that no human relations are adequate to human desires, but also to the disbelief in any further object for human desires than that which, being human, fails to satisfy them." The Grail was in mid-nineteenth-century art an attempt to postulate such an object; and the quest for that vision unites the poetry of baffled sadness to "the poetry of flight," a genre which Eliot distinguishes in quoting Baudelaire's "Quand partons-nous vers le bonheur?" and characterizes as "a dim recognition of the direction of beatitude."

So in Part V of *The Waste Land* the journey eastward among the red rocks and heaps of broken images is fused with the journey to Emmaus ("He who was living is now dead. We who were living are now dying") and the approach to the Chapel Perilous.

The quester arrived at the Chapel Perilous had only to ask the meaning of the things that were shown him. Until he has asked their meaning, they have none; after he has asked, the king's wound is healed and the waters commence again to flow. So in a civilization reduced to "a heap of broken images" all that is requisite is sufficient curiosity; the man who asks what one or another of these fragments means—seeking, for instance, "a first-hand opinion about Shakespeare"—may be the agent of regeneration. The past exists in fragments precisely because nobody cares what it meant; it will unite itself and come alive in the mind of anyone who succeeds in caring, who is unwilling that Shakespeare shall remain the name attached only to a few tags everyone half-remembers, in a world where "we know too much, and are convinced of too little."

Eliot develops the nightmare journey with consummate skill, and then manœuvres the reader into the position of the quester, presented with a terminal heap of fragments which it is his business to inquire about. The protagonist in the poem perhaps does not inquire; they are fragments he has shored against his ruins. Or perhaps he does inquire; he has at least begun to put them to use, and the "arid plain" is at length behind him.

The journey is prepared for by two images of asceticism: the brand plucked from the burning, and the annihilation of Phlebas the Phoenician. *The Fire Sermon*, which opens by Thames water, closes with a burning, a burning that images the restless lusts of the nymphs, the heirs of city directors, Mr. Eugenides, the typist and the young man carbuncular, the Thames-daughters. They are unaware that they burn. "I made no comment. What should I resent?" They burn nevertheless, as the protagonist cannot help noticing when he shifts his attention from commercial London to commercial Carthage (which stood on the North African shore, and is now utterly destroyed). There human sacrifices were dropped into the furnaces of Moloch, in a frantic gesture of appeasement. There Augustine burned with sensual fires: "a cauldron of unholy loves sang all about mine ears"; and he cried, "O Lord, Thou pluckest me out." The Buddhist ascetic on the other hand does not ask to be plucked out; he simply turns away from the senses because (as the Buddhist Fire Sermon states) they are each of them on fire. As for Phlebas the Phoenician, a trader sailing perhaps to Britain, his asceticism is enforced: "A current under sea picked his bones in whispers," he forgets the benisons of sense, "the cry of gulls and the deep sea swell" as well as "the profit and loss," and he spirals down, like Dante's Ulysses, through circling memories of his age and youth, "as Another chose." (An account of a shipwreck, imitated from the Ulysses episode in Dante, was one of the long sections deleted from the original *Waste Land*.) Ulysses in hell was encased in a tongue of flame, death by water having in one instance secured not the

baptismal renunciation of the Old Adam, but an eternity of
fire. Were there some simple negative formula for dealing
with the senses, suicide would be the sure way to regeneration.

Part V opens, then, in Gethsemane, carries us rapidly to
Golgotha, and then leaves us to pursue a nightmare journey
in a world now apparently deprived of meaning.

> Here is no water but only rock
> Rock and no water and the sandy road
> The road winding above among the mountains
>   Which are mountains of rock without water
>   If there were water we should stop and drink. . . .

The whirling, obsessive reduplication of single words carries
the travellers through a desert, through the phases of hallucination in which they number phantom companions, and closes
with a synoptic vision of the destruction of Jerusalem ("Mur-
mur of maternal lamentation" obviously recalling "daughters
of Jerusalem, weep not for me, but for yourselves and your
children") which becomes *sub specie aeternitatis* the destruction
by fire of civilization after civilization

> Jerusalem Athens Alexandria
> Vienna London
> Unreal

The woman at the dressing-table recurs:

> A woman drew her long black hair out tight
> And fiddled whisper music on those strings;

her "golden Cupidons" are transmogrified:

> And bats with baby faces in the violet light
> Whistled, and beat their wings
> And crawled head downward down a blackened wall

and where towers hang "upside down in air" stability is
imaged by a deserted chapel among the mountains, another
place from which the life has gone but in which the meaning
is latent, awaiting only a pilgrim's advent. The cock crows as

it did when Peter wept tears of penitence; as in *Hamlet*, it disperses the night-spirits.

> Then a damp gust
> Bringing rain.

There the activity of the protagonist ends. Some forty remaining lines in the past tense recapitulate the poem in terms of the oldest wisdom accessible to the West. The thunder's DA is one of those primordial Indo-European roots that recur in the *Oxford Dictionary*, a random leaf of the Sibyl's to which a thousand derivative words, now automatic currency, were in their origins so many explicit glosses. If the race's most permanent wisdom is its oldest, then DA, the voice of the thunder and of the Hindu sages, is the cosmic voice not yet dissociated into echoes. It underlies the Latin infinitive "dare," and all its Romance derivatives; by a sound-change, the Germanic "geben," the English "give." It is the root of "datta," "dayadhvam," "damyata": give, sympathize, control: three sorts of giving. To sympathize is to give oneself; to control is to give governance.

> Then spoke the thunder
> DA
> *Datta:* what have we given?
> My friend, blood shaking my heart
> The awful daring of a moment's surrender
> Which an age of prudence can never retract
> By this, and this only, we have existed.

The first surrender was our parents' sexual consent; and when we are born again it is by a new surrender, inconceivable to the essentially satiric sensibility with which a Gerontion contemplates

> . . . De Bailhache, Fresca, Mrs. Cammel, whirled
> Beyond the circuit of the shuddering Bear,

and requiring a radical modification of even a Tiresias' negative compassion.

> The awful daring of a moment's surrender . . .

> Which is not to be found in our obituaries
> Or in memories draped by the beneficent spider
> Or under seals broken by the lean solicitor
> In our empty rooms.

The lean solicitor, like the inquiring worm, breaks seals that in lifetime were held prissily inviolate; the will he is about to read registers not things given but things abandoned. The thunder is telling us what Tiresias did not dare tell Oedipus, the reason for the universal curse: "What have we given?" As for "Dayadhvam," "sympathize":

> DA
> *Dayadhvam:* I have heard the key
> Turn in the door once and turn once only
> We think of the key, each in his prison
> Thinking of the key, each confirms a prison

—a prison of inviolate honour, self-sufficiency, like that in which Coriolanus locked himself away. Coriolanus' city was also under a curse, in which he participated. His energies sufficed in wartime (Eliot's poem was written three years after the close of the Great War), but in peacetime it becomes clear that "he did it to please his mother, and to be partly proud." He is advised to go through the forms of giving and sympathy, but

> [Not] by the matter which your heart prompts you,
> But with such words that are but rooted in
> Your tongue . . .

After his banishment he goes out "like to a lonely dragon," and plots the destruction of Rome. His final threat is to stand

> As if a man were author of himself
> And knew no other kin.

He is an energetic and purposeful Prufrock, concerned with the figure he cuts and readily humiliated; Prufrock's radical fault is not his lack of energy and purpose. Coriolanus is finally shattered like a statue; and if

> Only at nightfall, aethereal rumours
> Revive for a moment a broken Coriolanus,

it may be only as the Hollow Men in Death's dream kingdom hear voices "in the wind's singing," and discern sunlight on a broken column. Do the rumours at nightfall restore him to momentary life, or restore his memory to the minds of other self-sufficient unsympathizing men?

> DA
> *Damyata:* The boat responded
> Gaily, to the hand expert with sail and oar
> The sea was calm, your heart would have responded
> Gaily, when invited, beating obedient
> To controlling hands

Unlike the rider, who may dominate his horse, the sailor survives and moves by co-operation with a nature that cannot be forced; and this directing, sensitive hand, feeling on the sheet the pulsation of the wind and on the rudder the momentary thrust of waves, becomes the imagined instrument of a comparably sensitive human relationship. If dominance compels response, control invites it; and the response comes "gaily." But—"would have": the right relationship was never attempted.

> I sat upon the shore
> Fishing, with the arid plain behind me

The journey eastward across the desert is finished; though the king's lands are waste, he has arrived at the sea.

> Shall I at least set my lands in order?

Isaiah bade King Hezekiah set his lands in order because he was destined not to live; but Candide resolved to cultivate his own garden as a way of living. We cannot set the whole world in order; we can rectify ourselves. And we are destined to die, but such order as lies in our power is nevertheless desirable.

> London Bridge is falling down falling down falling down
> *Poi s'ascose nel foco che gli affina*
> *Quando fiam uti chelidon*—O swallow swallow
> *Le Prince d'Aquitaine à la tour abolie*
> These fragments I have shored against my ruins

An English nursery rhyme, a line of Dante's, a scrap of the late Latin *Pervigilium Veneris,* a phrase of Tennyson's ("O swallow, swallow, could I but follow") linked to the fate of Philomel, an image from a pioneer nineteenth-century French visionary who hanged himself on a freezing January morning: "a heap of broken images," and a fragmentary conspectus of the mind of Europe. Like the Knight in the Chapel Perilous, we are to ask what these relics mean; and the answers will lead us into far recesses of tradition.

The history of London Bridge (which was disintegrating in the eighteenth century, and which had symbolized, with its impractical houses, a communal life now sacrificed to abstract transportation—

> A crowd flowed over London Bridge, so many,
> I had not thought death had undone so many.)

is linked by the nursery rhyme with feudal rituals ("gold and silver, my fair lady") and festivals older still. Dante's line focuses the tradition of Christian asceticism, in which "burning" is voluntarily undergone. Dante's speaker was a poet:

> Ieu sui Arnaut, que plor e vau cantan;
> Consiros vei la passada folor,
> E vei jausen lo jorn, que'esper, denan. . . .

"Consiros vei la passada folor": compare "With the arid plain behind me." "Vau cantan": he goes singing in the fire, like the children in the Babylonian furnace, not quite like Philomel whose song is pressed out of her by the memory of pain. The *Pervigilium Veneris* is another rite, popular, post-pagan, pre-Christian, welcoming in the spring and inciting to love: "Cras amet qui numquam amavit"; he who has never loved, let him love tomorrow; secular love, but its trajectory leads, via the swallow, aloft. Tennyson's swallow nearly two thousand years later ("Could I but follow") flies away from an earthbound poet, grounded in an iron time, and meditating "la poésie des départs." That poem is a solo, not a folk ritual. As for the Prince of Aquitaine with the ruined tower, he is one of the numerous *personae* Gérard de Nerval assumes in *El Desdichado:* "Suis-je Amour ou Phébus, Lusignan ou Biron?" as the speaker of *The Waste Land* is Tiresias, the Phoenician Sailor, and Ferdinand Prince of Naples. He has lingered in the chambers of the sea

> J'ai rêvé dans la grotte où nage la sirène . . .

and like Orpheus he has called up his love from the shades:

> Et j'ai deux fois vainqueur traversé l'Achéron
> Modulant tour à tour sur la lyre d'Orphée
> Les soupirs de la sainte et les cris de la fée.

So *The Waste Land* contains Augustine's cries and the song of the Thames-daughters; but de Nerval, the pioneer Symbolist, is enclosed in a mood, in a poetic state, surrounded by his own symbols ("Je suis le ténébreux,—le veuf,—l'inconsolé"), offering to a remembered order, where the vine and the rose were one, only the supplication of a dead man's hand, "Dans la nuit du tombeau," where "ma seule étoile est morte": under the twinkle of a fading star. It is some such state as his, these images suggest, that is to be explored in *The Hollow Men;* he inhabits death's dream kingdom. The mind of Europe, some time in the nineteenth century, entered an uneasy phase of sheer dream.

> These fragments I have shored against my ruins
> Why then Ile fit you. Hieronymo's mad againe.

Here Eliot provides us with a final image for all that he has done: his poem is like Hieronymo's revenge-play. Hieronymo's enemies—the public for the poet in our time—commission an entertainment:

> It pleased you,
> At the entertainment of the ambassador,
> To grace the king so much as with a show.
> Now, were your study so well furnished,
> As for the passing of the first night's sport
> To entertain my father with the like

> Or any such-like pleasing motion,
> Assure yourself, it would content them well.
> HIER: Is this all?
> Bal.:   Ay, this is all.
> HIER: Why then, I'll fit you. Say no more.
> When I was young, I gave my mind
> And plied myself to fruitless poetry;
> Which though it profit the professor naught,
> Yet is it passing pleasing to the world.

It profits the professor naught, like Philomel's gift of song; and pleases those who have no notion of what it has cost, or what it will ultimately cost them. Hieronymo goes on to specify:

> Each one of us
> Must act his part in unknown languages,
> That it may breed the more variety:
> As you, my lord, in Latin, I in Greek,
> You in Italian, and for because I know
> That Bellimperia hath practised the French,
> In courtly French shall all her phrases be.

Each of these languages occurs in *The Waste Land;* all but Greek, in the list of shored fragments. Balthasar responds, like a critic in *The New Statesman,*

> But this will be a mere confusion,
> And hardly shall we all be understood.

Hieronymo, however, is master of his method:

> It must be so: for the conclusion
> Shall prove the invention and all was good.

Hieronymo's madness, in the context provided by Eliot, is that of the Platonic bard. If we are to take the last two lines of *The Waste Land* as the substance of what the bard in his sibylline trance has to say, then the old man's macaronic tragedy appears transmuted into the thunder's three injunctions, Give, Sympathize, Control, and a triple "Peace," "repeated as here," says the note, "a formal ending to an Upanishad."

iii

Within a few months Eliot found himself responsible for a somewhat bemusing success. The poem won the 1922 *Dial* award; the first impression of one thousand copies was rapidly succeeded by a second; it was rumoured that the author had perpetrated a hoax; the line "Twit twit twit" was not liked; the "parodies" were pronounced "inferior" by Mr. F. L. Lucas; Arnold Bennett inquired of the author whether the notes were "a lark or serious," and was careful to specify that the question was not insulting. The author said that "they were serious, and not more of a skit than some things in the poem itself." Mr. Bennett said that he couldn't see the point of the poem. The *Times Literary Supplement* reviewer felt that Mr. Eliot was sometimes walking very near the limits of coherency, but that when he had recovered control we should expect his poetry to have gained in variety and strength from this ambitious experiment.

He had written a poem which expressed for many readers their sense of not knowing what to do with themselves; as he later put it, with Bradleyan subtlety, "their illusion of being disillusioned." He was credited with having created a new mode of poetic organization, as he had, though specific instances of the cinematic effect were as likely as not attributable to Pound's cutting. Also he was singled out as the man who had written an unintelligible poem, and *with notes*. The author and annotator of this "piece that passeth understanding" was not insensitive to the resulting climate of jest. Six years later he capped a comparison between Crashaw and Shelley by calling for elucidation of the "Keen as are the arrows" stanza of *To a Skylark:* "There may be some clue for persons more learned than I; but Shelley should have provided notes."

HOLLOW MEN

> A voice! a voice! It was grave, profound, vi-
> brating, while the man did not seem capable
> of a whisper.
>
> —*Heart of Darkness*

The Hollow Men aren't as dilapidated as one is tempted to suppose; they speak an admirably disciplined prose, rather closer to distinction than that of a *Times* leader:*

> Those who have crossed, with direct eyes, to death's other
> Kingdom, remember us—if at all—not as lost violent souls, but
> only as the hollow men, the stuffed men.

A principal verb is deferred with Gallic formality:

> Eyes I dare not meet in dreams in death's dream kingdom,
> These do not appear.

In the latter part of their discourse adverbial phrases adhere with nicely modified parallelism to a deferred conditional clause in a miniature Miltonic coruscation, urbane as a rolled umbrella in limbo:

> In this last of meeting places we grope together and avoid speech,
> gathered on this beach of the tumid river: sightless, unless the

---

*"I am less alarmed about the decay of English when I read a murder story in the appropriate paper, than when I read the first leader in 'The Times.' "—
T. S. Eliot, 1939.

· 157 ·

eyes reappear as the perpetual star, multifoliate rose, of death's
twilight kingdom: the hope only of empty men:

a sentence to fascinate a grammarian.

To call this prose is to identify its strength: it is an unaccus-
tomed formality of syntax that sustains the nerveless rhythms,
no line strong enough to encompass more than a few words,
each line beginning and ending, with the energy of bare sur-
vival, just at the points of grammatical articulation.

> We are the hollow men
> We are the stuffed men
> Leaning together
> Headpiece filled with straw. Alas!
> Our dried voices, when
> We whisper together
> Are quiet and meaningless
> As wind in dry grass
> Or rat's feet over broken glass
> In our dry cellar.

Only once, with that dangling "when," does the lineation
venture to evade the grammatical structure; and on that occasion not only does "when" receive a peculiar pathos of emphasis, but its exposed position brings it under the dominance of a
principle even more mechanical than syntax: rhyme: the sound
of "men" echoed with weary lyricism. Thereafter rhymes
occur in feeble permutation; "Alas!": "dry grass": "broken
glass"; "crossed": "lost" (almost inaudible); and in a stanza
tinged with romantic imagery, three sounds permuted with
sestina-like virtuosity: are, column, swinging; are, singing,
solemn; star. As we read naturally, however, the music whose
presence these rhymes certify is strangely difficult to locate,
though it suffuses dryness with a faint romance.

There is distinguished precedent for syntactic orthodoxy in
hell:

> Others more mild,
> Retreated in a silent valley, sing
> With notes Angelical to many a Harp

Their own Heroic deeds and hapless fall
By doom of Battle; and complain that Fate
Free Virtue should enthrall to Force or Chance.

The Hollow Men, however, are not in hell but in a place of gentility, where one does not think of protesting too much. They are Gerontions rubbed down and adjusted to one another, entered into a community where no contortion of the heroic line, no Senecan or Miltonic infatuation with the heroic individual ("white feathers in the snow") disrupts their urbane brotherhood. For the first time an Eliot poem articulates itself in the first person plural, a collective voice like a chorus of bankers, minor poets, and contributors to the *TLS:* not "Here I am, an old man . . ." but

> We are the stuffed men
> Leaning together.

They whisper together, and their voices are "quiet" (though "meaningless"): quiet as natural phenomena

> As wind in dry grass
> Or rats' feet over broken glass
> In our dry cellar.

The poem's first epigraph—"Mistah Kurtz—he dead"—suggests the increasing affinity the author of *The Waste Land* was discovering with Conrad's vision of subtle evisceration. "'And this also,' said Marlow suddenly"—he is speaking of London—"'has been one of the dark places of the earth.'" Conrad's spokesman goes on to describe the effect of another dark place of the earth on a man who has ambitions for improving the cultivation of its inhabitants.

> I think it had whispered to him things about himself which he did not know, things of which he had no conception till he took counsel with this great solitude—and the whisper had proved irresistibly fascinating. It echoed loudly within him because he was hollow at the core. . . .

We need not visit Kurtz's wilderness to experience this effect. It can occur in the Unreal City itself, of which Eliot once observed that it does not extend a rich odour of putrefaction, but merely shrivels like a little bookkeeper grown old.

Mistah Kurtz, now dead, was in life a person of unfailing eloquence. His words, like those in an Eliot poem, "were common everyday words—the familiar vague sounds exchanged on every working day of life. But what of that? They had behind them, to my mind, the terrific suggestiveness of words heard in dreams. . . ."

> "That corpse you planted last year in your garden,
> "Has it begun to sprout? Will it bloom this year?"

Kurtz resembles, in his "unextinguishable gift of noble and lofty expression," the central character of an Elizabethan play. A *community* of Kurtzes is unthinkable.

The second epigraph draws our attention to a contemporary of Shakespeare's and Donne's whose fate may have stirred the imagination of John Webster: an actual domestic incarnation of the stage Machiavel, a man who proposed to bring the world of King James I to an end in an explosion of gunpowder, who met his captors in a dry cellar beneath the House of Lords, and survived to name his co-conspirators under torture ("This is the way the world ends / Not with a bang but a whimper"). Guy Fawkes, who left his mark on the mind of England at thirty-six (Eliot's age when he finished the poem), has been celebrated in popular ritual ever since, his straw-stuffed effigy burned every fifth of November, to the accompaniment of fireworks financed by door-to-door solicitation: "A penny for the Old Guy." That the pyrotechnic rejoicing which in America attends the rebirth of the Republic each July should in England be devoted to commemorating a failure to produce an explosion, and that in the most dismal month of the English year, was a circumstance that would not have escaped Eliot's attention; nor would he have failed to perceive in the tall, auburn-bearded Fawkes a man whose zeal for the old religion led him unintentionally to provide the populace with an inferior religion wherein are preserved and perverted festivals of fire older than the church of Rome. Fawkes is a lurid parody of those, commended in *Four Quartets,* who do not think of the fruit of action, but fare forward; he was betrayed by the divided intentions of his collaborators, who allowed a humanitarian shadow to fall between the idea and the reality, and tipped off endangered friends with anonymous letters. And the burning of Fawkes is the one occasion for a ritual folk art in modern England; dummies are cheerfully rigged with sticks and stuffed with straw by people who complain, when they are shown an abstraction of Picasso's or a *Tyro* of Wyndham Lewis', that the likeness to a human being isn't very good and what are these modern artists trying to put over? But an aristocratic art, Eliot wrote in 1923, is the refinement, not the antithesis, of folk art.

This reduction of Renaissance individualism to a theme for lugubrious festivals, and this patriotic emotion released by the circumstance that on a certain historical occasion nothing happened, not only prompts reflections on the potentially compromising and over-simplifying nature of all action—such as the action Fawkes proposed to undertake; it also provides a historic perspective on modern England, where it is customary to draw comfort from the custom of non-interference with familiar arrangements which, if they cannot remain, can at least be left to change imperceptibly rather than dramatically. "We do not wish anything to happen," says the chorus in *Murder in the Cathedral;* and sure enough, in 1605 nothing did; hence these rockets and catherine wheels.

Hence this chorus of the respectable, condemned, partly by personal inertia and partly by the sanctions of a historic process reaching from the Renaissance, to inhabit "death's dream kingdom," not remembered, to be sure, as "lost violent souls," but, not on the other hand, even memorable. If Tiresias, morbidly fascinated by the behaviour of other people, is the epiphany of an over-knowing inability to respect their inviolate otherness, the Hollow Men, morbidly fascinated by their own lyric inertia, epiphanize the flaccid forbearance of an upper-middleclass twentieth-century community, where no one speaks loudly, and where the possession of an impeccably tailored uniform marks one as unlikely to disturb the silence:

> Let me also wear
> Such deliberate disguises
> Rat's coat, crowskin, crossed staves
> In a field
> Behaving as the wind behaves
> No nearer—

the scarecrow a mock crucifix, the dead rats and crows hung in symbolic admonition to rodent or corvine malefactors, as great sinners were once hung in chains.

In death's dream kingdom, as in the minor lyric verse of the nineteenth century, nothing happens, there are no confrontations;

> He is not here; but far away
> The noise of life begins again,
> And ghastly thro' the drizzling rain
> On the bald streets breaks the blank day.*

Hence there are no persons here besides ourselves, who are scarcely persons, only components in a modish surreal landscape by a Berman or a Chirico:

> Eyes I dare not meet in dreams
> In death's dream kingdom
> These do not appear:
> There, the eyes are
> Sunlight on a broken column
> There, is a tree swinging
> And voices are
> In the wind's singing
> More distant and more solemn
> Than a fading star.

And a half-page later,

> Here the stone images
> Are raised, here they receive

*Eliot has said of Tennyson that he faced neither the darkness nor the light in his later years; to that extent he seceded from the effort of the century's poets to construct a dream world.

The supplication of a dead man's hand
Under the twinkle of a fading star.

Death has some other kingdom, about which we can only
guess ("Is it like this?"). To death's other kingdom certain
persons have crossed "with direct eyes," "absolute for death,"
as the Duke said in *Measure for Measure;* but "there are no eyes
here." And the reappearance here of eyes, corresponding to the
assertion of a new iconograghy, not broken columns and stone
images but "the perpetual star, multifoliate rose," is, by a pro-
found ambivalence,

The hope only
Of empty men.

Men who have emptied themselves—for "the soul cannot be
possessed on the divine union, until it has divested itself of
the love of created beings"—are entitled to hope for this
metamorphosis of symbols. For the empty men who parody
those saints it is only a hope, and a forlorn one.

The Hollow Men parody the saints; in this poem Eliot
first ventures on the structural principle of all his later work:
the articulation of moral states which to an external observer
are indistinguishable from one another, but which in their
interior dynamics parody one another. We can judge a man's
actions, but we cannot judge the man by his actions. In art,
in drama, actions are determined by their objects; in morals,
they are determined by their motives, which are hidden:
hidden, often, from the actor. Thus there is no way for the
Knights who slew Becket to determine, since he opened the
door to their swords, that he did not commit suicide, or that
he was not a lost violent soul. As for the consequences of the
Knights' and the Archbishop's action, it is perfectly true, as
one of the Knights says, that if England is now arrived at a just
subordination of the pretensions of the Church to the welfare
of the State, it was they who took the first step. But this consequence cannot be traced back to the event and there rechrist-
ened a motive. Thomas, who had emptied himself of desire, is

in heaven a saint and a martyr; and the Knights, who were empty men and who may pass as benefactors to the modern world: as for them, it is they who inhabit in life death's dream kingdom:

> In the small circle of pain within the skull
> You still shall tramp and tread one endless round
> Of thought, to justify your action to yourselves,
> Weaving a fiction which unravels as you weave,
> Pacing forever in the hell of make-believe
> Which never is belief:

So the Hollow Men go round the prickly pear, wearing "deliberate disguises," though there is no sign that their pasts contain any action that requires justifying. There is also no sign to the contrary; it is precisely the index to their state, that what was done or undone in the past is irrelevant to it; that activity is irrelevant to it, and motive irrelevant to it; that like the souls in Paradise they inhabit a state which, however they came to merit it, is now that they have entered it immune from considerations of merit, of sequence and consequence. Their world of sunlight, a swinging tree and distant solemn voices parodies that of the blessed souls. The damned, as Dante discovered, tirelessly rehearse the irrevocable sequence of activities that brought them to damnation; and in purgatory a soul passes the stages of its age and youth; but heaven and the dream kingdom alike are timeless states untouched by any memory of time.

It is that, and yet it is modern England, and it is a moral state to which no one in any time or place has been immune. The poem explicates itself simultaneously on several levels.

> Between the idea
> And the reality
> Between the motion
> And the act
> Falls the Shadow
>   —For *Thine is the Kingdom*

"Lips that would kiss form prayers to broken stone," and

prayers are spoken on scaffolds, interrupted by the falling axe

> For Thine is
> Life is
> For Thine is the

The Mysterious Shadow falls with a gesture of decisive inhibition; Shakespeare's Brutus envisaged action at the far side of dream:

> Between the acting of a dreadful thing
> And the first motion, all the interim is
> Like a phantasma or a hideous dream;
> The Genius and the mortal instruments
> And then in council, and the state of man,
> Like to a little kingdom, suffers then
> The nature of an insurrection.*

Brutus undertook and carried through, an action not unlike Guy Fawkes', and on principles equally high; though an action less abstract; bearing a knife is a more personal crime than lighting a fuse beneath victims one cannot see. The "dream" for Brutus was an interim stage, to be passed through. The Shadow that fell for Fawkes took the form of sudden scruple among certain of his co-conspirators. He was detected and hanged. The Shadow for the Hollow Men falls apparently in the faculty of the will itself, impeding themselves alone; no one will know, in the absence of a produced "reality," that there was ever an "idea". They may lead, presumably, blameless lives. But they are neither worse than Brutus, or Fawkes, nor better.

The next phase of this litany parallels the first; conception is to creation as idea to reality, and emotion to response as motion to act. But there is development; the world of conception and creation, emotion and response, is a less abstract world, closer for instance to that of artistic procedure; the things that are not brought into being—as on the 5th of November there is celebrated an un-creation that did not occur

*I am indebted to Professor Grover Smith's book on Eliot for suggesting the relevance of this passage.

—are this time things closer to the senses and the blood. The third stanza carries the dialectic of "emotion" and "response" into Gerontion's universe of "history" as a supple minx, or the Thunder's injunction concerning a moment's surrender:

> Between the desire
> And the spasm
> Between the potency
> And the existence
> Between the essence
> And the descent
> Falls the Shadow
> —*For Thine is the Kingdom*

It may fall ("*For Thine is the Kingdom*") out of religious scruple, or acedia, or sheer impotence; it is one function of religions to interdict, in certain circumstances, certain modes of activity. But the Hollow Men's piety is a piety of incapacity, like Origen's; and the neo-platonic terminology of potency and existence, essence on the plane of inapprehensible ideal and descent to the plane of matter, parallels the motions of human birth with those motions by which, if at all, things get done or come to be.

In the dream kingdom desire, potency and essence remain as they are; nothing changes, comes to be or passes away; and there is no marrying nor giving in marriage. Morally, acedia; socially, entropy (the world ends with a whimper); not that it is *prima facie* desirable that it should end with a bang, as Fawkes proposed or as an Elizabethan Stoic would have liked. Social, moral, historical, and poetic vacuity are revolved before us in this remarkable poem which, in fewer words than *The Waste Land* has lines, articulates, one is convinced, everything remaining that *The Waste Land* for one reason or another omitted to say, and by rhythmic means enacts the failure of rhythm; and in inactivity protracts, for just as many lines as are required for full articulation, a poetic action.

IV. SWEENEY AMONG THE PUPPETS

Chronology

London, 1921–1927.

    Dial articles on contemporary London, 1921–1922.

    "Four Elizabethan Dramatists," 1924.

    Play about Sweeney conceived and drafted, 1924.

    Fragment of a Prologue published, 1926.

    Fragment of an Agon published, 1927.

    (The Fragments united under the title *Sweeney Agonistes,*
        1932)

    Essays on Seneca, 1927.

SUPPLEMENTARY DIALOGUE
ON DRAMATIC POETRY

X: We may speculate . . .

Y: Speak for yourself, X.

X: It is a curious speculation, why the poetic drama should make so powerful an appeal to poets. The form has been dead ever since the Puritans closed the theatres.

Y: That is why.

X: You refer to the challenge of getting the thing started again?

Y: And to the challenge of infinite possibility. The tradition is too remote to be confining. Our poet is at liberty to try anything whatsoever.

X: And what is in fact tried? A timid minuet of incidents, assisted by declamation, Macbeth in a morning coat. You have it all wrong, Y. A poet, like anyone else, shrivels at the prospect of liberty. Shakespeare has been dead for three and a half centuries. The tradition is too remote to be anything but confining. Poetic drama, like Greek tragedy, can never again be anything but an academic exercise, as the epic was in the Renaissance.

Y: You are not in love with the theatre.

X: I loathe the theatre. It is nothing but actors.

Z: I notice both of you assume that the impulse to write poetic drama has something to do with the theatre. I suspect that it has more to do with the nature of literary art. Did not James Joyce perceive a natural rhythm in the artist's development, lyric to epic to dramatic, the artist progressively effacing himself as his themes increasingly relate themselves to other people, increasingly separate themselves from his private experience and become components in some autonomous world which his imagination bodies forth and which demands independent articulation? And do not Eliot's "three voices of poetry" correspond to those phases?

Y: There is something in that. No writer of stature confines himself to the lyric for long.

X: You mean the short poem?

Y: I mean the poem, not necessarily short, which maintains an evident and immediate relationship to the poet's moods, impulses, and desires. It is frequently to be noted that the lyric impulse dies between the poet's thirty-fifth and fortieth years, if indeed it lives that long.

Z: As in Wordsworth.

Y: As in more poets than Wordsworth, and more varied ones. Tennyson after 1850 learned to imitate himself skilfully. There is nothing important in *The Princess* that we cannot find in the 1842 *Poems*. Yeats in his forties, having exhausted the self as every poet must, disdained to imitate himself but deliberately set about the creation of an antiself. Pound at thirty-four, in *Mauberley*, delicately separates himself from himself, and embarks on the *Cantos*. Eliot wrote that all art must draw on the accumulated sensations of the first twenty-five years; but he wrote that in 1917, when he was twenty-nine. Five years later we have him dissociating the unmistakable Voice with which he was endowed into the Voices of *The Waste Land;* in *The Hollow Men* he exhausts the last impulses quivering in the last fragments; by 1925, as he told John Lehmann thirty years later, he was convinced that he would write verse no more. The work that broke down was *Sweeney Agonistes;* he was struggling to make the transition from epic to drama when his invention failed.

X: So when the poet has nothing more to say, he can put in time by setting other characters talking?

Z: No, that is cynical. I think I understand what Y means. His recourse is to shift the centre of gravity still further away from his mere self. And as his sensations and impulses grow more complicated, it becomes necessary to divide them up among several personages who may then be set moving in a play.

X: As Eliot himself virtually says. I find him claiming in his essay on John Ford (1932) "that a dramatic poet cannot create characters of the greatest intensity of life unless his personages, in their reciprocal actions and behaviour in the story, are somehow dramatizing, but in no obvious form, an action or struggle for harmony in the soul of the poet." I am suspicious of this. Eliot, to be sure, in his last major poetry, does divide up his sensations and impulses among voices which he likens to the voices of a string quartet. *Four Quartets* is like a musical conversation, and it also mirrors some "struggle for harmony in the soul of the poet." Eliot was describing accurately the direction in which his own poetic development was to lie. But how can this be the formula for drama? Does not the dramatist, the most external of literary artists, work from the outside; does not he observe life?

Z: If you mean, does not he incorporate into his play bits of sound film, the answer is no. Does Sophocles? Does Shakespeare?

X: But Sophocles and Shakespeare do not subdivide their own souls; they offer us their unique understanding of other people.

Z: Let us not delude ourselves with that illusion of understanding. Eliot remarks apropos of Ben Jonson's opaque characters that the dramatist need not understand people, he need only be intensely aware of them. And I recall reading somewhere—not in Eliot—the observation that the one living reality that Shakespeare studied, all the years of his life that were not vanity, was the soul of the actor.

Y: Who on earth said that?

Z: I cannot recall. Some critic or other.

X: It sounds like the sort of thing I might say myself.

Y: It does; and I am going to rival its bravado. I am going to suggest that some five years' study of something corresponding to the soul of the actor was the proximate cause of Eliot's turning to drama.

Z: The soul of Tennyson?

Y: Good gracious, no; though I grant you they have both written plays about Becket. No, something more varied and accessible; the soul of the music-hall comedian.

Z: The music-hall comedian?

Y: Yes. I have seen that your studies are piled high with old books and periodicals, and that Mr. Gallup's *Bibliography* has been your unfailing guide. Now surely you both have read . . .

X: Not the "Marie Lloyd" essay?

Y: That is symptomatic, yes, but not what I had in mind. Have you read his "London Letters" in the *Dial?* Have you read a *Dial* article of 1920, reprinted in *The Sacred Wood*, "The Possibility of a Poetic Drama"? There—and mind you, just after writing that distillation of forty Elizabethan plays, *Gerontion*—he raises the question of why "the majority, perhaps, certainly a large number, of poets hanker for the stage." And in the course of discussing other problems he provides a sly unobtrusive answer. Here, read it for yourselves.

Z: ". . . To have, given into one's hands, a crude form, capable of indefinite refinement, and to be the person to see the possibilities—Shakespeare was very fortunate. And it is perhaps the craving for some such *donnée* which draws us on toward the present mirage of poetic drama." Yes, but he is arguing that in England there has been for some centuries no such traditional form. Most of the essay is devoted to demonstrating that neither Shaw nor Maeterlinck embodies a dramatic tradition, that they merely apply dramatic machinery to the statement of a fuzzily kinetic hybrid he calls "the idea-emotion," that in fact there is no such tradition, and that in consequence there is no poetic drama.

Y: Yes, but you have missed the end of the essay. It is there that he nominates a "crude form, capable of indefinite refinement," and lying ready to hand. Listen: "The majority of attempts to confect a poetic drama have begun at the wrong end; they have aimed at the small public which wants 'poetry.' . . . The Elizabethan drama was aimed at a public which wanted *entertainment* of a crude sort, but would *stand* a good deal of poetry; our problem should be to take a form of entertainment, and subject it to the process which would leave it a form of art. Perhaps the music-hall comedian is the best material. . . ."

X: A wry peroration. It is inconceivable that he meant it seriously.

Y: Not at all. Consider for a moment what we know about the conditions of Eliot's poetic activity in London. The author of *Prufrock*, identified with Harvard, is merely an aloof and somewhat superior person: superior, I mean, to his environment. That is why the Prufrockian irony is formless. London gave him an identity by depriving him of one. In London he discovered the indispensable condition of his art, a milieu whose camouflage he could adopt while remaining in its midst, secretively, the critical alien. It was a strategy he worked out while writing his great essays and pretending to be a member of the anonymous Establishment. That strategy turned his attention to the ideal impersonal poet, the committed being who is at the same time detached, and determined also his famous conception of tradition, that which (being an American) you can appropriate by labour but not (since it is English) inherit. It underlies *Gerontion*, where he is free from the opalescent language of the Jacobeans and so can manipulate their effects. It underlies *The Waste Land*, where he can turn into literature a world, a succession of worlds, that for him really exist chiefly as literature. And *The Hollow Men*, which arises from the anguish of almost-identification with that

London death which he is still permitted to *see*. Now, by 1920 he was visiting music halls; once again, like the literature of the English past, a fascinating phenomenon but not his inheritance.

X: You are making too much of a phrase or two. How much attention does he actually pay to music halls?

Y: So far as the English know, not much. But remember the duality of his role: he is willing to tell the Americans. In 1920 he becomes London correspondent for the *Dial*. And the first thing he writes for the *Dial* is "The Possibility of a Poetic Drama," with that terminal allusion to the music hall. Now listen to some of the things he discusses in his London Letters: where he is not, remember, exposing himself to Londoners. April, 1921: official English literary stupidity and dullness, the extinction of the middle classes, and—"The Palladium has at this moment an excellent bill, including Marie Lloyd, Little Tich, George Mozart, and Ernie Lotinga; and that provokes an important chapter on the Extinction of the Music Hall, the corruption of the Theatre Public, and the incapacity of the British public to appreciate Miss Ethel Levey." June, 1921: The Phoenix Society performance of *Volpone*, the abuse to which the press subjects that Society, the statement that "the appetite for poetic drama, and for a peculiarly English comedy or farce, has never disappeared"; and then four hundred words on Music Hall and Revue, with the judgement that "the music-hall comedian can still be seen to perfection." August, 1921: public stupidity, the decay of the official drama, instanced by the impending closure of eleven theatres ("considering the present state of the stage, there is little direct cause for regret"), musings about the possible influence of ballet on a new drama ("if a new drama ever comes"), and the statement that "what is needed of art is a simplification of current life into something rich and strange." May, 1922: The moral cowardice of literary London, "the nature of the peculiar torpor or deadness which strikes a denizen of London on his return," and a paragraph on Mistinguett in Paris, whose performance he found "a welcome reminder of London," since her role "would have been better understood and liked by an English music-hall audience that it was at the Casino de Paris. I thought of Marie Lloyd again; and wondered again why that directness, frankness, and ferocious humour which survive in her, and in Nellie Wallace and George Robey and a few others, should be odious to the British public, in precisely those forms of art in which they are most needed, and in which, in fact, they used to flourish." December, 1922: the obituary on Marie Lloyd, who "represented and expressed that part of the English nation which has perhaps the greatest vitality and interest," who "gave expression to the life of that audience, in raising it to a kind of art," and whose death (since she has no successor, and no other class has such an expressive figure) "is a significant moment in English history." And after that there are no more London Letters, though there is a review of Marianne Moore's poems in which fine art is said to be "the *refinement*, not the antithesis, of popular art," and ritual, whose condition all art emulates, is said to belong to the people, being like "aristocracy itself, a popular invention to serve popular needs."

Throughout the *Dial* series we find three themes intertwined, literary dullness, the experimental theatre, and the music hall. In short, there is no literary tradition in the Unreal City, the official drama is dead, in the *possibility* of drama one is nevertheless impelled to feel intense interest; and the music hall is the sole resource of dramatic vitality. There, I am talked out.

X: I have one instance to add. One time in a London publication he similarly commits himself, though to be sure the publication is Wyndham Lewis' *Tyro*, which the Establishment can be trusted not to read. And there he says (the date is 1922) that in the official theatre there is no Myth, no enlarged or distended projection of the actual; there is only the actual, "sometimes a little better dressed." He goes on to account for the power of Jonson: Jonson's *Volpone* "is made by the transformation of the actual by imaginative genius," and is thus a criticism of humanity far more serious than the play's conscious moral judgements; for "*Volpone* does not merely show that wickedness is punished: it criticises humanity by intensifying wickedness." Now this does not alter the lives of the audience, as cinema desperadoes have allegedly altered the lives of little boys who point loaded revolvers or tie their sisters to posts. Only a corrupt art alters the lives of the audience. Jonson's art simply allows the audience to "see life in the light of the imagination." "The Seventeenth Century populace was not appreciably modified by its theatre. The myth is based upon reality, but does not alter it. The material was never very fine, or the Seventeenth Century men essentially superior to ourselves, more intelligent or more passionate."

Z: I wish that statement could be stencilled on the brow of every reviewer who has contended that *The Waste Land* contrasts the present with an idealized past. Though everything in *The Waste Land* somehow becomes literary, and Eliot does credit the past with, at divers times, producing a more copious literature.

X: Quite; but let me continue. This transformation of the actual, and this criticism of the actual, he discovers to be operative in one department only of contemporary life (that is, in 1922). It is operative in—and the third of this short *Tyro* essay's five paragraphs is devoted to it—the music hall; though the music-hall audience are unaware of the compliment and criticism a performance by Little Tich or Marie Lloyd implies.

Y: I think I can see where this discussion is heading. You were saying, Z, that everything in *The Waste Land* becomes somehow literary; and if literature is not at present vital, is not even read, how can a transformation however radical of its present condition enjoy the status of that myth X was talking about, which "is based on reality, but does not alter it?" *The Waste Land* is based on reality, but a confined reality; it elevates to mythic stature only the world of people who "read much of the night, and go south in the winter." It transforms their world into something rich and strange. The point is not that they will not read it; I gather from X that since the seventeenth-century populace was not appreciably modified by its theatre, it matters very little for viable art whether anyone makes much of it after it is produced. The point is that their world—I do not mean their social sphere but their zone of consciousness—constitutes an insufficient portion of the artist's potential *subject*. I gather from all these asides of his about drama that Eliot was dissatisfied with *The Waste Land's* frame of reference at the very time when he was meditating that poem into being.

X: He hankered after status among a larger public.

Y: Not at all, though that is what somebody can always be counted on to say whenever the topic of Eliot's plays comes up.

X: I am glad not to have disappointed you. Are you going to tell us that he preferred a coterie public?

Y: Like any sensible poet, he would have preferred a state of society in which the public capable of taking an interest in poetry was larger. But that is not the point. You cannot change your society. No, his interest in the music hall depended on the perception that a homogeneous community of Londoners was also interested in it, a corporate culture not merely passive.

X: I see. To handle the music hall, to raise it to the condition of ritual, would be, not to appeal to the music-hall community, but to incorporate its vitality. He was looking not for an audience but for a subject.

Y: Let us say, a form: by which I mean not the décor or mechanics of the drama, but a scope for his art which should refresh it by contact with a variety of activities about which a determining number of people really cares.

Z: In 1921 he speaks of English literary culture: "A literature without any critical sense; a poetry which takes not the faintest notice of the development of French verse from Baudelaire to the present day, and which has perused English literature with only a wandering antiquarian passion, a taste for which everything is either too hot or too cold: there is no culture here." At the same time Marie Lloyd was expressing, with the most detailed technical knowledge, "that part of the English nation which has perhaps the most vitality and interest," and requiring for her appreciation a knowledge of "what objects a middle-aged woman of the charwoman class would carry in her handbag; exactly how she would go through her bag in search of something; and exactly the tone of voice in which she would enumerate the objects she found in it." This knowledge widely diffused in her milieu is exactly comparable to that knowledge of, for instance, the development of French verse from Baudelaire to the present day, which Eliot wished was diffused among literary people. If a determining number of people had such knowledge, then they would be different people, and a poetry springing, as Eliot's does, from such knowledge would share their lives whether or not they understood or even read it, instead of having to refresh itself out of so many books which remain, explicitly, unknown books. *The Waste Land* is in part about the fact that the literary heritage is not active knowledge but a jumble of quotations from books people do not read. That is why the people in it receive none of the life of the poem, why only the flowing crowd and the automatic hand will come within its scope. In a piece of literature, which by the very nature of literature must be founded on the current state of literature, London is merely the Unreal City; but in a drama which should discover modes of contact with the music hall, human concerns, not human unconcern, could become the point of departure for that myth which is based on reality without altering it. I express myself badly.

Y: As well as anyone could. The subject is elusive. But I think we have discovered why Eliot was suddenly so strongly attracted to the drama, and a music-hall drama at that. The Invisible Poet was seeking a new relation with the milieu in which he made it his continual business to remain anonymous. Furthermore, the camouflage he had been perfecting for some years was growing too perfect. He sensed, perhaps, that he was becoming too much like a denizen of the literary world to retain his fructive detachment in that sphere.

X: Hence *The Hollow Men*. See the vitality dwindle in his prose as he grows, between *The Egoist* and the *TLS*, more and more like the thing he was pretending to be! Like Harcourt-Reilly, he is most impressive as The Unidentified Guest. I wonder if *The Cocktail Party* may not in part be about the process by which its author was gradually found out. Reilly retains his ascendancy, after his anonymity has been punctured, by insisting on his professional role, and Eliot took to editing *The Criterion*, and emitting with firm authority *dicta* not less commonplace than some of Reilly's. The Professional Reilly informs us that half of the harm that is done in this world is due to people who want to feel important. The Unidentified Reilly could make gnomic remarks like "You can't tell the truth on the telephone," as the invisible Eliot could gravely draw the attention of literary people to a filament of platinum, or assert that *Hamlet* was an artistic failure.

Z: Really, X, this is frivolous. But since you bring up *The Cocktail Party*, I want to know what happened to that music-hall drama. Those drawing-room plays have nothing to do with the music hall.

Y: What happened to it was that the music hall died out.

Z: But *Sweeney Agonistes* died half-written before the music hall did.

X: Actually, there is a gap between Eliot's documented interest in the music hall and our first intimations of *Sweeney*. It was two years after the *Dial* series, in September, 1924, to be exact, that Eliot told Arnold Bennett he had definitely given up *The Waste Land* form of writing ("form" is barbarous, but I am quoting Bennett's *Journals*) and was now "centred on dramatic writing." By Bennett's account, "He wanted to write a drama of modern life (furnished-flat sort of people) in a rhythmic prose 'perhaps with certain things in it accentuated by drum-beats.' We agreed that he should do the scenario and some sample pages of dialogue." The rhythmic prose became verse and incorporated its own drum-beats. And what we have is precisely some sample pages of dialogue.

Y: Between those pages and the music hall I can see only this explicit connexion, that both deal with low life.

Z: You forget that the music-hall "turn" isn't drama. It was something that required to be indefinitely transmuted before anything resembling a play should emerge. And there are other connexions: the songs, the minstrel-show stylization of the chorus (indebted, of course, to the author's American background), the exact depiction ("elevated to the condition of ritual") of two women engaged in furnished-flat activities, discussing a guest-list, dealing with the telephone, reading the cards.

Y: And he contrives to cut a path clear around Shakespeare. At one end, the minstrel show, the music hall, the revue; at the other end, Aristophanes. The Greek theatre is his other great source. Even when he has abandoned the walk-up flat for the country house and the consulting room he remains indebted to Greece. *Sweeney* was to be an "Aristophanic Melodrama," and Eliot subsequently bases plays on the *Oresteia,* the *Alcestis,* the *Ion,* the *Oedipus at Colonus.*

X: They are too remote to be "sources," and too thinly handled. He doesn't, like Cocteau, give us an X-ray image of the classic. They are convenient plots, nothing more, as the *Menaechmi* was for Shakespeare.

Y: Quite; and in that connection I recall Eliot's most pregnant remark about Greek drama: "behind the drama of words is the drama of action, the timbre of voice and voice, the uplifted hand or tense muscle, and the particular emotion." Now I notice two things about that; first, that the "drama of action" is apparently static, "the uplifted hand or tense muscle": nothing unrolls, reveals, gathers up, and resolves itself. His imagination sees the Greek theatre imagistically, in tableaux, like the details of his own poems: "A woman drew her long black hair out tight."

Z: We shouldn't labour a chance remark; he's simply making a point against Seneca, not laying all things Greek before us.

Y: But consider the other thing that I notice: in no Eliot play, with the possible exception of *Murder in the Cathedral,* is there an action, that *sine qua non* for the sake of which, Aristotle said, the characters should exist. *Sweeney* is two scenes, and the sole difference between them is that the second is the first disturbed, because Sweeney has entered. It's a fragment, granted. But in the finished plays, though the plot gets more accomplished, the action is either aborted or unintelligible. Can you tell me what happens in *The Family Reunion?*

X: For that matter, can you tell me what happens in *Prufrock?*

Y: Well asked. Granted there is nothing we would want omitted, further granted that the mermaid passage makes what is called "a strong ending," yet ideally that ending could have come much earlier in the poem without interrupting anything that is taking its course and needs time to declare itself. *Prufrock* is static. So is *Gerontion.* So, really, is *The Waste Land.* Not that they are padded (what Pound cut out of *The Waste Land* was, I suppose, material that would have been padding had it stayed in). But neither does anything happen before our eyes, nor at the end of *Prufrock* or *Gerontion* do we know more than we did when we started. There is neither an overt action, as in *Sir Patrick Spens* nor an intellectual action, as in *A Slumber Did My Spirit Seal,* where the second stanza transmutes the chance phrase "she seem'd a thing . . ." with such appalling force of explication. We linger in the chambers of the sea, that is all.

Z: We linger there long enough for . . .

X: For what?

Z: For an emotion to articulate itself, to expand, comprehend and invest the universe of the poem, and spend its force. It is the way of gnosis, not cognosis.

X: Wholly undramatic. A poet whose gifts lie that way should stay clear of the theatre.

Z: Perhaps. But since he has not stayed clear of it, I want to hear more about what he does in the theatre. You said, Y, that his plotting gets steadily more accomplished.

Y: Plotting, the carpentry of events. *That* he works at. The final scene of *The Confidential Clerk* is a show-piece of Revelations, Reversals, Recognitions, the 3 R's of French farce. But what unbroken line of meaning runs from Sir Claude's plans in the first ten minutes to Colby's abdication in the last ten? And it is a line of meaning that, if I understand him, Aristotle means by the action, the *muthos,* that, and not what we generally mean by "plot"; that, and not the provision of linkages whereby each event initiates the next like dominoes tipping over.

X: It is called the action, furthermore, because the difference between the stage and a book is that on the stage people are visible in action. Shall I put a sharper point on Y's remarks? The Eliot characters do not act. They are voices. You have the whole play on a set of phonograph records, as you do not for instance have the whole of *Waiting for Godot,* another play in which nothing seems to be happening, on a set of phonograph records.

Y: They are voices. So is Prufrock. So are the personages in *The Waste Land.* So are the Hollow Men, lifting up their bleak antiphon. Eliot himself, with a few bare shifts of pace and accent, gives on a phonograph record a finer performance of the *Fragment of an Agon* than any cast on a stage is likely to manage.

Z: Do you notice that when Eliot writes about the poetic drama it is about the *language* that he writes? It seems to be the great practical problem and the one requiring the utmost deliberation, because he has set himself the problem of explaining (I quote from the "Spencer Memorial Lecture") "whether and if so why poetic drama has anything potentially to offer the playgoer, that prose drama cannot." The minute you start thinking of it as a problem in making the playgoer stand for verse, or even offering him something extra, you are lost. The playgoer comes to witness the inevitable, like an audience at an execution. All of *Coriolanus* is a seamless inevitability, from the entrance of a rabble with clubs to Aufidius' frigid remorse two hours later. All of it holds us, not the story or the speeches or the fights, all, *including* the unalterable language. If Shakespeare had troubled himself about how the audience would like his language . . . !

Y: Eliot would not disagree. He spends half the lecture to which you were referring in explaining from many angles how the verse "must justify itself dramatically, and not merely be fine poetry shaped into a dramatic form."

Z: Ah, but he thinks of the dramatic as an interplay of speeches. He is capable of inspecting *At the Hawk's Well* or *The Dreaming of the Bones* and saying only that they are "poetic prose plays with important interludes in verse," and hence that "they do not solve any problem for the dramatist in verse." That is like listening only to the songs in *Hamlet*, and then saying that it does not solve any problems for the composer of opera. It is in the folding of the cloth by masked figures, the old man moving marionette-like to the taps of a drum, the dance of the Guardian of the Well, or (especially) the revelation that beneath her cloak her dress suggests a hawk, that *At the Hawk's Well* declares itself; but Mr. Eliot evidently sees the play as existing only while people are *talking*.

Y: He is, of course, not a man of the theatre. One supposes that like most of us he received his formative impressions of drama from the printed page, where the most critical action is represented by a line or two of italics. I admit that he often behaves as though he had received them from the radio.

X: You are wrong both times. He behaves as though he had received his formative impressions of the drama from Shakespeare.

Y and Z: What?!

X: From Shakespeare. Who else handed our whole drama over to the spoken word? What plays before his have never a silent moment? He alone had the power to have rectified and made ceremonious that impossible hodgepodge of theatrical opportunisms in which he immersed his dyer's hand. He might have purged it; he was content to transfigure it. He questioned nothing; he merely did with imperial ease and un-rivalled power what his contemporaries would have done if they could. They were straining, in "artistic greediness" (it is Eliot's own phrase) after "every sort of effect together." Their aim of realism (Eliot again, speaking out of a moment of withering illumination) "was unlimited." The wooden O with is uncurtained forestage was an opportunity for ritual intensi-ties; he was content to adorn the taste that called for cramming on to it the Battle of Agincourt, and then apologising for the poverty of the representation,

> Four or five most vile and ragged foils
> Right ill dispos'd in brawl ridiculous.

Yeats said of the dancer before severed heads, that the heads should not be carved; "if the dancer can dance properly no wood-carving can look as well as a parallelogram of painted wood"; but the severed head of Macbeth dangles by its hair. It is in the first place to assist this drive toward unlimited realism that there is so much talk; we must conjure up with words what we have not the resources to show. Shakespeare cannot make what Aeschylus would have made of bare pillars; words must adorn them with jutty, frieze, buttress, coign of vantage, and the nest of the temple-haunting martlet. And committed to this realism, Shakespeare, having to bring a play to a climax with a man smothering his wife, so conceives the situation that the man must talk for twenty mortal lines, and hold dialogue with her for sixty more, until the act when it comes merely illustrates the words (it is radio drama) and there is not a dry eye in the house.

Z: Enough, X, enough; Y is stopping his ears.

Y: I am not; I heard every word. I even heard the acknow-ledgements to Eliot. What is more, I can place them. What X has been paraphrasing with his own inimitable intensity is the argument of "Four Elizabethan Dramatists," that preface to an unwritten book with which Eliot tantalized the readers of the *Criterion* in 1924. And it puzzles me that Eliot the dramatist, who derived so misleading a notion of drama from an Elizabethan whose genius has sanctified all the bad taste of the Renaissance, should not have learned from Eliot the critic, who desired that the imitation of life should be circumscribed, and deplored the fact that the banalities of contemporary drama were the faults of Elizabethan drama extrapolated.

X: I can give you three reasons. The first is that, however accurately the critic can perceive the nature of what has occurred and is occurring, the craftsman, however gifted, only does what he can. The second is that "Four Elizabethan Dramatists" was written in 1924, and the plays a decade or two decades or three decades later, on the far side of that crisis of the will through which Eliot passed, like so many poets, about his fortieth year. And the third is that even in "Four Elizabethan Dramatists" the analysis is insufficiently radical. He has much of the utmost pertinence to say about convention, about the self-consistency of the work of art, about the virtue of having actors trained within several centuries of strict form, and about the interpenetration of the poetic and the dramatic impulse, but nothing to discredit the assumption that drama is essentially an affair of language. He does not perceive that the bias towards talk is itself an expression of the Elizabethan greed for explicitness. (That, Y, was my own contribution. Not everything that I said against Shakespeare was paraphrased from Eliot.) In "The Three Voices of Poetry" a quarter-century later we can detect him using a betraying verb: "when we *listen* to a play by Shakespeare." Throughout his career he takes for granted that drama is talk, and wants the talk formed, abstracted, circumscribed. But he nowhere asserts the primacy of a dramatic action, of something that shall *happen* in the course of the play.

Z: I think I see. And consequently we observe of *Sweeney Agonistes* that the talk is indeed formed, abstracted, circumscribed, that it is enclosed within a convention, or the parody of a convention; and we also observe that nothing whatever is happening.

Y: Which explains, no doubt, its unfinished condition. Because it was not going anywhere, there was nowhere for it to go. The advent of Sweeney in the second scene is intensely dramatic, according to that understanding of the dramatic which Eliot displays in his essays. But there is nothing more that can happen. Sweeney's talk simply prolongs the effect produced by his arrival, and when that effect has been fully explicated the scene closes on a full chorus. *Sweeney Agonistes* is a drama about a man no one else on the stage can understand; exactly as is *The Family Reunion*. And while *The Family Reunion* is written through to its conclusion, nothing is more difficult than to explain just what revelation frees Harry, and allows him to take his departure. It is, as Eliot himself later said, a good first act, followed by more of the same. The original conception, which we may trace back to *Sweeney*, was radically undramatic because inactive.

Y: In fact the original conception, so far as we can judge it from what is accessible, was the conception—the intuition, rather—of an emotional tone and a situation. And these, pondering as he always does on problems of language, he has brilliantly rendered, inventing for them the appropriate rhythms, the appropriate words. That pair of fragments is a unique, grotesque invention.

X: Quite so. I might summarize the three reasons I gave you a moment ago by saying that Eliot has failed to reform English drama because he is not a poet—the sort of being a survey of whose operations is codified in Aristotle's *Poetics*—but a phenomenon almost as rare, a superlative *writer* of poetry.

Y: You are being paradoxical again.

X: You are being obtuse again. The poet constructs an action. Eliot perfects a surface, or rotates an intuition. Take *Prufrock* or *Gerontion* or *The Waste Land* or *The Hollow Men*, and work out its structure (which has often been done; a whole smokeless industry has been devoted to it); you will not persuade yourself that what you have diagrammed elucidates the poem? We have agreed that one cannot tell what happens in *Prufrock*. But take five words together, or twenty-five, and you have seamless writing, phrases that seem to have written themselves prolonging themselves in indissoluble cadences. You can persuade yourself that he is the greatest writer who ever handled English verse, the firmest coercer of language, the humblest before the autonomy of concerted words. There have been great verse writers before this, but none who has so often brought off the trick of curving a long passage of verse until by its very integrity it resembles a poem.

Z: Tennyson brought it off a few times: look at *Mariana in the Moated Grange*. Eliot noted that when Tennyson wrote "The blue fly *sung* in the pane," he avoided ruining the line by writing "sang." It is the sort of detail Eliot himself takes pains over; and *Mariana* is a whole by the same criteria we apply to *Prufrock*, and only by those.

Y: One ruined line—one "sang" in place of "sung"—would have given the show away. We should have been aware that we were merely in the presence of written words.

X: It is an intensely dramatic performance: I mean that we undergo the half-conscious suspense of wondering how it can be sustained.

Z: Yet it has nothing to do with the acted drama. I wish the word "dramatic" did not cover so many things. Eliot uses it in yet a third sense when he maintains that all poetry is dramatic. I think he means that it somehow relates to an imagined speaker, and implies an imagined situation, whether social (as in *Prufrock*) or moral (as in *Gerontion*). But none of this has anything to do with what Aristotle means when he talks of constructing an action.

X: Naturally, Eliot's kind of poetry and Aristotle's conception of drama tend to separate from one another. Consider *The Rock,* where Eliot was simply given a scenario to fill out, and where he moves with lame decency except at the static moments when he has the opportunity to write choruses. He naturally conceives the dramatist's whole problem as one of keeping the audience's attention; in 1938 he writes to Pound that everything Aristotle and others say about plot and character is secondary to that capital problem, and adds that if the audience gets its strip tease it will swallow the poetry.

Y: Perfectly good sense, of course, since if it cannot hold the attention of the audience your play may as well not exist.

X: He also writes that if you lose their attention "you got to get it back QUICK." That seems good sense too.

Z: But if the action is not so contrived as to hold their attention, even when nothing exciting is going on at the moment, then there can be no artistic validity to any contrivances by which, having momentarily lost it, you get it back QUICK. There should have been no possibility of losing it.

Y: An Olympian counsel. Dramaturgy is an art of the possible. I agree with you, though, that concern with the audience's attention is misplaced. It leads to plays written for an audience who will swallow the poetry if they get their Noel Coward; it leads to the West End stage and Mr. Martin Browne; it leads to plays more dignified, literate, and intelligent than the West End stage has supported in its time, or than Broadway has commonly occasion to mount; but not to that "new drama (if a new drama ever comes)" which was to owe something to the music hall and the ballet and the invention of a new form, elevating contemporary life into something rich and strange. "To have, given into one's hands, a crude form, capable of indefinite refinement, and to be the person to see the possibilities. . . ." He may have decided in the 1940's that the drawing-room comedy was such a crude form. But if so, he was betrayed; for the drawing-room comedy is not a form but nothing more than a series of devices for holding the attention of the audience.

Q: Good afternoon.

Y: Where did *you* come from?

Q: I have been reading. I thought I ought to put in an appearance to help hold the attention of the audience. I heard you mention drawing-room comedy. Were you discussing Eliot's late plays?

Z: We are coming to the end of our subject; for we seem to be discovering that the late plays do not complete a continuous concern for inventing a new drama, but rather bring to an existing drama—precisely, that official theatre of manners which in 1922 Eliot found so barren—certain themes it was not aware it could handle, and a suppleness of language developed by several decades' practice in subduing the most structureless of civilized tongues. "English," Eliot noted long ago, "imposes less upon the writer than French, but demands more from him. It demands greater and more constant variation; every word must be charged afresh with energy every time it is used; the language demands an *animosity* which is singularly deficient in those authors who are most publicly glorified for their style." That is why *style* in colloquial dialogue is so intensely difficult to achieve, that is why the language of the West End theatre is flat and common; that is why *The Cocktail Party* seems the first *written* play to have made a popular success in our generation. To have brought sinew and limpidity together to extended passages of dialogue in a popular theatre is not to have reformed the drama, but it is to have done much.

Q: Bravo! The party line of our literary bureaucracy's more benevolent wing. I have never heard it better stated. But I should advise you not to settle yourselves into it too comfortably. You may be embarrassed to discover that Eliot has done more than you suppose with the West End stage. While the three of you were talking I was looking at the end of the book.

X: What book?

Q: Why this book, what other? The book in which the four of us are appearing.

X: How on earth could you do that?

Q: I have not been a student of Bradley's for nothing. But let me suggest to you that, as for the themes of the late plays, the way to approach them is not by way of their author's interest in the drama, but by way of his poetic development from *Sweeney* onward.

Y: What do you mean by that?

Q: I mean that the two fragments printed as *Sweeney Agonistes* are not really fragments of a play at all, but a pair of remarkable *poems*. Are they really fragmentary, any more so than *Prufrock*? Do you really feel, taking them on their own terms, that anything is missing? There are a thousand possible chains of efficient causality that might lead into the *Prufrock* situation, or the *Gerontion* situation, and as many that might lead out of it; but we are not moved to speculate what they might have been. The Prologue and Agon seem to me self-sufficient in the same way.

Y: So in reading them we can put out of our minds all that Playwright Eliot did not do, then and later.

X: In that case, let us turn to *Sweeney*. . . .

SWEENEY AND THE VOICE

No one on stage has the faintest idea what Sweeney is talking about. He proposes the cannibal isle as a milieu of macabre purity, like an egg—

> There's no telephones
> There's no gramophones
> There's no motor cars
> No two-seaters, no six-seaters,
> No Citroën, no Rolls-Royce.

—divesting himself, in fact, of the love of created beings; and the chorus supposes that it is reinforcing this lurid asceticism when it croons a shop-assistant's daydream. He affirms the terrible compulsion "to do a girl in," and his hearers advert to the cosy sensationalisms of the weekend press. He sketches the moral limbo of the man who has joined the company of the lost violent souls, having performed an act which cannot be undone; and they articulate a second-hand nightmare. Nothing is strange to them, nothing appals, because everything drops into familiar categories, and forms the substance of familiar songs. The song of the bamboo tree paraphrases a nugatory ditty popular at the time of the St. Louis World's Fair; the "morning . . . evening . . ." *diminuendo* is adapted from "Ain't We Got Fun"; the nightmare song—

When you're alone in the middle of the night and you wake in a
  sweat and a hell of a fright

—is sanctioned by the Lord Chancellor's patter in *Iolanthe*

When you're lying awake with a dismal headache, and repose is
    taboo'd by anxiety,
I conceive you may use any language you choose to indulge in,
    without impropriety;

which presumably licenses Wauchope, Horsfall, Klipstein, and
Krumpacker to take the name of hell in vain. The lopsided
percussion of an idling four-cylinder Ford establishes the beat
within which they permute their ragtime formulae.* As
Tennysonian cadences conceal his own meaning from Prufrock, so the insistent four-stress rhythm protects the personnel
in this jazz-age walk-up from any confrontation with reality.
War, for instance:

KRUMPACKER: We were all in the war together
                 Klip and me and the Cap and Sam.
KLIPSTEIN: Yes we did our bit, as you folks say,
                 I'll tell the world we got the Hun on the run
KRUMPACKER: What about that poker game? eh what Sam?
                 What about that poker game in Bordeaux?
                 Yes Miss Dorrance you get Sam
                 To tell about that poker game in Bordeaux.

Not that the human condition has been exorcised from a grass-
hopper's paradise; "birth, and copulation, and death," the
triple foci (as Sweeney observes) of mystery and tension, exist,
and admonish, but are prevented from involving them; from
these vortices of the imponderable they draw adrenal stimula-
tion, as a caged man may grimace at a tiger. Thus murder
occurs, but not as it occurred for Raskolnikov; it occurs in the
papers; and murderers walk, but at a distance, their very
liberty something to prompt sensations of ambient profundity.

SWARTS: These fellows always get pinched in the end.
SNOW: Excuse me, they dont all get pinched in the end.
           What about them bones on Epsom Heath?
           I seen that in the papers

*Eliot suggested in 1926 that contemporary perception of rhythm had been
affected by the internal combustion engine.

> You seen it in the papers
> They *dont* all get pinched in the end.
>
> DORIS: A woman runs a terrible risk.

If there were no terrible risks (abstract, though, and encapsulated; Doris is repeating the ritual formulae of the penny dreadfuls), life would be pallid. It is essential to suppose that crisis lurks offstage, safely offstage.

It is the same with the ritual of the cards. The cards do not touch fact, but it is essential to suppose that they mime fact, as coins mime increase. It is essential also to suppose that their fall mimes the incidence of that which is ineluctably coming to be, because if we know what is to happen we can prepare our nervous systems for it. The belief that the future can be foretold implies that it is preordained; curiosity about it implies Stoicism; and Stoicism, Eliot has noted, is "a philosophy suited to slaves." As he wrote in connection with Seneca, whose rhythms underlie much of the *Prologue* and *Agon,*

> Stoicism is the refuge of the individual in an indifferent or hostile world too big for him; it is the permanent substratum of a number of versions of cheering oneself up.

Thus the fall of the two of spades induces momentary panic—

> DUSTY: The *two* of *spades*
> THAT'S THE COFFIN!!
> DORIS: THAT'S THE COFFIN?
> Oh good heavens what'll I do?
> Just before a party too!

which modulates instantly into lyric resignation:

> DUSTY: Well it needn't be yours, it may mean a friend.
> DORIS: No it's mine. I'm sure it's mine.
> I dreamt of weddings all last night.
> Yes it's mine. I know it's mine.
> Oh good heavens what'll I do.

They lack, however, the nerve for Stoicism, whatever the attractions of flirting with the stoical attitude. An exit presents itself: perhaps the cards ordain rather than predict?

> Well I'm not going to draw any more,
> You cut for luck. You cut for luck.
> It might break the spell. You cut for luck.

Not being dummies, they must play with fire; but not being courageous, they must will away its burning. The crisis dissipates itself in musing stichomythia:

> DUSTY: It's a funny thing how I draw court cards
> DORIS: There's a lot in the way you pick them up
> DUSTY: There's an awful lot in the way you feel
> DORIS: Sometimes they'll tell you nothing at all
> DUSTY: You've got to know what you want to ask them
> DORIS: You've got to know what you want to know
> DUSTY: It's no use asking them too much
> DORIS: It's no use asking more than once
> DUSTY: Sometimes they're no use at all.

With which compare,

> Fatis agimur; cedite fatis.
> non sollicitae possunt curae
> mutare rati stamina fusi.
> quidquid patimur mortale genus,
> quidquid facimus venit ex alto,
> servatque suae decreta colus
> Lachesis nulla revoluta manu.
> omnia secto tramite vadunt;
> primusque dies dedit extremum,

lines quoted by Eliot in 1927 from the *Oedipus* of Seneca. The future they interrogate and evade; as for the actual, it can also be evaded, if we are connected with it by nothing more immediate than a telephone wire:

> Say what you like; say I'm ill,
> Say I broke my leg on the stairs
> Say we've had a fire

This is metrically indistinguishable from the statement of the telephone itself—

> TELEPHONE: Ting a ling ling
> Ting a ling ling

DUSTY: That's Pereira
DORIS: Yes that's Pereira
DUSTY: Well what you going to do?
TELEPHONE: Ting a ling ling
                  Ting a ling ling

And the counterpointed rhythm patterns develop, as Ezra Pound noted long ago, a hint picked up from Seneca:

Rex est timendus.
                    Rex meus fuerat pater.
Non metuis arma?
                    Sint licet terra edita.

It is on this locked, dreaming world that Sweeney impinges; and the simple device of shifting the initial stress from the first syllable of the line to the second conveys in his first words an irrupting urgency:

SWEENEY: I'll carry you off
            To a cannibal isle.

The cannibal isle, clearly, is no Gauguinesque paradise nor yet a Thoreauvian retreat, but the objective correlative of a terrible thirst for metaphysical purity. Sweeney has passed through some fire on the other side of which telephones, gramophones, and motor cars, the enduring things of this life, have become as shadows. It is not clear whether in divesting himself of the love of created things he is preparing his soul, as one of the epigraphs hints, for the divine union, though he does propose to consume the body and blood of Doris, duly converted by the transubstantiating process of savage ritual into "missionary stew." The traditional missionary who underwent this conversion had thought to nourish the cannibal's soul on a sacramental Body, but the cannibal, whose tom-toms beat out for his sensibility a protective prison not radically different in function from the ragtime rhythms of Dusty and Doris, interprets this teaching less esoterically.

Sweeney has reduced the unredeemed life to its sufficient essentials

> Birth, and copulation, and death.
> That's all, that's all, that's all, that's all,
> Birth, and copulation, and death.

DORIS: I'd be bored.

SWEENEY: You'd be bored.

> Birth, and copulation, and death.
> That's all the facts when you come to brass tacks:
> Birth, and copulation, and death.
> I've been born, and once is enough.
> You dont remember, but I remember,
> Once is enough.

We have been enjoined that we must be born again; Sweeney's single birth, whether the remembered trauma publicized in the 1920's by Otto Rank, or the process of his disastrous initiation into his bleak reductive universe, has been sufficiently catastrophic to inhibit another. He is in precisely the same condition as the Magi of Eliot's 1927 poem, who had seen a sight that left them

> . . . no longer at ease here, in the old dispensation,
> With an alien people clutching their gods,

having lost all appetite for

> The summer palaces on slopes, the terraces,
> And the silken girls bringing sherbet.

The Magus, however, says, "I should be glad of another death." He has died once. Sweeney is under the illusion that he has been born once.

Sweeney, in fact, has undergone the process Eliot characterizes as "the frightful discovery of morality." Middleton's *Changeling*, he wrote in 1927, is about

> an eternal tragedy, as permanent as *Oedipus* or *Antony and Cleopatra;* it is the tragedy of the not naturally bad but irresponsible and undeveloped nature, caught in the consequences of its own action. In every age and in every civilization there are instances of the same thing: the unmoral nature, suddenly trapped in the inexorable toils of morality—of morality not made by man but by Nature—and forced to take the consequences of an act

which it had planned light heartedly. Beatrice is not a moral creature; she becomes moral only by becoming damned.

Ten years earlier he had put the same theme more picturesquely:

> In Gopsum street a man murders his mistress. The important fact is that for the man the act is eternal, and that for the brief space he has to live, he is already dead. He is already in a different world from ours. He has crossed the frontier.

The lost violent souls are somewhere; they are damned. It is a recurrent theme of Eliot's in those years. Baudelaire, he wrote in 1930, "walked secure in this high vocation, that he was capable of a damnation denied to the politicians and the newspaper editors of Paris."

It is, however, impossible to say what experience it is that has brought Sweeney to his savage conviction that "Life is death." He "knew a man once did a girl in," but there is simply no telling whether he is himself that man. "One of the unhappy necessities of human existence," Eliot said in the Baudelaire essay, is "that we have to 'find things out for ourselves,'" which one would be tempted to combine with Sweeney's

> Any man might do a girl in
> Any man has to, need to, wants to
> Once in a lifetime, do a girl in,

did not an ambiguity radiating from the image of a drowned woman suffuse *The Waste Land* and recur as an explicit motif in *The Family Reunion*. According to the needs of the poem in question, the ambiguity takes various forms: whether the drowned woman is fact or fantasy, whether the account of her demise is coming from a confidant or an expediter, whether she fell or was pushed. She is part of the public mythology of an era when one of the police-court shamans of the British people was the man who drowned a succession of wives, by a method which left no marks of struggle, in order to realize their insurance money. Eliot may well have speculated, as he did concerning the cult of Guy Fawkes, on the roots of such passionate interest in the case of the Brides in the Bath. His disavowal of having himself on any occasion done a girl in (at least up to May, 1933) is a matter of public record. It was made before an audience of Vassar students, after a performance of *Sweeney Agonistes*, in response to a question. He stated that he was not the type.

In the *Agon* that evasiveness about what actually happened, which we have seen to be characteristic of the man who wrote *Appearance and the Objects of Knowledge in the Philosophy of Francis Herbert Bradley*, constitutes an embarrassment for which the earlier poetry does not prepare us. The strategy of the poems is to coerce the reader by a hundred precise indirections into a kind of co-naturality with some moral phase. This phase the reader, who has arrived at familiarity with it, knows as he knows the air in his room, neither discursively nor explicitly but with the immediacy of an emotion intensely undergone. It is related (in the reader's mind) to sensuous experience, but not to sensations variously recollected: rather, to the substantiality of words on the tongue, and of cadences invading the sensibility's obscure musculature. *The Waste Land* or *Gerontion* in this way approach the condition of music, that they evoke rather than create their constituent vignettes, evade rather than resist explication, and live in performance: verse to read rather than to have read to one. "A master of miniature," wrote Nietzsche of Wagner, intuiting the method of the long Eliot poem.

The dramatist, however, must commit himself to something: to the presence of certain people in a located place, to their interaction, to the speaking under defined circumstances of intelligible words. Hence it distressed Eliot, as it might not have distressed Dryden, that whereas in writing a poem like *Gerontion* "the way it sounds when you read it to yourself is the test," in writing verse for the theatre "the problem of communication presents itself immediately. You are deliberately writing verse for other voices, not for your own, and you do not know whose voices they will be." For the word, in

Eliot's imagination, relates itself most immediately not to any object which it names, not to the dictionary or to a system of discourse, but to the Voice which is the persisting reality, the entranced self-expending *élan vital* of which each word is a momentary modulation, each word "communicating," because it is not an atom of meaning but a renewed occasion for the Voice, "before it is understood." But when you write for actors "you do not know whose voices they will be."

The *Agon* simply dramatizes this difficulty by thrusting Sweeney, a being for whom, like the author of *The Hollow Men*, "the question of communication, of what the reader will get from it, is not paramount," into the midst of six people who are both transfixed and bewildered by his verbal carrying-on.

> I gotta use words when I talk to you

says Sweeney,

> But if you understand or if you dont
> That's nothing to me and nothing to you.

"The poem can wait a little while; the approval of a few sympathetic and judicious critics is enough to begin with; and it is for future readers to meet the poet more than half way."

Sweeney, like the generic finite centre described by Bradley, articulates an experience which falls within his own circle, a circle closed on the outside; and, with all its elements alike, his sphere is opaque to the others which surround it. "In brief, regarded as an existence which appears in a soul, the whole world for each is private and peculiar to that soul." It is therefore perfectly pointless for us to think of extricating, when Sweeney does not, the fate of the girl and the identity of her assailant from the gestures of Sweeney's voice exteriorising his fusion of boredom and horror:

> I knew a man once did a girl in
> . . .
> Well he kept her there in a bath

With a gallon of lysol in a bath

. . .

This went on for a couple of months
Nobody came
And nobody went
But he took in the milk and he paid the rent

—like a poet living with an unfinished poem, or like the man
in *The Waste Land* who came back, late, from the Hyacinth
garden,

Your arms full, and your hair wet, I could not
Speak, and my eyes failed, I was neither
Living nor dead, and I knew nothing. . . .

This man of Sweeney's acquaintance too knew nothing:

He didn't know if he was alive
and the girl was dead
He didn't know if the girl was alive
and he was dead
He didn't know if they both were alive
or both were dead
If he was alive then the milkman wasn't
and the rent-collector wasn't
And if they were alive then he was dead.

This is tense, diagrammatic, and uncommunicative; indeed,
the whole point (for Eliot is brilliantly evading the difficulties
of the stage) is that it is uncommunicative. "I gotta use words
when I talk to you," and though I am not unskilful in the
manipulation of words my resources are limited. Philomel's
song, born out of harsh and bitter experience, entrances ears
which have accustomed themselves to mark conventional
trills and intervals. She has to use song when she talks to us,
and hence is mistaken for a musician. In the same way,
Sweeney's audience mistake him for an inexpert manipulator
of conventional images. They know to what context tropical
isles belong—

Where the Gauguin maids
In the banyan shades
Wear palmleaf drapery.

They know with what sentiments it is customary to envelop "birth and copulation and death"—

> *My little island girl*
> *My little island girl*
> *I'm going to stay with you*
> *And we wont worry what to do. . . .*

They know perfectly well what passes through the mind of a murderer—

> And you wait for a knock and the turning of a lock for you
>   know the hangman's waiting for you.
> And perhaps you're alive
> And perhaps you're dead. . . .

Sweeney's case, in fact, is easily diagnosed: he is undergoing a bout of the hoo-has; and it is useless for him to protest, with the Orestes of the epigraph, "You don't see them, you don't —but *I* see them; they are hunting me down, I must move on."

The growth of *Sweeney Agonistes* into a completed play appears to have been inhibited by Eliot's two interrelated difficulties with the drama, his reluctance to conceive drama as primarily an orchestrated action, and his bias toward a poetry that exteriorizes but does not explicate the locked world of the self. The former is not even partially solved until, in *The Confidential Clerk,* the dénouement readjusts the values of five people: the first real modification of Eliot's generic Lazarus plot in which the man who returns from the dead, Prufrock or some other, passes across the stage possessed by his own doom and merely sets surfaces rippling. The second difficulty inheres in the Lazarus plot itself, for this plot turns on the fact that Lazarus, however he may ache for communion, cannot "tell you all" (though if a lady, "settling a pillow by her head, should say: 'That is not what I meant at all,' " he can always adopt Sweeney's solution and drown her). It comes to be solved only in appearance, by making the verse so light that we seem to see through it. The characters of the later, finished plays remain inviolable monads, and (making a virtue of this necessity) the theme of the plays, like that of *Sweeney*, depends on the fact that they are inviolate. If some of them change, it is they who will that change. Eliot becomes very resourceful in giving them means of making conversation, one reason why he prefers a drawing-room milieu and a convention of urbane chit-chat more varied, though no less confining, than the *Sweeney* jazz-matrix.

Subduing these two inherent contradictions between his poetic method and the nature of the acted drama afforded Eliot a programme for thirty years' intermittent work with the stage. He conceived in addition another outstanding obligation, which was to finish the unfinished *Sweeney Agonistes* itself. It was ultimately finished after some fifteen years, rewritten from beginning to end and entitled *The Family Reunion*.

V. THAT THINGS ARE AS THEY ARE

Chronology
    1927–1935

        Essay on Lancelot Andrewes, 1926.

        Confirmation in the Church of England, 1927.

        Journey of the Magi, August, 1927.

        Salutation (i.e., part II of *Ash-Wednesday*), December, 1927.

        Perch'io non spero (i.e., part I of *Ash-Wednesday*), Spring, 1928.

        A Song for Simeon, September, 1928.

        Som de l'escalina (i.e., part III of *Ash-Wednesday*), Autumn, 1929.

        "Dante," September, 1929.

        Animula, October, 1929.

        Ash-Wednesday, March, 1930.

        Marina, September, 1930.

        Triumphal March, October, 1931.

        Difficulties of a Statesman, Winter, 1931.

        Selected Essays, 1932.

        The Use of Poetry and the Use of Criticism, 1933.

        After Strange Gods, 1934.

        The Rock, 1934.

        Murder in the Cathedral, 1935.

ARIEL POEMS

In the years between *The Waste Land* and *A Song for Simeon* we discern Eliot shifting his attention from project to project, with evident difficulty and indecision. *Doris's Dream Songs*, three lyrics apparently constructed out of *Waste Land* remnants, appeared in November, 1924. The title suggests that they may have been intended for the play about Dusty and Doris on which he was then working. The play in turn was perhaps a delayed by-product of an attempt at translating the *Agamemnon*, into which Pound had spurred him four years earlier. This translation never appeared, though a draft of it seems to have been mailed to Pound in December, 1921.* One of the "Doris" lyrics was incorporated into *The Hollow Men*, two became *Minor Poems*, and the published dramatic fragments are devoid of "dream songs." These dramatic fragments appeared in print in 1926 and 1927, ascribed to a work entitled *Wanna Go Home, Baby?* No more was heard of this work. "Four Elizabethan Dramatists. I: A Preface" was published in February, 1924: six years later it was reprinted in *Selected Essays* as "A Preface to an Unwritten Book." Plainly about 1924 a co-ordinated critical and creative activity, embracing

---

*See Pound, *Guide to Kulchur*, p. 92. The following month Pound wrote back, "Aeschylus not so good as I had hoped, but haven't had time to improve him yet." In the same correspondence we find a convalescent Eliot reporting that he is "trying to read Aristophanes." *The Letters of Ezra Pound*, pp. 170–1.

poetry, the drama, and the contemporary "panorama of anarchy and futility" was set advancing on several fronts; plainly, too, it disintegrated rapidly, yielding as its only finished work that Pyrrhic victory of the lyric impulse, *The Hollow Men*, which became available for public inspection as the terminal work in the collected *Poems: 1909–1925*. This volume did not include the dramatic fragments, which received their present title (*Sweeney Agonistes: Fragments of an Aristophanic Melodrama*) seven years later in a pamphlet, the appearance of which marked Eliot's ultimate concession that the play did not lie within his power to finish.

Poems: 1909–1925 was one of the first publications of Faber & Gwyer Ltd., the founders of which, at the instigation of Hugh Walpole, had invited Eliot to associate with them in a business capacity. It is quite on the cards that Mr. F. V. Morley's whimsical memoir of Eliot's association with Faber is at this point to be taken at its face value: when he came to the new firm from the foreign department at Lloyd's Bank, it was not at all as a literary adviser. "It isn't even as if his colleagues at Faber & Gwyer were acknowledged or ardent admirers of Eliot's literary judgement. In 1925 I doubt if any of them saw any particular reason to defer to him in literary matters. What then were his assets? He was a gentleman; he was literate; he was patient; he got on well with difficult people; he had charm; and, he had been in the City. He had good qualifications for a man of business, and it was as a man of business, I suggest, that he was taken on."

A photograph of the period shows Eliot before the doorway of Faber & Gwyer Ltd., slim and impeccable in full City uniform, spats, bowler, Malacca cane, and double-breasted suit, clutching a paper parcel with jaunty aplomb, smiling at the camera an intent Gioconda smile: a strikingly young-looking man of thirty-eight, at liberty within his own anonymity. He was at that time a member of a minor publishing firm, the editor of an intensely respectable magazine which in the palmiest of its seventeen years was never to acquire more than eight hundred subscribers, and a frequent contributor of unsigned reviews to the *Times Literary Supplement*. He had previously served for brief periods as London correspondent for *The Dial* in New York and for *La Nouvelle Revue Française* in Paris. These were, from the point of view of, say, Arnold Bennett's public, activities esoteric to the point of being negligible. The Bloomsbury cenacle he was also known to frequent, a fact known chiefly to its initiates. Another photograph shows him in the informal company of Lord David Cecil, Leslie Hartley, Anthony Asquith, and Edward Sackville-West, and we learn from Virginia Woolf's *Diaries* that a word from "Tom, great Tom" sufficed to unsettle the complacency with which she would have preferred to contemplate the "illiterate, underbred" *Ulysses*. He agreed with her, however, that people were now afraid of the English language, and thought that Macaulay had spoilt English prose. It was necessary now, so went his salon talk, "to be a very first rate poet to be a poet at all. When there were great poets, the little ones caught some of the glow, and were not worthless." But there had been no poet that interested him since the time of Jonson. "Browning he said was lazy: they are all lazy he said," and Mrs. Woolf took pains to record his remarks. The polemic intensity of the *Egoist* articles is absent from these pronouncements, the sense of a present in which new modes of perception were stirring; and the ceaseless book-reviewing (mainly for the *TLS*) displays a readiness to bandy abstractions which would have distressed the critic who once parodied that very manner. He had acquired in fact, as Ezra Pound was to note with benevolent acerbity a decade later, a niche inside the system; a system, it should be remembered, of influential and often interlocking minorities.

These facts are not unconnected with the torpor of his muse; the editor of *The Criterion*, for instance, was compelled to spend his time supervising a good many contributors and composing a great deal of copy, little of it more than topical. With but two exceptions, none of the hundred-odd essays and reviews

Eliot wrote for *The Criterion*—not to mention some sixty editorial "Commentaries"—is to be found in *Selected Essays*. At one time we find him reviewing sixteen detective novels, at another time six books of popular theology, and on a third occasion two books on the history of the dance. He was publicly managing an institution, obligated both to take account of everything that was going on, and to transpose it all to a plane of desiccated urbanity which from time to time could only be protected—as in the review of the complete Sherlock Holmes stories—by the conventions of the family joke. These were inauspicious conditions for a man who had done his best work when no one was paying any attention to him. And it is relevant to mention that Ezra Pound, the very personification of revolutionary vigour, the mentor who discerned cause for complaint in the fact that within the Establishment the very best men, the men who aren't for sale, "get a little, just a little, good-natured or perhaps only humorous" —Pound had given up London for lost and moved to the continent.

At any rate, the play faltered, the subversively purposeful book on Elizabethan drama dissipated itself in commissioned articles for the *TLS*, and *Poems: 1909–1925* seemed likely to slip ineluctably into the past as the complete poetical works of T. S. Eliot. He was convinced that the poet in him would never write another line. He wrote his next lines of poetry in 1927, as a result of a definite commission, by the Faber firm, for a poem to be included in a series of shilling greeting-cards entitled *Ariel Poems*.

Journey of the Magi, then, was written, as no previous Eliot poem had been, explicitly for publication, as an object to be purchased by—it was hoped—a relatively large number of people of taste. It has even a proper Christmas card theme— Wise Men and Camels. As in his later stage-verse, so here, he can be seen deliberately thinning out his customary opacities of image and tying his effects to a running line of consecutive statement:

"A cold coming we had of it,
Just the worst time of the year
For a journey, and such a long journey:
The ways deep and the weather sharp,
The very dead of winter."

If this is prosy, it is not the prosiness of Macaulay who spoilt English prose, nor that of the official British journalese whose enervated decorousness supplies so much of the syntactic ordonnance of *The Hollow Men*. It is a prose that contrives to knit itself without contortion and advance itself without dissipation, each sentence moving with impeccable sureness to its full stop, incorporating in its progress just so much variety of cadence and formality of apposition as will sustain the structure of the poetic line. We may inspect its behaviour in the Christmas sermon of Bishop Lancelot Andrewes (1555–1626) from which Eliot adapted the first sentence of the poem:

> It was no summer progress. A cold coming they had of it at this time of the year, just the worst time of the year to take a journey, and specially a long journey in. The ways deep, the weather sharp, the days short, the sun farthest off, *in solstitio brumali*, "the very dead of winter."

It is not the specific borrowing that is noteworthy—Andrewes, for that matter, had supplied *Gerontion* with "the word within a word, unable to speak a word" and "Christ the tiger" —but the mode of organizing the progress of a sentence so that the lineation of verse will coincide with its very bones. This, and not the Bishop's gift for the flashing phrase, pre-occupied Eliot during the rereading of Andrewes that preceded a *TLS* tercentenary article of 1926. In this article, two years later reprinted, along with one on Bradley and six others, in a volume significantly entitled *For Lancelot Andrewes: Essays on Style and Order*, Eliot quotes, and characterizes as "a paragraph of admirable criticism," an earlier critic's account of the work-ing of Andrewes' *Preces Privatae*. "The internal structure is as close as the external. . . . He does not expatiate, but moves forward: if he repeats, it is because the repetition has a real force of expression; if he accumulates, each new word or phrase represents a new development, a substantive addition to what he is saying. He assimilates his material and advances by means of it. His quotation is not decoration or irrelevance but the matter in which he expresses what he wants to say. . . . The prayers are arranged, not merely in paragraphs, but in lines advanced and recessed, so as in a measure to mark the inner structure and the steps and stages of the movement. . . ."

Such an account was capable of suggesting to an acute reader in 1926 a new means of organizing extended passages of English verse. It may also have suggested ("he does not expatiate, but moves forward") a new line of development for a poet who had been accustomed to concatenating succulent auditory vignettes. The paragraph about the yellow fog in *Prufrock* adapts the syntax to the lineation with composed variety of cadence and formality of apposition, but it does not move forward, it expatiates. The syntax of *Gerontion* moves forward, but the reader's attention arrests itself among phrases which *caesurae* and enjambment serve to energize. The quotations in *The Waste Land* are not decoration or irrelevance, but neither are they "the matter in which he expresses what he wants to say": rather they are points of adhesion, wholly literary in their bearings, concerning which there is nothing that needs to be said.

For these poems exhaust a tradition, or as much of the tradition as lay within the compass of their author's purposes. Milton and Dryden, when they "triumphed with a dazzling disregard of the soul," introduced a century in which "poets revolted against the ratiocinative, the descriptive; they thought and felt by fits, unbalanced; they reflected"; not solely because a dissociation of sensibility had set in, but also because the example of Milton and Dryden licensed a verse which could first be written out in prose and then "intensified," its intensity answering to no internal structure, and its internal structure a mechanical distribution of emphasis, by inversion, enjambment,

and *caesura,* within a garrulity that would not inherently de-
mand verse were not this an occasion on which verse is called
for.

> To whom mild answer Adam thus return'd.
> Sole Eve, Associate sole, to me beyond
> Compare above all living creatures deare,
> Well hast thou motion'd, well thy thoughts imployd
> How we might best fulfill the work which here
> God hath assign'd us. . . .

Thus Milton without "poetry." Put the poetry in, and you
get a poetic of resonant epithets:

> Him the Almighty Power
> Hurld headlong flaming from th' Ethereal Skie,
> With hideous ruine and combustion, down
> To bottomless perdition, there to dwell
> In Adamantine Chains and penal Fire,
> Who durst defie th' Omnipotent to Arms.

Reflect that the syntax is rhetorical mechanism, a deliberate
rearrangement of the declarative sentence so as to bring its
nodes into coincidence with the means of emphasis Milton's
metric affords, dismiss the syntactic formality in irritation, and
you get (omitting various intermediate steps),

> By Hakagawa, bowing among the Titians;
> By Madame de Tornquist, in the dark room
> Shifting the candles; Fräulein von Kulp
> Who turned in the hall, one hand on the door.

And of this method we may remark, in Eliot's practice, that
it will not yield extended passages except by diffusion, as in
much of *Prufrock,* and that with its post-symbolist emphasis on
static irradiation, it progresses from theme to theme by discontinuous means, as in *The Waste Land.* Examine a passage of
the most regular end-stopped iambic pentameter:

> A rat crept softly through the vegetation
> Dragging its slimy belly on the bank
> While I was fishing in the dull canal
> On a winter evening round behind the gashouse

> Musing upon the king my brother's wreck
> And on the king my father's death before him.
> White bodies naked on the low damp ground
> And bones cast in a little low dry garret
> Rattled by the rat's foot only, year to year.

The rat, the canal, the gashouse, the king, the bodies, the bones, each item produces the next at the prompting of a casual association, whose phases the verse impartially measures out. If verse, to invoke an early test of Eliot's, should be at least as well written as prose—and this verse is—then it is a nerveless prose that it presupposes, one possessing no inner capacity to "assimilate its material and advance by means of it."

Journey of the Magi, on the other hand, has behind it the prose of Andrewes, "which appears to repeat, to stand still, but is nevertheless proceeding in the most deliberate and orderly manner." The syntax is often informal—

> Then the camel men cursing and grumbling
> And running away, and wanting their liquor and women,
> And the night-fires going out, and lack of shelters . . .

but nothing dissipates the spare, intent forward movement; if the accumulations of detail seem static, they are the stases of a spinning top which may suddenly leap:

> At the end we preferred to travel all night,
> Sleeping in snatches,
> With the voices singing in our ears, saying
> That this was all folly.

This is writing of such distinction that it succeeds in incorporating without disaster the theme's essential aridity and enervation. As for the theme, it is as we have noticed already the theme of *Sweeney Agonistes:* the impact of an experience which has rendered quotidian pleasures meaningless, and protracted life a preliminary death. Or rather, it is Sweeney's theme baptized; though Sweeney has been born, "and once is enough," the Magus says unequivocally, even amidst perplexity at his own satisfaction, "I would do it again."

The thing they saw has also changed the world, but the world has yet to apprehend its own change. Every detail in the "temperate valley," the three trees, the leaves of the true vine of which my Father is the husbandman, the dicing, the pieces of silver, the wineskins into which no one puts new wine, everything here is already charged with potential symbolism not yet explicated. The transfiguring presence is already on earth, and after thirty-three years "pieces of silver" will never signify quite what they did before. There is occurring, on the plane of redemption, that process which Eliot has accustomed us to take stock of on the plane of artistic creation: "for order to persist after the supervention of novelty, the *whole* existing order must be, if ever so slightly, altered." The temperate valley sounds as though it ought to be the goal of their journey, but it is only an earthly paradise, where people are kind to old white horses; and its most innocent details are trembling, in these first moments of the Christian era, on the brink of total symbolic transfiguration.

The Magus, however, is unaware of all this; he has passed through what we can see to be a landscape crying out with significations of ministry and passion, and can ascertain only that there is no information.

> But there was no information, and so we continued
> And arrived at evening, not a moment too soon
> Finding the place; it was (you may say) satisfactory.

The place they found he cannot trouble to describe; the place he describes he fancies he describes because it exerted such a lure to the fatigued senses, though we are free to note that he is telling us more than he knows.

The third part exhibits to the fullest advantage the method of Andrewes, not expatiating but moving forward, and repeating, if he repeats, because the repetition has a real force of expression.

> All this was a long time ago, I remember
> And I would do it again, but set down
> This set down

This: where we led all that way for
Birth or Death? There was a Birth, certainly,
We had evidence and no doubt. I had seen birth and death,
But had thought they were different; this Birth was
Hard and bitter agony for us, like Death, our death.

Though this has the virtues and the vocabulary of prose it does not ask to be printed as prose; to destroy the verse form is to deprive it not of emphasis ("Him the Almighty Power . . .") but of substantial articulation, which entails the verse divisions without depending on them.

On completing *Journey of the Magi* Eliot turned his hand immediately to a complementary poem of about the same length, with the same three-part structure, in which the second death for which the Magus wished has been accorded, the desert (now blossoming, in fulfilment of the prophecy, like a rose) has been invested with a supernal quiet, its sand a blessing and the day now cool. "These kingdoms" of the old dispensation have given place to

the land which ye
Shall divide by lot. And neither division nor unity
Matters. This is the land. We have our inheritance.

Salutation, with its precise and ritual interpenetration of vision, symbol, and Scriptural allusion, seems meant for a companion poem to the reminiscence of the cold coming. The discomforts of the journey have their ritual parallel in the dismemberment of the speaker by three white leopards; the "temperate valley," redeemed and elevated by visionary process to a place outside of time, is now "the Garden where all loves end"; and the "alien people clutching their gods" become, now that the bones of Ezekiel's dry valley have quickened, the tribes restored from captivity dividing their inheritance. *Salutation*, however, ultimately found its place in the sequence entitled *Ash-Wednesday*, where *Journey of the Magi* would not fit; and *Journey of the Magi* acquired as companion-piece a second Ariel poem on the theme of acquiescent renunciation, *A Song for Simeon*.

It is clear that the author of these poems has one eye on his own earlier poems, which he proposes not to retract but to complete. The three white leopards at their leisurely ritual of dismemberment transpose Gerontion's tiger from the plane of melodrama to that of vision. The journey of the Magi sanctifies that undertaken in Part V of *The Waste Land*—

> Here is no water but only rock
> Rock and no water and the sandy road

—terminating in a place merely "satisfactory" as the Waste Land journey terminated in an empty chapel where portentous questions waited to be asked. But the Waste Land journey entails panic and flight and the destruction of cities, a fleeing from the wrath to come; and the interval of time in which it occurs, that between the Crucifixion and the Resurrection, when Christ had withdrawn himself from the world, is related to the time of the Magi's reminiscence, when Christ had rendered irrelevant the old world without yet revealing the new, as neurosis is related to renunciation. *A Song for Simeon* employs in the same way a paradoxical lacuna in time, dramatizing the plight of the old man for whom, because he had been promised that he should not die until he saw the Saviour, the sight of the Saviour was to mean death, and it returns still more deliberately to earlier themes; it is an explicit and purposeful parallel to *Gerontion*.

Its first word is the vocative "Lord," its first subject the disposition of a nature external to the speaker:

> Lord, the Roman hyacinths are blooming in bowls and
> The winter sun creeps by the snow hills;
> The stubborn season has made stand.

Gerontion opens,

> Here I am, an old man in a dry month . . .

the season, like everything else in the poem, a virtual attribute of himself. Simeon goes on,

> My life is light, waiting for the death wind,
> Like a feather on the back of my hand.

> Dust in sunlight and memory in corners
> Wait for the wind that chills towards the dead land,

a self-assessment we are meant to contrast with that of the

> old man driven by the Trades
> To a sleepy corner

who awaits annihilation by the cleansing blast:

> Gull against the wind, in the windy straits
> Of Belle Isle, or running on the Horn,
> White feathers in the snow . . .

determined to pretend that he is capable of dying heroically (rebelliously) and that this is important. What Gerontion has never done—

> I was neither at the hot gates
> Nor fought in the warm rain
> Nor knee deep in the salt marsh, heaving a cutlass,
> Bitten by flies, fought,

cheats us by its rocking rhythms and the abrupt *caesurae* into supposing that something more impressive has occurred than Simeon's lifelong unobtrusive achievement:

> I have walked many years in this city,
> Kept faith and fast, provided for the poor,
> Have given and taken honour and ease.
> There went never any rejected from my door.

Though Gerontion's old age is of a piece with his former evasions, yet between

> Bitten by flies, fought

and

> My house is a decayed house . . .

what the changing pace of the verse insists on is an illusion of contrast: after such glory, what a shabby finish! It is Simeon who is really in a position to issue such a complaint; but the contrast between his deserts and the foreseen fate of his descendants is negated by a level transition without even a stanza break, for events are events and the just man claims no credit:

. . . There went never any rejected from my door.
Who shall remember my house, where shall live my children's
    children
When the time of sorrow is come?
They will take to the goat's path, and the fox's home,
Fleeing from the foreign faces and the foreign swords.

Gerontion "*sees himself* in a dramatic light," and to clarify this is the functional use of rhetoric; while Simeon is not regarding himself at all: hence a conspicuously unrhetorical poem. Simeon's

Not for me the martyrdom, the ecstasy of thought and prayer,
Not for me the ultimate vision

is instantly retrieved from self-pity by the calmly juxtaposed

                Grant me thy peace.

In the same way, one of the most stirring moments in *Gerontion*,

    Signs are taken for wonders. "We would see a sign!"
The word within a word, unable to speak a word,
Swaddled with darkness. In the juvescence of the year
Came Christ the tiger

is in *A Song for Simeon* emptied of its rhetorical intensity to assist poignancy of a wholly different kind:

    Now at this birth season of decease,
    Let the Infant, the still unspeaking and unspoken Word,
    Grant Israel's consolation
    To one who has eighty years and no to-morrow.

The lithe tiger in the darkness has no place in Simeon's glamourless calm.

    The verse of *A Song for Simeon* does not await the emphatic fall of stresses, nor linger over polysemous words. The steady production of meaning, attended by a chilly vitality, enables it to define a moral state of which the more powerful and impressive writing in *Gerontion* produces only the parody. We have already seen Eliot work in this way, making the vacuity of the Hollow Men misrepresent the saint's willed emptiness, or the annihilation, by a death, of Sweeney's savour in Sweeneyesque pleasures parody the Magi's disenchantment with their kingdoms on witnessing a Birth. We shall see him do it again: the distinction between opposed moral states with virtually identical symptoms provides the plot of *Murder in the Cathedral*, and a four-parted minuet of apposites achieving specious reconciliations which foreshadow true ones constitutes the internal dynamic of *Four Quartets*. The method works by a delicate opposition of styles, the clue to which leads back to that early essay on Rostand, "Rhetoric and Poetic Drama." It is at once Eliot's most sophisticated contribution to the art of poetry, and the fulfilment of a method of systematic parody to which his instinct led him when, "working out the implications of Laforgue," he presented J. Alfred Prufrock as a John the Baptist who has been executed, having denounced no adultery, a Lazarus who fears to return from the dead lest he be misunderstood, a Falstaff who resembles the gross knight only in being a butt and growing old, a Hamlet who is all soliloquies and no heroism, fustily annihilated like Polonius: in every way a caricature of his exemplars, who were "absolute for death."

In this method of pairing early poems with late ones and late ones with one another, Eliot found means of evading the impeachment he aimed in 1920 at an unfortunate phrase of Paul Valéry's. Valéry had suggested that the modern poet aims to produce in us a *state*, "et de porter cet état exceptionnel au point d'une jouissance parfaite." To this Eliot retorted that a state, in itself, is nothing whatever.

> The poet does not aim to excite—that is not even a test of his success—but to set something down; the state of the reader is merely that reader's particular mode of perceiving what the poet has caught in words.

This remark is contained in the essay on Dante which rounds out *The Sacred Wood;* Eliot notes that "no emotion is contemplated by Dante purely in and for itself," for what the poet sets down for us to inspect, he also assists us to locate in relation to other things set down.

> The emotion of the person, or the emotion with which our attitude appropriately invests the person, is never lost or diminished, is always preserved entire, but is modified by the position assigned to the person in the eternal scheme. . . .

He also distinguishes "the eternal scheme" perceived by Dante from the technical scheme employed by Dante. "The emotional structure within the scaffold is what must be understood—the structure made possible by the scaffold. This structure is an ordered scale of human emotion"; and as for the scaffold, it was merely the framework entailed by "a poem of so vast an ambit," its centre of gravity "more remote from a single action, or a system of purely human actions, than in drama or epic."

It should be possible, then, especially in an *oeuvre* conceived on a smaller scale, to register such a scheme, and within it elements in an ordered scale of human emotions, without employing allegorical machinery. This possibility seems to have lain dormant in Eliot's mind until, in 1929, his attention had circled back to Dante, on whom he issued a small book now incorporated in *Selected Essays*. It was at about that time that he appears to have begun contemplating his own poetic enterprise as a single work, in which sundry emotional phases, appertaining to poems the readers of which had supposed, with some reason, that they were written in order to induce a *state*, should be "placed" in relation to comparable emotional phases, and so located in an eternal scheme.

The principle of differentiation between these emotional phases is simple; what is always excessive in the ones that belong toward the negative end of the scale is *self*. Gerontion iterates the pronoun "I," Prufrock is imprisoned within experiences that come to him merely as attributes of his selfhood. Toward the positive end of the scale we find serene but unexciting qualities: intelligence, perception, peace.

Here as in Eliot's criticism, however, we are not to conceive the "scale of values" as resembling the marks on a ruler, a set of graduations achieved in isolation from anything to be measured, but as resembling the scale of C, a group of sounds so arranged as to clarify their relations. The scale comes into existence as the sounds are enunciated. In the same way, whatever Eliot the New England moralist may have thought of various human predispositions, Eliot the poet does not write poems to illustrate his rigid view of life, but to illuminate his other poems. The next Ariel poem, *Animula*, traces the career of a soul: not any soul, but one whose life is both unexciting (like Simeon's) and static (like Prufrock's). For these qualities can exist in combination; we are not to suppose that the only antithesis to Simeon is Gerontion. *Animula* may be taken as a brief commentary on *Prufrock*. The soul in question has never made the discovery of morality; from its childhood,

> Advancing boldly, sudden to take alarm,
> Retreating to the corner of arm and knee,

it has moved by uninterrupted process ("day by day, week by week") to an increasing perplexity "With the imperatives of 'is and seems,'" never really deserting the phase in which a child

> Confounds the actual and the fanciful,
> Content with playing-cards and kings and queens,
> What the fairies do and what the servants say.

It will ultimately subscribe to *The Times;* we observe it occupied with that other compendium of organized illusion, the *Encyclopaedia Britannica*.

> Issues from the hand of time the simple soul
> Irresolute and selfish, misshapen, lame,
> Unable to fare forward or retreat,
> Fearing the warm reality, the offered good,
> Denying the importunity of the blood,
> Shadow of its own shadows, spectre in its own gloom:

measuring out its life with coffee spoons, and reflecting that it grows old. This is one earthly career. The last six lines of the poem remind us that more spectacular earthly careers than Prufrock's can mask a comparable vacuity:

Pray for Guiterriez, avid of speed and power,
For Boudin, blown to pieces,
For this one who made a great fortune,
And that one who went his own way.
Pray for Floret, by the boarhound slain between the yew trees,
Pray for us now and at the hour of our birth.

It is *univocally* true of such souls, as it is *analogically* true of souls that have succeeded in entering while still on earth the universe where good and evil have meaning, that they "live first in the silence after the viaticum."

Triumphal March swarms with simple souls, through whose "flat world of changing lights and noise" is passing a splendid, interminable pageant which incorporates a Roman general's triumph, Christ's entry into Jerusalem, the Lord Mayor's show, the pageant in *Purgatorio,* Canto XXIX, the viceregal cavalcade in *Ulysses* ("bronze by gold . . ."), 5,800,000 rifles and carbines, the still point of the turning world, and a cast of thousands.

This ideal Event is timeless, so we are not surprised to hear a British inflection in the narrative ("Will it be he now? No.") or to observe "the Mayor and the Liverymen" marching in the same procession with "virgins bearing urns" and the "*société gymnastique de Poissy.*" We are even treated to some of the statistics with which the newspapers are accustomed to adorn accounts of public ceremonies; for if "the natural wakeful life of our Ego is a perceiving," that is a property it shares with the natural wakeful life of a ciné camera, less well adapted for judging *what* it is that has been perceived than for inspecting the passage of 53,000 field and heavy guns or 1,150 field bakeries ("What a time that took!").

These armaments of course are the spoils the victorious general has brought back from the wars; Eliot is in fact transcribing a list of things surrendered or destroyed by the

Germans after Versailles,* and so contrasting the booty of ancient campaigns with modern war's mass transfers of useless property, superintended by appropriate book-keeping. Roman spoils were dedicated in a temple. What happens to thousands of trench mortars, ammunition wagons, and field kitchens it is difficult to say.

When the general at length rides by, it is possible that he occupies "the still point of the turning world," at any rate of the turning world of power. It is equally possible that he does not. The absence of interrogation, the indifferent eyes, may signify plenitude or vacancy. The natural wakeful life of our Ego has no way of telling. It is plain however that there is another turning world whose still point he does not inhabit: the dove's wing and the palm tree at noon transfer our attention from a Roman or an English city to the Palestinian Triumphal March in the course of which flowers were strewn before the feet of a donkey. The General's entry parodies that of Jesus, though a casual spectator of the latter, disappointed by the lack of eagles and trumpets, would have said just the opposite.

Tucked away in a corner of the poem we discern a promising lad to whose mode of consciousness everything that has been transacted corresponds exactly. "Young Cyril," when he was taken to church (he had to be taken somewhere, and Easter Day his parents didn't get to the country), heard a bell ring and "said right out loud, *crumpets.*" The bell was rung at the consecration of the Host, and when young Cyril thought of something to eat he was on the right track. The muffin-man's casual pedagogy has conditioned him perfectly, and the widely publicized dogs of Professor Pavlov, who salivated when a bell was rung, are no better trained than he. In a city refreshed by the empty passage of opaque spectacles

> (And the flags. And the trumpets. And so many eagles.
> How many? Count them.)

*I am indebted for this information, as for many other oddments of fact, to Professor Grover Smith Jr.'s book, *T. S. Eliot's Poetry and Plays.*

young Cyril may be expected to grow into a satisfactorily qualified citizen.

In *Difficulties of a Statesman*, sure enough,

Arthur Edward Cyril Parker is appointed telephone operator
At a salary of one pound ten a week rising by annual increments
 of five shillings
To two pounds ten a week; with a bonus of thirty shillings at
 Christmas
And one week's leave a year.

So he is still employing his talent for responding to bells, and memorable occasions in his life still coincide with festivals of the Christian religion. The Statesman, on the other hand, is crying "all flesh is grass," entangled in bureaucratic pomposities ("The first thing to do is to form the committees") and like Caius Marcius Coriolanus ejaculating "Mother mother": not however at the moment of broken pride, but in sheer weariness of spirit. It is as though Mussolini had turned into Ramsay MacDonald.

Four years after writing these two pieces, Eliot brought them together under the title *Coriolan* in the "Unfinished Poems" department of his 1935 collection. He had planned, as he later divulged, a sequence of scenes in the life of "young Cyril," that indomitable speck of detail. Had the sequence been finished, with its finely hammered externality of presentation, it could, one imagines, have richly complemented *Ash-Wednesday*, which may have been what the author had in mind.

ASH-WEDNESDAY

What then, shall I continually "fall" and never "rise"? "turn away" and not once "turn again"? Shall my rebellions be "perpetual"?

—Lancelot Andrewes.

. . . a beautiful and ineffectual angel, beating in the void his luminous wings in vain.

—Matthew Arnold.

A thin, firm minor music, of ceremonious intricacy, dissolving the world of Tiresias, Hamlet, and Mrs. Equitone, creating in the zone vacated by that world "a place of solitude where three dreams cross"; a visionary precision in which a symbolic stair has (incidentally) a banister, and three symbolic leopards sit quietly because their stomachs are full; a wholly transparent network of allusions, tacitly nourished, like a nervous system, from secret sources among which research will discover nothing irrelevant; a religious poem which contains no slovenly phrase, no borrowed zeal, no formulated piety: this improbable achievement subsumes for good the secular Eliot whose traces of Original Richard Savage precipitated in his poems an arresting residue of gritty substantiality. We are to hear no more of how

> Apeneck Sweeney spreads his knees
> Letting his arms hang down to laugh,

nor will such a detail as "rats' feet over broken glass" momentarily usurp the world.

> And a time for the wind to break the loosened pane
> And to shake the wainscot where the field-mouse trots,
> And to shake the tattered arras woven with a silent motto.

In these lines from *East Coker* we see images from one of Eliot's familiar constellations functioning in a new way. The trotting field-mouse is a figure in a poemscape, not like the rat in *The Hollow Men* the synedoche of some omnipresent world. The most arresting images now *recede;* intensity inheres in the design of the whole passage, not in the immutable phrase. His former idiom had tended toward opacity. Its savour lay in the gestures of real speech exactly caught. The vice that menaced it was a certain succinct impenetrability ("this broken jaw of our lost kingdoms"). The language after *Ash-Wednesday* is characteristically open, even tranquil, its aim a ritual translucency, its lapses into facility and small talk. Some withdrawal from individual speech has occurred, which resembles a loss of vigour, though the vigour is rather dispersed than evaporated. This poetry is related less intimately now to the speaking voice than to renovated decorums of the impersonal English language. Its substance even becomes to some extent its own decorousness

>   —every phrase
> And sentence that is right (where every word is at home,
> Taking its place to support the others, . . .
> The common word exact without vulgarity,
> The formal word precise but not pedantic,
> The complete consort dancing together),
> Every phrase and every sentence is an end and a beginning,
> Every poem an epitaph.

This points to the animating principle of *Ash-Wednesday*, its own autonomous virtuosity in a universe implying adjacent spiritual states, but wholly compounded of verbal suggestions. From node to node of its own structure, from zone to zone, the poem moves swiftly like a swallow, and without flutter. Arrived in each zone, it circles and searches before passing on, making its way in this fashion from the zone of feeling dominated by "Because . . ." to the domain of "although . . . ," from a ratiocinative submission ("Because I know . . ." "Consequently I rejoice . . .") in the place where "there is nothing again," to a tension among substantial presences ("And the weak spirit quickens to rebel / For the bent golden-rod and the lost sea smell") that has no use for "because" and "consequently."

What is achieved—we are driven to impersonal summary —is a tension: more than the Magus achieved. He arrived at a disenchantment which "another death" might make right. Sweeney too lost the taste for created things. The centre of perception that moves through *Ash-Wednesday* (a focal point as specific as an "I" can be, but too wholly absorbed in its own spiritual states to be called a protagonist:), the "I," the Voice, the "finite centre," begins where the Magus left off, and moves on: not at the last merely "no longer at ease here, in the old dispensation," but installed in a realm of superior wakefulness where

> . . . the lost heart stiffens and rejoices
> In the lost lilac and the lost sea voices
> And the weak spirit quickens to rebel
> For the bent golden-rod and the lost sea smell
> Quickens to recover
> The cry of quail and the whirling plover
> And the blind eye creates
> The empty forms between the ivory gates
> And smell renews the salt savour of the sandy earth.

Here every noun, verb and adjective pulls two ways. The heart is lost to the world and lost in the world. It stiffens with life and with rebellion. The lilac is lost in belonging to the world that has been renounced, and the heart "rejoices" either to applaud its departure or to bring it back transfigured: this last a thin possibility inhering only in the overtone emphatic placement confers upon "rejoices," a possibility so nearly illusory that the phrase "weak spirit" remains appropriate in its presence. The senses, by the same implication of trans-figuration and recovery, renew "the salt savour of the sandy earth"; but the parallel with the delusions created by the "blind eye" and the doubtful force of "sandy" (Is it really fruitful earth? What are its relations with "the desert in the garden" of Part V and with the desert of "the blessing of sand" in Part II?) increase the tension of implicit delusion. From which follows—

> Suffer us not to mock ourselves with falsehood
> Teach us to care and not to care
> Teach us to sit still
> And even among these rocks,
> Our peace in His will
> And even among these rocks
> Sister, mother
> And spirit of the river, spirit of the sea,
> Suffer me not to be separated
> And let my cry come unto Thee.

"Teach us to care and not to care." The tension itself is a good. This line and its companion have not the context of resignation that sponsored their first appearance in Part I; or rather, the resignation is of greater purity. The ambivalent "separated" rejects internal separation as well as separation from God. Without specifying what evades specification, it is permissible for commentary to suggest that the opposite pull of the senses and the devotional spirit—of God's creation and God—is to be maintained as a fruitful and essential equivocalness, not "solved" by relegating one half of the being to the earth and the other half to heaven, nor yet, as in the Buddhist Fire Sermon, by becoming "weary of the knowledge of the visible" and so "empty of desire." A temptation to deny the senses must be resisted, rather as Becket in *Murder in the Cathedral* contends with the temptation to appoint himself martyr.

That is where the poem goes. It arrives there by a climbing of stairs, a vision, and a vertigo of assonances where

> . . . the unstilled world still whirled
> About the centre of the silent Word.

Before the stairs, it undergoes a dismemberment of all corporeality, by three white leopards; over this scene of macabre tranquillity presides the goodness of a Lady who subsequently withdraws herself

> In a white gown, to contemplation, in a white gown.

The composition of this strange scene includes a juniper tree, bones, and a desert, dreamily static like an invention of the Douanier Rousseau's. It is evidently the first phase of that which is constructed "upon which to rejoice," according to the proposal in the first section of all:

> Because I cannot hope to turn again
> Consequently I rejoice, having to construct something
> Upon which to rejoice
>
> And pray to God to have mercy upon us
> And I pray that I may forget
> These matters that with myself I too much discuss
> Too much explain

The middle sections of the poem, consequently, neither discuss nor explain, but pursue that "logic of the imagination" for which in his Introduction to Perse's *Anabase* Eliot in 1930 claimed a status coequal with that of the familiar logic of concepts. The first part, however, allies itself to that zone of consciousness where discussion is carried on, and with the aid of a form which suggests a strict form in echoing the melodic freedom of the Cavalcanti *ballate*, it adapts the ceremonious wraith of a syllogism to the uses of an ideal self-examination.

> Because I do not hope to turn again
> Because I do not hope
> Because I do not hope to turn
> Desiring this man's gift and that man's scope
> I no longer strive to strive towards such things
> (Why should the agèd eagle stretch its wings?)
> Why should I mourn
> The vanished power of the usual reign?

"Perch'io non spero di tornar gia mai . . ." so Guido Cavalcanti expecting to die in exile commences the dialogue with the Ballata he is sending to his distant lady: the dialogue with the Ballata is the Ballata itself, much as Eliot's resolve to construct something upon which to rejoice is itself an element in the construction.

> Because no hope is left me, Ballatetta,
> Of return to Tuscany,
> Light-foot go thou some fleet way
> Unto my Lady straightway,
> And out of her courtesy
> Great honour will she do thee.*

With Cavalcanti's plight is associated the mood of Shakespeare, one of his hundred moods:

> When in disgrace with fortune and men's eyes,
> I all alone beweep my outcast state
> And trouble deaf heaven with my bootless cries,
> And look upon myself and curse my fate:
> Wishing me like to one more rich in hope,
> Featured like him, like him with friends possessed,
> Desiring this man's art and that man's scope. . . .

This English Renaissance fit of the sulks, readily cured by thinking of something else ("haply I think on thee . . ."), is transcended by Cavalcanti's irremediable plight just as Cavalcanti's is transcended by the metaphysical despair of Ash-Wednesday, when the Christian universe examines its own unworthiness. The *Ash-Wednesday* language bears a similar relation to Shakespeare's: it is emptied of irrelevant specificity: the speaker does not quaintly "trouble deaf heaven" but moves as if through the phases of some liturgy, in an unpunctuated *stil nuovo*, cadenced rather than counted, pre-Elizabethan, not mediaeval, a language never spoken anywhere, though never remote in its deliberate bare elegance from the constructions (if not the energies) of actual speech. Though the cadences swing with the untrammelled gravity of a Foucault pendulum,

*Ezra Pound's translation.

the idiom is devoid of copiousness: when we come upon "the infirm glory of the positive hour" we are aware of "infirm" and "positive," two deliberate words, neither one resonant, each salient in the grave nerveless ambience. So with "the one veritable transitory power": these rare polysyllables bring with them an air of exactness without momentum. The energy of the line has precisely expended itself in establishing two precise words, and there is none left over to propel the next line to some rhetorical pitch. The next line is simply, "Because I cannot drink."

The other dimension of the opening is an insistent melli-fluousness, nearly Tennysonian, located in the long vowels and associating itself with the recurrent pairings of identical words ("I no longer strive to strive towards such things"; "Because I know I shall not know") and with the liturgical repetition of constructions, phrases, and whole lines. It is this quality that sets the language of *Ash-Wednesday* at a remove from speech, so much so that we are driven for analogy as far as the Laureate's *Holy Grail:*

> Then every evil word I had spoken once,
> And every evil thought I had thought of old,
> And every evil deed I ever did,
> Awoke and cried, "This Quest is not for thee."
> And lifting up mine eyes, I found myself
> Alone, and in a land of sand and thorns,
> And I was thirsty, even unto death;
> And I too cried, "This Quest is not for thee."

This Victorian ceremony of iterations is crude beside Eliot's austere gestures of withdrawal and submission; nevertheless, it appears to have been under his eye. A few lines later Sir Percivale is telling of the delusions that beset him on his quest; he came to a brook with apple trees,

> But even while I drank the brook, and ate
> The goodly apples, all these things at once
> Fell into dust and I was left alone
> And thirsting in a land of sand and thorns.

which may be the source of

Because I cannot drink
There, where trees flower, and springs flow, for there is nothing
again

Percivale proceeds to encounter what Eliot calls "the infirm
glory of the positive hour," in the shape of a knight

> In golden armour with a crown of gold
> About a casque all jewels; and his horse
> In golden armour jewell'd everywhere;

he likewise fell into dust. Later in *The Holy Grail* Sir Lancelot
climbs stairs towards a vision—

> up I climb'd a thousand steps
> With pain: as in a dream I seem'd to climb
> For ever;

the vision when he encounters it is veiled.

By way of Tennyson, *Ash-Wednesday* is united with certain
Waste Land themes: the quester, the Chapel Perilous, the elusive
vision associated with a lady. By way of Dante, the lady, appearing on three planes, gathers divinity. In the desert she is
withdrawn to contemplation, like the earthly Beatrice. In the
vision that follows the scene on the stairs, she appears veiled in
white and blue, capable of making strong the fountains and
fresh the springs, functioning in the economy of the poem
somewhat as Beatrice does in Canto XXX of the *Purgatorio*.
Though she goes "in Mary's colour" she is not Mary; yet she
is perhaps also "the veiled sister" of Part V, who may pray
"for those who wait in darkness," and who in the finale of the
poem is so closely associated with the "holy mother" as to be
virtually identified with her.

When we first become aware of her, she is not, however,
a wholly settling presence; there is even something a little
sinister in the indifference of her withdrawal ("in a white
gown, to contemplation, in a white gown") after the leopards
have completed their feast. She is in more than one way a
"Lady of silences," and if she is "Calm and distressed / Torn

and most whole," those are qualities not only of supernatural compassion, but of natural derangement, proper to the sphere of the Hyacinth girl's unnerving simplicity, and to the fact that the positive hour's glory ("looking into the heart of Light, the silence") is "infirm." Not that these vaguely troubling implications are of any salience; the remote, cool ritual verse obliterates all but our most determined attention to the normal range of certain words. In Part II, with its "I who am here dissembled" and its willed forgetting, we inhabit a *protective* peace, dreamlike, just below the threshold of a less soothing wakefulness. Parts III and IV are not so fragile; the "devil of the stairs" and the "cloud of tears" do not menace a dream, they are components of a vision.

Plainly the speaker is in some unspecifiable way thrusting past experiences into the destructive element of symbol, though it is pointless to fuss about the poem's sequence of events, or to determine which of its scenes may be recollections, which presences. It is true that the verbs in Parts II, III and IV are chiefly in the past tense, but Eliot's tenses are frequently opportunisms, as in *Triumphal March*, for dimming or vivifying. Grammatically, five minutes ago is as much in the past as twenty years ago. In Part IV, however, we hear of "the years that walk between," and are at liberty to suppose that the lady who once enlivened the Waste Land, "made cool the dry rock and made firm the sand," did so on the far side of those years, in "the positive hour," perhaps, and that the injunction "Sovegna vos," if we are to press the parallel with Arnaut's speech in *Purgatorio*, Canto XXVI, is addressed to her out of a present metaphorical fire. For the years restore her:

Here are the years that walk between, bearing
Away the fiddles and the flutes, restoring
One who moves in the time between sleep and waking, wearing
White light folded, sheathed about her, folded,
The new years walk, restoring
Through a bright cloud of tears, the years, restoring
With a new verse the ancient rhyme. . . .

The parallel with the iterated participles that introduce *The Waste Land* seems deliberate: on that occasion, a "covering" and an umbilical "feeding" that resist the Spring's breeding, mixing, and stirring; on this occasion, a welcoming of what the new years bring even as they seem to be taking gratifying things away. They restore "with a new verse, the ancient rhyme," not only enhancing the present but bestowing meaning on the neutral past. As we are to be told in *The Dry Salvages,*

> approach to the meaning restores the experience
> In a different form, beyond any meaning
> We can assign to happiness.

The "white gown" of her faintly unsettling withdrawal in Part II is now "white light," as she moves in the time between sleep and waking. The function of her departure and restoration is somewhat explicated in *Marina*, an Ariel Poem published a few months after *Ash-Wednesday*. Here an epigraph from Seneca's *Hercules Furens* tugs against the explicit parallels with Shakespeare's *Pericles* sufficiently hard to arouse a slight but stubborn possibility that the speaker may be mocking himself with falsehood. The epigraph, spoken by a man who has slaughtered his children and is now recovering sanity, tends to align certain motifs of *Pericles* with the Eliotic sequence of perhaps-drowned women, though it is true that when Shakespeare's hero threw his queen into the sea he supposed her already dead. In the shipboard scene (V:i) in which the king's lost daughter is restored to him as prelude to the recovery of his wife, Pericles supposes for a time that he is enjoying only "the rarest dream that e'er dull sleep did mock sad fools withal." He asks the apparition,

> But are you flesh and blood?
> Have you a working pulse? And are no fairy?

Eliot's speaker asks,

> What is this face, less clear and clearer
> The pulse in the arm, less strong and stronger—
> Given or lent? more distant than stars and nearer than the eye.

The pulse may be his own, the face a vision; he next evokes

> Whispers and small laughter between leaves and hurrying feet
> Under sleep, where all the waters meet.

The sleeping and waking worlds are equivocally mingled throughout the poem, and we are not required to suppose someone passing, as Pericles did, from one to the other. A curious passage intermingling the decrepitude of his ship ("the rigging weak and the canvas rotten") with his realization that the dream-child was of his making leads into the evocation of

> This form, this face, this life
> Living to live in a world of time beyond me; let me
> Resign my life for this life, my speech for that unspoken,
> The awakened, lips parted, the hope, the new ships.

New life, new ships, and the daughter belong to the same perhaps illusory dispensation. "I made this," in the same way, points both to the ship and to the child: "between one June and another September" may or may not be a nine-month interval. The "bowsprit cracked with ice and paint cracked with heat"* suggests some such lurid journey as the Ancient Mariner's, now "become unsubstantial." The daughter, or the possibility of her presence, at least for the duration of Eliot's most elusive poem, suspends nervewracking actualities:

> What seas what shores what granite islands towards my timbers
> And woodthrush calling through the fog
> My daughter.

In *Ash-Wednesday* the woman who "moves in the time between sleep and waking" comes like the daughter in *Marina* out of the past to bestow a transitory happiness which can transfigure the world, and which after its pleasure has faded like music, leaves the world, past and present, better understood. This is the reverse of Eliot's Lazarus plot, in which someone's passing through leaves the ambience troubled. It is an

---

*La glace qui les mord, les soleils qui les cuivrent,
Effacent lentement la marque des baisers.
—Baudelaire, *Le Voyage.*

event he never represents as happening at the behest of present actuality: always at the bidding of an awakened memory. Present actuality is the actuality of *Triumphal March*, or if it is subtler than that it is Bradley's "immediate experience," a circle closed on the outside.

> This is the use of memory:
> For liberation—not less of love but expanding
> Of love beyond desire, and so liberation
> From the future as well as the past . . .
> . . . See, now they vanish,
> The faces and places, with the self which, as it could, loved them,
> To become renewed, transfigured, in another pattern.
> (*Little Gidding*)

What we are entitled to prize in the natural present is "tension." A new verse may perhaps restore the ancient rhyme, and a verse is not only something added to a poem but etymologically a turning again; nevertheless the last section of *Ash-Wednesday* begins "Although I do not hope to turn again. . . ." The emphasis of the final prayer,

> Suffer us not to mock ourselves with falsehood
> Teach us to care and not to care
> Teach us to sit still,

is explicated by Eliot in specific terms five years later, in the play about the Canterbury Bishop who was tempted not to resist his enemies, and finally succeeded in not resisting them, but not as he had been tempted. There are ways of not caring and of sitting still that constitute mocking ourselves with falsehood. The function of the journey detailed in *Ash-Wednesday* is to arrive at a knowledge of the modes and possibilities of temporal redemption sufficient to prevent our being deluded by a counterfeit of the negative way. The 1920's were full of elegant sceptics, and T. S. Eliot was one of their heroes, but he does not return the compliment.

MURDER IN THE CATHEDRAL

Murder in the Cathedral, the drama of a solitary man, retraces in specific terms the zone traversed by *Ash-Wednesday*. Becket, elusive however articulate, moves like the Voice who does not hope to turn again from the "because" of a determined Wheel to the "although" of one who has "lost his will in the will of God, not lost it but found it, for he has found freedom in submission to God." These states differ very subtly indeed, since the Wheel and the Will of God both bear him toward the same violent death; they determine, however, whether that death will belong to the world's categories, Murder or even Suicide, or whether it will constitute a Martyrdom enjoined by God's love. Becket readily puts aside three Tempters, whose function resembles that of the visions left behind on the *Ash-Wednesday* stairs; indeed one of them recalls to "old Tom, gay Tom" the attractions of

> Fluting in the meadows, viols in the hall,
> Laughter and apple-blossom floating on the water,
> Singing at nightfall, whispering in chambers,

in language Tom Eliot's readers seem meant to connect with

> . . . a slotted window bellied like the fig's fruit
> And beyond the hawthorn blossom and a pasture scene
> The broadbacked figure drest in blue and green
> Enchanted the maytime with an antique flute.
> (*Ash-Wednesday*, III)

But the Fourth Tempter, whom he does not expect, shakes his composure; what the Fourth Tempter proposes is that he rejoice that things are as they are. He has only to comply with the lethal will of his persecutors and he shall be a martyr.

THOMAS: What is your counsel?
TEMPTER: Fare forward to the end.
            All other ways are closed to you
            Except the way already chosen. . . .
            Think, Thomas, think of enemies dismayed,
            Creeping in penance, frightened of a shade;
            Think of pilgrims, standing in line
            Before the glittering jewelled shrine,
            From generation to generation
            Bending the knee in supplication. . . .
THOMAS: I have thought of these things.

He has thought of these things, and they are precisely, as the audience knows, the things that have in fact happened. That they have in fact happened has nothing to do with the direction of Becket's will; they are the world's ceremonial, adorning what the world understands to have been a dramatic death. Becket may undergo death in the knowledge that the world will reward his memory. But certain knowledge of the consequences of an act, were it possible, would be the most depraved conceivable motive for willing that act; it would deprive the act of that faith which sanctifies action; would concede that what I do is dignified only in its unravelling consequences, exists only in its consequences; for in a world where everything is foreseen the particular willed act has neither moral status nor existence. The finger of the man who turns on the light, in turning on the light abandons itself to the causalities of a switching system; but to turn on a light is a moral act when we do not know what we shall see.

For Eliot this theme is as old as Prufrock, who was demeaned by the knowledge that he was going where he must go: "I have known them all already, known them all." As he walks he puts streets behind him, and what he measures off behind him now "follows" him,

> Streets that follow like a tedious argument
> Of insidious intent
> To lead you to an overwhelming question.

This man's past, as it accumulates, presses him toward his future: towards that future, however, his election of which has made his past what it is. The nightmare quality of the theme is diminished by Dusty and Doris with their cards, and by Mme. Sosostris' client; these devotees of "living and partly living" are not interested in the consequences of their own actions, because they do not contemplate action; they are merely interested in knowing what they must undergo. The Cumaean Sibyl, however, undergoes the torment of knowing, as a result of her deliberate bargain with Apollo, how many, many years she has still to endure.

So the Fourth Tempter seeks, for a start, to lock Becket's will to its own foreseeable consequences. But he does not stop there; he reminds Becket of other distractions he has entertained, like the protagonist of *Ash-Wednesday*,

> . . . sometimes at your prayers,
> sometimes hesitating at the angles of stairs,
> And between sleep and waking, early in the morning,
> When the bird cries . . .

Becket on such occasions has reflected "that nothing lasts, but the wheel turns." Indeed his answer to the First Tempter, who offered to renew the lighthearted past, employed this precise image:

> We do not know very much of the future
> Except that from generation to generation
> The same things happen again and again.
> Men learn little from others' experience.
> But in the life of one man, never
> The same returns. Sever
> The cord, shed the scale. Only
> The fool, fixed in his folly, may think
> He can turn the wheel on which he turns.

This is a very subtle temptation, analogous with that of the

Ash-Wednesday protagonist who renounced hope for "the infirm glory of the positive hour," those flowers and those trees, and consequently proposed to "construct something upon which to rejoice." Becket has only to construct for himself a martyrdom, shrugging off the world because he perceives that in the world, characteristically, "there is nothing again," and he may have his hands on the enduring crown.

> Seek the way of martyrdom, make yourself the lowest
> On earth, to be high in heaven.
> And see far off below you, where the gulf is fixed,
> Your persecutors, in timeless torment,
> Parched passion, beyond expiation.

There is nothing so dangerous as denying the world; and it is the Four Tempters in chorus who speak the paraphrase of *Animula*—

> Man's life is a cheat and a disappointment;
> All things are unreal,
> Unreal or disappointing:
> The Catherine wheel, the pantomime cat,
> The prizes given at the children's party,
> The prize awarded for the English Essay,
> The scholar's degree, the statesman's decoration.
> All things become less real, man passes
> From unreality to unreality. . . .

The main moral action of the play, the purification of Becket's will, is insufficiently analyzed. It is invisible, because there is no way that it can express itself in action. The action, not preventing himself from being killed, would appertain equally to an unregenerate Becket. And it is inaudible, because rhetorical force, importing the vigorous rhetorizing Self, would adulterate. After an interval we are merely told that it has occurred—

> THOMAS: Now is my way clear, now is the meaning plain:
> Temptation shall not come in this kind again.
> The last temptation is the greatest treason:
> To do the right deed for the wrong reason. . . .

—and subsequently in the Christmas Sermon we learn in some detail how martyrdom is never the design of men.

During the interval preceding this announcement the Chorus of Women has demonstrated how life can be regarded as something more than a cheat and a disappointment, though without excessive optimism. They do not pass from "unreality to unreality";

We are not ignorant women, we now what we must expect and
   not expect.
We know of oppression and torture,
We know of extortion and violence,
Destitution, disease,
The old without fire in winter,
The child without milk in summer . . .

This catalogue of misfortunes does not suggest to them a facile disillusionment:

> And meanwhile we have gone on living,
> Living and partly living,
> Picking together the pieces,
> Gathering faggots at nightfall,
> Building a partial shelter,
> For sleeping, and eating and drinking and laughter.

The Tempters, more knowing than these but less conscious than Becket, inhabit that dangerous middle zone where formulae of negation assemble themselves with unresisted fluency. Their parts, in Eliot's original arrangement of the play, were to be doubled with those of the Knights, whose Shavian facility of presentation can cope with anything. The Knights, having slaughtered the Archbishop with swords, regret the necessity for violence, and the Fourth Knight argues that the Archbishop has really killed himself. This is his solution to the Archbishop Murder Case: "Suicide while of Unsound Mind. It is the only charitable verdict you can give, upon one who was, after all, a great man."

Plainly, one function of the play is to distinguish analytic cleverness from wisdom, and enterprising good sense from conformity of one's will to the will of God. And Eliot's great dramatic problem is that the distinctions he wishes to dramatize do not terminate in distinct actions, but in the same action. In this dilemma he has recourse to the unexploited contrast lurking in every detective story, the contrast between actions as they were performed, a step at a time into the unknown, will intersecting with will, hidden desire belying overt conduct, and the same actions as the Sleuth glibly recounts them in his context of omniscience. A detective story is a twice-told tale; it is the second telling that we think we understand. The second telling—the one in the last chapter—establishes this illusion by reducing person to purpose and behaviour to design. Eliot's ingenious stratagem was to give the first telling the substantiality of dramatic exhibition, and produce the glib summing-up as a fatuous anticlimax. That is why the Fourth Knight begins his reconstruction by installing us in the world of Mrs. Christie: "What I have to say may be put in the form of a question: *Who killed the Archbishop?*" That is also why several lines from a Sherlock Holmes story are dovetailed into Becket's dialogue with the Second Tempter, and why his exchange with the Third Tempter opens with the figure of rhetoric the late Rev. Ronald Knox christened the Sherlockismus:

THIRD TEMPTER: I am an unexpected visitor.
THOMAS: I expected you.

(With which compare,
    "How do you know that?"
    "I followed you."
    "But I saw nothing."
    "That is what you may expect to see when I follow you."
                —Sir Arthur Conan Doyle, "The Devil's Foot.")

That is also why Eliot proposed calling the play *The Archbishop Murder Case*, a way of playing at Possum in the very citadel of Shakespeare and Aeschylus.

Unhappily, three things combine to sidetrack this extremely promising device for throwing into dramatic relief the changed orientation of Becket's will. The first is the effectiveness of the second act, which so impresses us with Becket's human force, his energetic fortitude before death, that the interchange with the Fourth Tempter is obliterated from memory, and thus rendered inaccessible to the Fourth Knight's suicide verdict which ought to have recalled it and brought it viably into salience at the climax of the play. The second is opportunism; for Eliot did not deny his Third Knight a chance to score against the twentieth-century audience.

> But, if you have now arrived at a just subordination of the pretensions of the Church to the welfare of the State, remember that it is we who took the first step.

This is the one part of the Knights' speeches the audience is likely to take seriously; in the film version, indeed, it is forced into prominence, as the Knight suddenly stands in darkness and speaks to the cinema audience:

> . . . ask yourselves, who is more representative of the thing you are: the man you call a martyr, or the men you call his murderers?

—an excellent point, but one pertinent to a different play. And the third thing that muffles the dramatic scheme of *Murder in the Cathedral* is the language of the Chorus.

The language of the Chorus: their ululating logorrhea, doubling and tripling the image, assailing and bewildering the mind with that reduplication of epithets that caused Ezra Pound to turn off his radio in Rapallo with a despairing, "Oh them cawkney woices." ("I stuck if fer a while, wot wiff the weepin and wailin. Mzzr Shakzpeer *still* retains his posishun.")

The horror of the effortless journey, to the empty land
Which is no land, only emptiness, absence, the Void,
Where those who were men can no longer turn the mind
To distraction, delusion, escape into dream, pretence,
Where the soul is no longer deceived, for there are no objects, no
    tones,
No colours, no forms to distract, to divert the soul
From seeing itself, foully united forever, nothing with nothing,
Not what we call death, but what beyond death is not death. . . .

"The effortless journey, to the empty land" is a fine line, as yet unsalvaged. The rest is dissipated through being said four times over.

Eliot had first written choruses the year before, for a pageant-play entitled *The Rock;* and had quite possibly discovered that when enunciated simultaneously by seven men and ten women the most crisp and athletic verse he had it in him to write became unintelligible three rows from the footlights. Hence, one may conjecture, his new and counter-Eliotic tactic of accumulating epithets around a simple emotion, syntactic structure left in abeyance. The choruses of *Murder in the Cathedral* have this merit, that they are perfectly intelligible even when spoken by elocutionists. Furthermore, the most notable achievement of the choruses in *The Rock*, the sustained tone of surgically impersonal admonition—

> O weariness of men who turn from GOD
> To the grandeur of your mind and the glory of your
>   action . . .
> Exploiting the seas and developing the mountains,
> Dividing the stars into common and preferred,
> Engaged in devising the perfect refrigerator,
> Engaged in working out a rational morality. . . .

—this tone was quite useless for a chorus of poor women, hysterically apprehensive concerning

> Ths strain on the brain of the small folk who stand to the doom
>   of the house, the doom of their lord, the doom of the world
>   . . .

Indeed no stable tone presents itself; the Women, "Living and partly living," squander dozens of arresting phrases in a tumult of unfocused concern. This absence of focus, of course, inheres in Eliot's conception of their function; "They know and do not know," as Becket says, and they flounder among images because their emotions, like those of a talented second-rate poet, lack an objective correlative. A tragedy adequate to their apprehensions is produced before them, and draws their tumult into its order, and the last Chorus is spoken with composure. They remain a poetic embarrassment.

There are in fact three motifs in *Murder in the Cathedral*, not intertwined but competing for prominence: the change in the orientation of Becket's will, which makes the play so useful a commentary on *Ash-Wednesday;* the strife, still active in Eliot's poetic imagination because not wholly realized in *The Rock*, between secularism and the will of God; and that motif which the mere conditions of acted drama could not but thrust into prominence, the death of a valiant man. It is a remarkable first play, containing enough chaos to animate three more plays. It animated instead, in the same year, a remarkable meditative poem that stirred into life among the play's unrealized motifs and rejected scraps: *Burnt Norton.*

VI. INTO OUR FIRST WORLD

Chronology

FOUR QUARTETS

In the summer of 1934 Eliot, vacationing at Chipping Campden in Gloucestershire, visited an uninhabited mansion, erected on the site of an earlier country house two hundred years burnt, and wandered in its deserted formal garden.

>   Other echoes
> Inhabit the garden. Shall we follow?
> Quick, said the bird, find them, find them,
> Round the corner. Through the first gate,
> Into our first world, shall we follow
> The deception of the thrush? Into our first world.
> There they were, dignified, invisible,
> Moving without pressure, over the dead leaves,
> In the autumn heat, through the vibrant air,
> And the bird called, in response to
> The unheard music hidden in the shrubbery,
> And the unseen eyebeam crossed, for the roses
> Had the look of flowers that are looked at. . . .

This experience catalyzed certain fragments which *Murder in the Cathedral* did not finally incorporate, and provided him with the terminal poem to *Poems: 1909–1935*, where it follows and transfigures the *Choruses from "The Rock."*

    Burnt Norton terminates Eliot's most fluent poetic years. The sinuous easy gravity, the meditative poise, the pellucid certainty

of cadence and diction, draw strength from two years' un-
remitting work with stage verse, which if it permitted diffuse-
ness exacted clarity or the show of clarity, and which brought
to his disposal techniques for generating with cool assurance
an air of unemphatic meaning.

Many small things draw the mind forward through this
verse. The syntax beckons just a little ahead of our attention,
never delivering over everything to some resonant line on
which we can come to rest.

> And the bird called, in response to
> The unheard music hidden in the shrubbery,
> And the unseen eyebeam crossed, for the roses
> Had the look of flowers that are looked at:

which is utterly different from the characteristic movement of
The Waste Land:

> In this decayed hole among the mountains

an achieved quotable line, followed by

> In the faint moonlight, the grass is singing

another self-sufficient line, after which comes

> Over the tumbled graves, about the chapel

—followed in turn by the next item in this accumulation of
strong lines

> There is the empty chapel, only the wind's home.

The sentence in *Burnt Norton* goes so delicately about its business that we forget to be puzzled by the "unseen eyebeam";
it takes its place on the plane of half-apprehensible fact where
the inhabitants of "our first world" move without pressure.
The Waste Land, working by accumulation, cannot afford to
relax its mantic intensity. Its obscurities envelop themselves
in folds of sound, dogmatically impenetrable:

> Revive for a moment a broken Coriolanus.

"Broken" is a luminescent enigma, its alternative connotations of moral defeat and a shattered statue not central to the line but by-products of the presence in the line of a word with a suitable open vowel. In *Burnt Norton* we are not detained in that way. "Our first world," by not insisting, establishes itself in a pattern of meaning, whether we accept it as the world of childhood and "they" as departed elder presences, or as the garden of Eden and "they" as our first parents, or as the garden at the Burnt House in ceremonial use, and "they" as seventeenth-century spectres whom the imagination conjures into a scene now deserted. These connotations detach themselves, but the words themselves are innocently transparent, untouched by rhetoric:

> Through the first gate
> Into our first world.

"First" twice takes meaningful stress; we cannot be sure what the meaning is, but the structure of discourse is seamless, like that of superb conversation imperfectly heard. In the same way, the otherwise precarious mystery of "music hidden in the shrubbery" is neutralized by a tactful "unheard":

> And the bird called, in response to
> The unheard music hidden in the shrubbery.

The responding bird call, again, establishes the reality of "unheard music" on some plane of consciousness in which we can believe though we do not at the moment share it. And as for the "unseen eyebeam," invisible presences and unheard music prepare us for it, and the roses, we are told, respond to its crossing:

> for the roses
> Had the look of flowers that are looked at.

That *we* are looking at them seems irrelevant, so tactfully have we by this time been effaced, so substantial have the inapprehensible presences become.

The four-stress line in this passage is manipulated with a new easy authority; admitting as it does four unobtrusive opportunities for emphasis, it selects without insisting just those components of the vision that will sustain one another:

> Móving without préssure, over the déad léaves,
> In the áutumn héat, through the vibrant áir.

Dead leaves and autumn heat the senses can testify to; vibrant air and pressureless movement acquire by association a comparable authority.

Eliot was a long time settling on this characteristic four-beat measure, which can relax toward colloquial intimacy—

> There would be nó dánce, and there is ónly the dánce

or contract in meditative deliberation—

> Tíme pást and tíme fúture.

We first encounter it in *Journey of the Magi*, then find it in the *Choruses from "The Rock,"* accommodating within its hortatory firmness an unexpected wit:

> "Here were decent godless people:
> Their only monument the asphalt road
> And a thousand lost golf balls."

—in *Murder in the Cathedral*, spanning a scale from doggerel to exaltation; now in *Burnt Norton*, the unassertive Eliotic measure framing verse that, for the first time, we suppose to be selflessly transparent. The development of this measure, in the course of eight years or so, was Eliot's last feat of technical innovation.

To devise a measure is to devise a voice, and the appropriate range of expressive content the Voice implies. Of this Voice we may remark first of all its selflessness; it is Old Possum's last disappearing-trick. No *persona*, Prufrock, Gerontion, Tiresias or the Magus, is any longer needed. The words appear to be writing themselves:

> Footfalls echo in the memory
> Down the passage which we did not take
> Towards the door we never opened
> Into the rose-garden.

This is not a troubling Prufrockian "Let us go"; "we," like the French *on*, is devoid of specificity, so much so that the first person singular—

> My words echo
> Thus, in your mind.

—intrudes with dry Puritanic mischief, compounded by the gesture of pedagogic despair that follows:

> But to what purpose
> Disturbing the dust on a bowl of rose-leaves
> I do not know.

This mimics a lecture-room trick without personifying the trickster; it serves to locate in the Harvard graduate seminar the dozen lines of speculation concerning Time present and Time past with which *Burnt Norton* opens, slyly justifying their austere exactness without allowing us to suppose that a didactic poet is on his high horse. Prufrock's "There will be time, there will be time" is by comparison a forensic toying with syllables.

This mimicry of the dynamics of personal intercession, the Voice moving from exposition through intimacy to reminiscence, passing through lyric, expending itself in over-heard meditation, without ever allowing us to intuit the im-purities of personal presence, transforms at last into self-sus-taining technique the anonymity which Eliot always devised, by one means or another, as the indispensable condition of his poetry. He had employed masks, he had employed styles; he had manipulated ventriloqually the effects of respected poets; in *Ash-Wednesday* he had allowed a discontinuous *poésie pure* to imply a moving zone of consciousness. In *Ash-Wednesday* the relation between speaker and reader—indeed the speaker's very mode of existence—is made to seem artless by an extreme of artifice, like the perspective in some pastiche of Fra Angelico. In *Burnt Norton* such problems are not so much solved as caused to vanish, as Euclid or the author of *Thirty Days hath September* caused them to vanish. The man holding the pen does not bare his soul, but on the other hand we feel no compulsion to posit or pry into some *persona*. The motifs of the poem simply declare themselves; and when we come upon the line,

> I can only say, *there* we have been: but I cannot say where.

the first person pronoun prompts no curiosity.

We never know quite where we are in the poem, but all possible relevant experiences are congruent. When

> Footfalls echo in the memory
> Down the passage which we did not take
> Towards the door we never opened
> Into the rose-garden,

we are at liberty to suppose that this is a picturesque evocation of "what might have been," or to recall the White Rabbit's footfalls and the garden which Alice had to traverse the whole of Wonderland in order to enter. A moment later it is the formal garden of the Burnt House, and when we move

> Along the empty alley, into the box circle,
> To look down into the drained pool

there is no harm in allowing "the box circle" to remind us of a theatre as well as a hedge. The lotus, sure enough, moves rather like a ballerina of Diaghilev's—

> Dry the pool, dry concrete, brown edged,
> And the pool was filled with water out of sunlight,
> And the lotos rose, quietly, quietly,
> The surface glittered out of heart of light,
> And they were behind us, reflected in the pool.

This is—to complicate matters further—ideal water and an imagined lotus:

> Then a cloud passed, and the pool was empty.

This garden now disenchanted resembles Eden transformed into a place where the soil must be tilled:

> Go, go, go, said the bird: human kind
> Cannot bear very much reality.
> Time past and time future
> What might have been and what has been
> Point to one end, which is always present.

We have very nearly stepped into some world where happenings are simultaneous, the past actual, what might have been really so, our first world still here, "that vanished mind of which our mind is a continuation" sensibly co-present with our restricted sphere of experience. But this would be reality, of which human kind cannot bear very much, so it is as a concession to our weakness that we are shut up in the present moment. This motif is first announced by Becket, minutes before his death. The Chorus has smelt the death-bringers, and has perceived that

> What is woven on the loom of fate
> What is woven in the councils of princes
> Is woven also in our veins, our brains.

And when it has taken upon itself the guilt for what might have been and what will be, Becket assures it—

> Peace, and be at peace with your thoughts and visions.
> These things had to come to you and you to accept them.
> This is your share of the eternal burden,
> The perpetual glory. This is one moment,
> But know that another
> Shall pierce you with a sudden painful joy
> When the figure of God's purpose is made complete.
> You shall forget these things, toiling in the household,
> You shall remember them, droning by the fire,
> When age and forgetfulness sweeten memory
> Only like a dream that has often been told
> And often been changed in the telling. They will seem unreal.
> Human kind cannot bear very much reality.

It is a much quieter revelation in the Burnt Norton garden, that becomes unbearable, but a revelation so rich in its promise that the whole of *Four Quartets* exfoliates from it. The next lines move into a lyric extrapolation from the Women of Canterbury's discovery that what is woven on the loom of fate is woven also in their veins and brains:

> The dance along the artery
> The circulation of the lymph
> Are figured in the drift of stars.

A harmonious circling order comprehends all movement:

> Ascend to summer in the tree
> We move above the moving tree
> In light upon the figured leaf
> And hear upon the sodden floor
> Below, the boarhound and the boar
> Pursue their pattern as before
> But reconciled among the stars.

Since the whole passage unites mundane and celestial phenomena, there is no need for its opening lines,

> Garlic and sapphires in the mud
> Clot the bedded axle-tree,

to occasion puzzlement. The axle-tree appears to be that of the turning heavens, its lower end, like the bole of Yggdrasill, embedded in our soil. A moment later the image of the axle-tree gives place to an abstract equivalent, and the measure expands to accommodate meditation picking its way:

> At the still point of the turning world. Neither flesh nor fleshless;
> Neither from nor towards; at the still point, there the dance is,
> But neither arrest nor movement. And do not call it fixity,
> Where past and future are gathered.

This is the philosophers' paradox of the Wheel, the exact centre of which is precisely motionless, whatever the velocity of the rim. Though one may imagine the centre as a point of cancellation, Aristotle presented it (*De Anima:* III: 10) as the energizing point:

> Except for the point, the still point,
> There would be no dance, and there is only the dance.

The still point confers meaning; G. K. Chesterton remarked that since the time of Chaucer human society had been converted from a dance into a race. And it is some apprehension of the still point, where past and future are gathered, that has occurred in the garden—

> both a new world
> And the old made explicit, understood

In the completion of its partial ecstasy,
The resolution of its partial horror.

This is consciousness, not the consciousness which philosophers
think about, but a consciousness as enveloping and undiscussible
as the Bradleyan "immediate experience"; and, "To be conscious is not to be in time."

There is however something that does occur in time, and
that is memory. Memory is to be cherished and resorted to
because one cannot often expect to be conscious. And memory
which occurs in time is our weapon against Time:

> But only in time can the moment in the rose-garden,
> The moment in the arbour where the rain beat,
> The moment in the draughty church at smokefall
> Be remembered; involved with past and future.
> Only through time time is conquered.

These speculations have all grown out of the experience of
déjà vu in the garden. They generalize that strange concurrence
of sensations, supply it with meaning not merely eerie, and
unite its gravity with that of the meditative life. The third
part of *Burnt Norton* provides a second experience, located not
in the Garden but in the City, or rather beneath the City, on an
underground platform, no doubt of the Circle Line. The
Underground's "flicker" is a mechanical reconciliation of
light and darkness, the two alternately exhibited very rapidly.
The traveller's emptiness is "neither plenitude nor vacancy." In
this "dim light" we have

> neither daylight
> Investing form with lucid stillness
> Turning shadow into transient beauty
> With slow rotation suggesting permanence
> Nor darkness to purify the soul
> Emptying the sensual with deprivation
> Cleansing affection from the temporal.

There is rotation, but it does not suggest permanence; there is
darkness, purifying nothing; there is light, but it invests nothing

with lucid stillness; there is a systematic parody of the wheel's movement and the point's fixity—

> Men and bits of paper, whirled by the cold wind
> That blows before and after time,

not like the souls of Paolo and Francesca, who were some-where in particular throughout eternity for a particular reason known to them, nor even like de Bailhache, Fresca, and Mrs. Cammel, who were disintegrated; but simply

> . . . the strained time-ridden faces
> Distracted from distraction by distraction
> Filled with fancies and empty of meaning
> Tumid apathy with no concentration.

Light and darkness are opposites, apparently united by this flicker. Their actual reconciliation is to be achieved by "des-cending lower," into an emptier darkness:

> Descend lower, descend only
> Into the world of perpetual solitude,
> World not world, but that which is not world,
> Internal darkness, deprivation
> And destitution of all property,
> Desiccation of the world of sense,
> Evacuation of the world of fancy,
> Inoperancy of the world of spirit;
> This is the one way . . .

Opposites falsely reconciled, then truly reconciled: in the central section of the poem its central structural principle is displayed. The false reconciliation parodies the true one, as the Hollow Men parody the saints, as Gerontion parodies Simeon, as Becket suicide would have parodied Becket martyr, as the leader's eyes in which there is no interrogation parody that certainty which inheres "at the still point of the turning world."

In this Underground scene, curiously enough, the in-structed reader may catch a glimpse of the author, sauntering through the crowd as Alfred Hitchcock does in each of his films. For its locale, Eliot noted, sharing a private joke with his brother in Massachusetts, is specifically the Gloucester Road Station, near the poet's South Kensington headquarters, the point of intersection of the Circle Line with the Piccadilly tube to Russell Square. Whoever would leave the endless circle and entrain for the offices of Faber & Faber must "descend lower," and by spiral stairs if he chooses to walk. "This is the one way, and the other is the same"; the other, adjacent to the stairs, is a lift, which he negotiates "not in movement, but abstention from movement." As Julia Shuttlethwaite observes in *The Cocktail Party*, "In a lift I can meditate."

After this whiff of the Possum's whimsey, Part IV displays the flash of the kingfisher's wing, to offset an instance of the Light which rests. The sun is the still point around which the earth turns, and light is concentrated there; it subtly becomes (for Eliot does not name it) a type of the still point where every variety of light inheres, which transient phenomena reflect. And Part V presents language itself as a transience on which sufficient form may confer endurance. The poem ends with a reassertion of the possibility, and the significance, of timeless moments:

> Sudden in a shaft of sunlight
> Even while the dust moves
> There rises the hidden laughter
> Of children in the foliage
> Quick now, here, now, always—
> Ridiculous the waste sad time
> Stretching before and after.

In this elusive vision the moving dust in sunlight suggests the conditions of human existence, dust sustained and made visible by whatever power enamates from the still point; "quick" means both instantaneous and alive; here and now acquire momentarily the significance of "always"; and the "before and after" which for Shelley contained those distracting glimpses of "what might have been," cease to tantalize: they are merely aspects of "the waste sad time" which the timeless moment has power to render irrelevant.

This remarkable poem, which no one, however well acquainted with Eliot's earlier work, could have foreseen, brings the generalizing style of the author of *Prufrock* and the austere intuitions of the disciple of Bradley for the first time into intimate harmony. Suggestion does not outrun thought, nor design impose itself on what word and cadence are capable of suggesting. It was a precarious unobtrusive masterpiece, which had for some years no successor. Having recovered *Burnt Norton* from the chaos of one play, Eliot concerned himself not with a successor to *Burnt Norton* but with another play, which ought to have been a securer achievement that it is. In 1939 he published *The Family Reunion*.

ii

Approaching *The Family Reunion* not as Eliot's first play for the commercial stage, but rather as his next poem after *Burnt Norton*, we discover a woman who has attempted for eight years to enforce, at a country house named Wishwood, a protracted artificial timeless moment ("Nothing has been changed. I have seen to that"); a man who is more dogmatically convinced than the musing voice at the *Burnt Norton* opening that

> all past is present, all degradation
> Is unredeemable,

but who has nonetheless returned to his first world to seek out the presences that move without pressure over its dead leaves; and a chorus of strained, time-ridden faces, distracted from distraction. The man who has come back recalls a life transacted in a more lurid facsimile of the *Burnt Norton* underground

> The sudden solitude in a crowded desert
> In a thick smoke, many creatures moving
> Without direction, for no direction
> Leads anywhere but round and round in that vapour—
> Without purpose, without principle of conduct
> In flickering intervals of light and darkness. . . .

In this subterranean void he has willed a deed of violence, which he has incurred the obligation of expiating; for he has discovered that he cannot simply leave the past behind, just as his mother needs to discover that she cannot simply keep it with her.

Through time, however, time is conquered. He gains the means of liberation from his nightmare past by acquiring, in Wishwood, insight into a still earlier past which he had never comprehended. His father, a presence out of his first world, becomes intelligible to him, "dignified, invisible," and his own crime, which he had been concerned to expiate in isolation, turns out to be simply the present cross-section of a family crime projected through generations. As he has willed to kill his wife, so his father, it turns out, had once willed to kill his.

> The trilling wire in the blood
> Sings below inveterate scars
> And reconciles forgotten wars;

and Harry, the purpose of his visit to the great house with its garden now accomplished, takes his departure.

It is easy to see the application to Harry's plight of the enigmatic epigraphs from Heraclitus which Eliot affixed to *Burnt Norton:* "Though the law of things is universal in scope, most men act as though they had insight of their own"; and "The way up and the way down are one and the same."

> Whether in Argos or England,

The *Family Reunion* Chorus proclaims,

> There are certain inflexible laws
> Unalterable, in the nature of music.

Harry has supposed himself the centre of a totally sick world which has arranged itself around his unique malaise. When he tell his impercipient uncles and aunts that they have gone through life in sleep, never woken to the nightmare, and that life would be unendurable if they were wide awake, it is because he supposes himself a privileged person, habituated to "the noxious smell and the sorrow before morning." But though it is true that

> . . . the enchainment of past and future
> Woven in the weakness of the changing body,
> Protects mankind from heaven and damnation
> Which flesh cannot endure,

nevertheless the "inflexible laws, unalterable, in the nature of music," are not the iron chains Harry supposes them to be; like the laws of music, they define the conditions of freedom.

> Only by the form, the pattern,
> Can words or music reach
> The stillness, as a Chinese jar still
> Moves perpetually in its stillness.

By approaching it from *Burnt Norton*, we see the intelligible play Eliot was attempting to write. Looking at it as a first night audience, we are more likely to behold an impenetrable screen of symbols that do not declare themselves and events that do not occur. The ending is particularly troublesome. Harry goes,

> the consciousness of [his] unhappy family,
> Its bird sent flying through the purgatorial flame,

and where he is going and what he proposes to do, what will be the nature of his liberated existence, these are of obvious dramatic importance. But *Burnt Norton* does not carry things that far, and the fundamental thinking for the play is what is contained in *Burnt Norton*. The problem is in fact a pseudo-problem, forced upon the play by the exigencies of dramatic construction; for, as we learn from subsequent poems, the state promised in the garden at *Burnt Norton* is, like the reorientation of Becket's will, not reducible to terms of exhibited action, but rather an invisible inflection of whatever action one performs. If this consideration spoils *The Family Reunion*, it lends itself intimately to further meditative poems; and in 1940, the year after the performance of the play, Eliot published *East Coker*. While working on it, he conceived the sequence of four poems to which *Burnt Norton* was ultimately transferred, and by 1942 had completed *Four Quartets*.

iii

The series title suggests a further insight into the language developed in *Burnt Norton;* it is string music, more closely analogous to the human voice than any other instrumentation, but still not to be confused with either quotidian discourse or with a particular person speaking. The *Quartets* muse, they traverse and exploit a diversity of timbres and intonations, interchange themes, set going a repetitive but developing minuet of motifs. *The Waste Land* is by comparison a piece of eloquence. Like the voices of a string quartet, the lyric, didactic, colloquial, and deliberative modes of these poems pursue in an enclosed world the forms of intent *conversation;* the occasional voice that rises above the consort does so tentatively, mindful of the decorum in which there is no audience to address, but only the other voices. We are not addressed, we overhear.

Like instruments, the voices have stable identities. *East Coker* introduces them in turn: the inhabitant of England, with a family, a past, and a penchant for visiting significant landscapes; the lyric poet; the sombre moralist, intermittently Christian; and the man of letters, "trying to learn to use words." We may enumerate them in this way without implicating the now wholly effaced Invisible Poet, who composed the score, but is only figuratively present in the performance.

There is an empty custom of referring here to the "late" quartets of Beethoven, a parallel which impedes understanding by suggesting that the *Quartets* offer to be an Olympian's transfinite testament. Eliot is reported to have said that he was paying attention chiefly to Bartok's Quartets, Nos. 2–6.★

The title also implies that the deliverances of the poem will be as formal and as elusive as music, which they are; and that something resembling a strict form is going to be observed,

★I owe this information to Mr. M. J. C. Hodgart of Pembroke College, Cambridge.

as it is. The five-parted dialectic of *Burnt Norton* is exactly paralleled three times over, and so raised by iteration to the dignity of a form.

Or so one would say, were not *Burnt Norton*, surprisingly enough, the exact structural counterpart of *The Waste Land*. That form, originally an accident produced by Pound's cutting, Eliot would seem by tenacious determination to have analyzed, mastered, and made into an organic thing. *Burnt Norton*, terminating the 1935 *Collected Poems*, appears meant to bear the same relation to *The Waste Land* as Simeon to Gerontion. Its rose-garden, for instance, with the passing cloud and the empty pool, corresponds to the Hyacinth garden and the despondent "*Oed' und leer das Meer*," while "the heart of light, the silence" that was glimpsed in the presence of the hyacinth girl is the tainted simulacrum of that light which "is still at the still point of the turning world."

Each *Quartet* carries on this structural parallel. The first movement, like *The Burial of the Dead*, introduces a diversity of themes; the second, like *A Game of Chess*, presents first "poetically" and then with less traditional circumscription the same area of experience; the third, like *The Fire Sermon*, gathers up the central vision of the poem while meditating dispersedly on themes of death; the fourth is a brief lyric; the fifth, a didactic and lyric culmination, concerning itself partly with language, in emulation of the Indo-European roots exploited in *What the Thunder Said*.

Numerous other formalities resemble in function those conventions of musical structure that distinguish a Quartet from an improvization. The poems concern themselves in turn with early summer, late summer, autumn, and winter; with air, earth, water, and fire, the four elements of Heraclitus' flux; their brief fourth movements celebrate successively the Unmoved Mover, the redeeming Son, the Virgin, and the Holy Ghost; and each poem is named after some obscure place where the poet's personal history or that of his family makes contact with a more general Past.

East Coker is the village in Somerset where Eliots or Elyots lived for some two centuries, before the poet's ancestor Andrew Eliot emigrated in 1667 to found the American branch of the family. On that act depends T. S. Eliot's status, an almost assimilated Englishman, nowhere at home, whose first twenty-five years were spent in "a large flat country." Whether, on the other hand, if Andrew Eliot had remained in England his family would have boasted an eminent man of letters, must remain

> a perpetual possibility
> Only in a world of speculation.

This poem deals with the pastness, beyond significant recall, of the irrevocable past, and with its irrevocability. Andrew and various other ancestors have done what they have done, and

> In my beginning is my end.

Like *Burnt Norton*, the poem begins by leading us from a meditation of sombre principles, through a landscape into a vision. The landscape is ominously static:

> And the deep lane insists on the direction
> Into the village, in the electric heat
> Hypnotised. In a warm haze the sultry light
> Is absorbed, not refracted, by grey stone.
> The dahlias sleep in the empty silence.
> Wait for the early owl.

The vision presents not a polysemous "first-world," but a dancing of sixteenth-century peasants around a midsummer fire,

> Leaping through the flames, or joined in circles,
> Rustically solemn or in rustic laughter
> Lifting heavy feet in clumsy shoes,
> Earth feet, loam feet, lifted in country mirth
> Mirth of those long since under earth
> Nourishing the corn.

A native of East Coker, Sir Thomas Elyot, had discussed in *The Boke named the Gouvernour* (1531) "wherefore in the good

ordre of daunsinge a man and a woman daunseth to gether,"
and four centuries later his collateral descendant weaves phrases
from *The Boke* into his poem:

> Two and two, necessarye coniunction,
> Holding eche other by the hand or the arm
> Whiche betokeneth concorde.

As the spelling indicates, that past lives but quaintly; and the
emphasis falls on the decay of so many transient bodies,

> ashes to the earth
> Which is already flesh, fur and faeces,
> Bone of man and beast, cornstalk and leaf.

If "daunsinge" has signified "matrimonie—A dignified and
commodious sacrament," matrimony in the universe of "flesh,
fur and faeces" is governed by

> The time of milking and the time of harvest
> The time of the coupling of man and woman
> And that of beasts. Feet rising and falling.
> Eating and drinking. Dung and death.

This dance, though it comes to us in a vision, is not the one
containing "neither arrest nor movement" which is located
"at the still point of the turning world." It is merely a Tudor
festival of fire, now superseded: an incident in the unecstatic
rhythm of peasant life.

In succeeding passages *Burnt Norton*'s perpetual possibilities
are refuted by "what has been." The intimate identity between
"the dance along the artery" and "the drift of stars" gives
place to a universe which is all of a piece only in being pointed
towards destruction. The presences in the rose-garden become
"the quiet-voiced elders" who have nothing to tell us,

> The serenity only a deliberate hebetude,
> The wisdom only the knowledge of dead secrets
> Useless in the darkness into which they peered
> Or from which they turned their eyes.

Indeed not only traditional wisdom but one's own past seems
of limited value;

The knowledge imposes a pattern, and falsifies,
For the pattern is new in every moment
And every moment is a new and shocking
Valuation of all we have been.

Part III, like the third part of *Burnt Norton*, invites us to "descend lower":

be still, and wait without hope
For hope would be hope for the wrong thing. . . .

Part IV introduces Christ the Wounded Surgeon; Part V, under His aegis, a reconsideration of apparent personal failure. The "twenty years largely wasted" were

. . . perhaps neither gain nor loss.
For us, there is only the trying. The rest is not our business.

Hence it is relevant to continue trying, and not to count on

the long looked forward to,
Long hoped for calm, the autumnal serenity
And the wisdom of age.

The cemetery of East Coker takes its place in the pattern which is new in every moment; for it is of the nature of human life to complicate endlessly its relations with the dead and the living:

. . . a lifetime burning in every moment
And not the lifetime of one man only
But of old stones that cannot be deciphered.

Hence "old men ought to be explorers," and Andrew Eliot's enterprise becomes both a justification and a precedent, itself justified.

We must be still and still moving
Into another intensity
For a further union, a deeper communion
Through the dark cold and the empty desolation,
The wave cry, the wind cry, the vast waters
Of the petrel and the porpoise. . . .

The "wounded surgeon" enters this communion, and so does

the dead ancestor; the poem ends by reversing its initial despairing motto, and aligning it with the words which Mary Queen of Scots had embroidered on her Chair of State:

In my end is my beginning.

There is no faking in this reversal; *East Coker* stays within its own dark ambit, not Eliot's least animated poem, but the one least touched by possibilities of animation. In its presence even *The Hollow Men* seems to an imponderable degree satiric, the circuit round the prickly pear posititively facetious. It is not a depressed poem, though depression has entered it ("twenty years largely wasted"). The presence of *Ecclesiastes* within ten lines of the opening serves to remind us that the pervasive sombreness is more than personal, that it is a view of the world that has seemed tenable to men in every generation. It weights, moreover, the redeeming elements when they enter. We hear of Good Friday, not of the Love that moves the sun and the other stars; the concluding forward journey passes "through the dark cold and the empty desolation" to a "further union" not specified;* the very "laughter in the garden", when it makes its brief appearance, simply points "to the agony of death and birth."

Moods change, but a man's stable moods correspond to the things he chooses to regard as important. Unless the disparity of emotion between *Burnt Norton* and *East Coker* can be resolved, they become alternative ways in which the mind responsible for their existence deceives itself. As the next phase in the programme of the *Quartets*, a reconciliation of opposites seems in order.

But Eliotic opposites may be resolved in contrary ways. Of certain opposites presented in *Burnt Norton* itself, the Underground world in Part III is a parody-reconciliation, its dominating natural force Gerontion's wind. Its "flicker" combines darkness and light, plenitude and vacancy, in a barrenly mechanical way; the mechanically ordered movement of the pas-

*But compare *Marina*.

sengers, restless but predictable on its "metalled ways," combines stillness and dancing. But this relationship of three terms, the third falsely combining the first and second, is the poet's means of localizing a fourth: the darkness which is still further from natural darkness than is the eternal half-light of the tube, and which is hence introduced by a spatial gesture:

> Descend lower, descend only
> Into the world of perpetual solitude,
> World not world, but that which is not world.

And this "world not world," described always positively yet always with circumstantial tact in terms of what it is not, really does, we are given to understand, perform the function which the place of the flicker only pretends to perform. The light and darkness with which it has affinity are the opposites it reconciles.

This is diagrammatic; in *Burnt Norton* it is diagrammatically presented. The diagram, however, points up the manner in which, from first to last, *Four Quartets* deals with opposites first falsely, then truly, reconciled, exactly as suicide and martyrdom, superficially identical, were the false and true modes by which Becket's plight could be resolved. It should not surprise us, therefore, that *The Dry Salvages* moves off from the first two *Quartets* in a direction not wholly commendable, dwelling on the poet's merely personal past by the Mississippi and the Atlantic seaboard, and plucking its conciliating formulae from those mazes of Hindu metaphysics in which, he once remarked, he spent some years at Harvard "in a state of enlightened mystification." *The Dry Salvages* is a poem of *opinion:* "I do not know much about gods; but . . . ," or "I sometimes wonder if that is what Krishna meant. . . ." In Part V we hear the voice of Eliot playing one of his public roles, the anxious social commentator; haruspication on the Edgware Road is filtered through this medium, not allowed to establish its own melancholy identity. And in Part II he nearly expostulates with us, urges us to follow an argument which he is having difficulty in formulating satisfactorily.

> I have said before
> That the past experience revived in the meaning
> Is not the experience of one life only
> But of many generations—

He has *not* said this before: it has said itself, with unselfconscious authority:

> . . . a lifetime burning in every moment
> And not the lifetime of one man only
> But of old stones that cannot be deciphered.

But the voice we hear in *The Dry Salvages* is using this poetic illumination, or his own leaden paraphrase of it, as a datum in a laboured construction. The rhythms are cumbrous, the phraseology has neither grace nor pith—

> the latter a partial fallacy,
> Encouraged by superficial notions of evolution;

the instances lack sureness—

> Fruition, fulfilment, security or affection,
> Or even a very good dinner;

the second sentence in the passage loses its direction and its syntactic identity entirely; and the laboured "I have said before" has none of the ironic grace of the comparable detail in Part III of *East Coker*. *The Dry Salvages* contains enough detachable mannerisms to have permitted the only successful parody of an Eliot manner, Henry Reed's *Chard Whitlow:*

> . . . I think you will find this put,
> Far better than I could ever hope to express it,
> In the words of Kharma: "It is, we believe,
> Idle to hope that the simple stirrup-pump
> Can extinguish hell."
> Oh, listeners,
> And you especially who have switched off the wireless. . . .

It is the necessary false truce in the economy of the *Quartets,* the necessary phase of satisfaction with what our own capacity for insight can deliver, from which the taut revelations of *Little Gidding* are later distinguished.

Not that he has deliberately written a second-rate poem; *The Dry Salvages* not only contains the most powerfully articulated passage he has ever published, the twenty-three-line sentence that enumerates the sea's voices

> . . . The menace and caress of wave that breaks on water,
> The distant rote in the granite teeth. . . .

but it also provides, in the course of its attempts to mediate between recurrent illumination and pervasive failure, several formulae of both structural and exegetical utility:

> We had the experience but missed the meaning,
> And approach to the meaning restores the experience
> In a different form, beyond any meaning
> We can assign to happiness.

Or,

> . . . do not think of the fruit of action.
> Fare forward.

Or,

> . . . time is no healer: the patient is no longer here.

These it can provide by virtue of its persistent inquiry within the sphere where such formulations are arrived at. There is nothing in the last three-quarters of *The Dry Salvages*, not the materials handled, the mode of ideation, nor the process by which instance yields formulation, that is beyond the scope of a sensitive prose essayist. The function of the verse is not to leap gaps, but simply to establish and sustain the meditative tone, sufficiently remote from the idiom in which you address other people to obviate the lengthy and distracting ceremonial by which the prose writer assures his readers that he isn't leaving them behind. The poem leads us *out of* "poetry"—the river and the sea—down into small dry air in which to consider in an orderly fashion what "most of us" are capable of. The saints are capable of more:

> to apprehend
> The point of intersection of the timeless

> With time, is an occupation for the saint—
> No occupation either, but something given
> And taken, in a lifetime's death in love,
> Ardour and selflessness and self-surrender.

We who are not saints may from time to time enjoy hints of that apprehension—

> the unattended
> Moment, the moment in and out of time,
> The distraction fit, lost in a shaft of sunlight,
> The wild thyme unseen, or the winter lightning
> Or the waterfall, or music heard so deeply
> That it is not heard at all, but you are the music
> While the music lasts.

If these seem familiar experiences, that is the point of the passage. For "These are only hints and guesses, hints followed by guesses"; and

The hint half guessed, the gift half understood, is Incarnation.

This is literally meant; such a "moment in and out of time" as occurred in the *Burnt Norton* garden is not the saint's beatitude, but the temporary translation of that beatitude into a more familiar medium, into a mode of experience available to human kind. This is what our least time-ridden moments can give us, not timelessness but a glimpse of it; hence to decide that we live for those moments is to be content with the parody of the real. *The Dry Salvages*, similarly, is what our capacity for orderly generalization from experience can give us, not the continual apprehension of the still point but an account of how our experience would be related to such an apprehension if we could have it. To repose in such an account is to be free from irrelevant desires; but it may also be to wonder, with the student of Francis Herbert Bradley, what it was we wanted and why we ever supposed we wanted anything. The poem's last formulation is one from which no agnostic propounder of a free man's worship would dissent. No one succeeds, the thing is to try; our efforts "fructify in the lives of others," and we ourselves enrich the ground. This is very close to the social gospel of ants; and the final line empties of inconsistent optimism a Ruskin-like cliché about "significant toil":

> For most of us, this is the aim
> Never here to be realized;
> Who are only undefeated
> Because we have gone on trying;
> We, content at the last
> If our temporal reversion nourish
> (Not too far from the yew-tree)
> The life of significant soil.

Thus the parody-reconciliation, the collective voice of the late nineteenth century, urging us to strive without personal hope, to consider how we are placed in a cosmos whose dimensions dwarf us on an earth whose soil at least knows how to make use of us, seeking our fulfilment in a collective endeavour, and our religious support in "religious experiences" which are likely to be experiences of nature—"the winter lightning / Or the waterfall"—or of music, and not really distinguishable from the fulfilment of "a very good dinner." It is some ideal Matthew Arnold's road out of East Coker.

iv

Upon this decent self-abnegation bursts the "midwinter spring" of *Little Gidding*, a poem of paradox, metamorphosis, and climax. Snow on the hedgerow,

> a bloom more sudden
> Than that of summer, neither budding nor fading,
> Not in the scheme of generation,

asserts in the midst of death ("no earth smell / Or smell of living thing") not the wistful apprehension of invisible presences in a rose-garden but the possibility of

> the unimaginable
> Zero summer.

This time suspended in time, "zero" because heat is cancelled, though not by cold, and because movement is ended, though not in immobility, this actuality toward which we are admonished by "pentecostal fire" flaming on ice, comes shockingly against our senses to subsume many tedious abstractions, "neither from nor towards," "concentration without elimination," and the rest of it. Our next surprise is to discover that the place associated with this vision is a place accessible to anyone, distinguished, at the end of a rough road, by a pig-sty, a dull façade, and a tombstone. It is a place where intentions alter:

> what you thought you came for
> Is only a shell, a husk of meaning
> From which the purpose breaks only when it is fulfilled
> If at all,

thus rendering irrelevant the curiosity which "searches past and future and clings to that dimension"; a place which is in many senses "the world's end," though similar to other such places,

> some at the sea jaws,
> Or over a dark lake, in a desert or a city.

These were all zones of combat in 1942, where many men encountered the world's end. They are also places associated with saints; in a note for his brother, Henry Ware Eliot, the author cited the isles of Iona and Lindisfarne, associated with St. Colomba and St. Cuthbert; St. Kevin's lake of Glandalough; the Thebaid of St. Anthony (who is also the tempted "word in the desert" of *Burnt Norton*); and the Padua of the other St. Anthony. But this place has been celebrated neither by canonized saints nor by topical warriors. It is a place "where prayer has been valid," and as to what may happen there,

> . . . what the dead had no speech for, when living,
> They can tell you, being dead: the communication
> Of the dead is tongued with fire beyond the language of the living.

This place is Little Gidding in Huntingdonshire. Like the Burnt House, the Little Gidding chapel is a restoration of an earlier place destroyed. Cromwell's soldiers sacked it in 1647, and scattered the saintly community. Charles I took refuge there after Naseby, "very privately, in the darkness of night."

If *East Coker* brings the Eliot family from England to America, and *The Dry Salvages* brings T. S. Eliot from the "nursery bedroom" to the phase in which he was a student of Bradley's and a disciple of Irving Babbitt's, *Little Gidding* returns him to England, and the Church of England, and brings the temporal cycle round from the sixteenth century to a disastrous Now. In *Burnt Norton* a formal garden centuries old, in *East Coker* a village life centuries gone, briefly allow the present to participate; in *Little Gidding*, similarly, the loop in time incorporates into an England menaced by Stuka bombers

> (The dove descending breaks the air
> With flame of incandescent terror)

the achievement of a place where "prayer has been valid" for three centuries.

This place arose from the ashes of the Civil War; so when in the litany of the Four Elements that initiates Part II we encounter a reference to its destruction,

> Water and fire shall rot
> The marred foundations we forgot,
> Of sanctuary and choir,

we may take it that all the modes of death in that Litany are likewise redeemable. These deaths—

> Dust in the air suspended
> Marks the place where a story ended

—prompt instances from the bombing of London; no other *Quartet* is so explicitly located in time as this one in which time is conquered. The ghost is encountered on a London street, by a fire-spotter dazed after an air raid, "at the recurrent end of the unending," and the horn on whose blowing he fades (by analogy with the dawn which removed the ghost of Hamlet's father) is the "all-clear".

This ghost (whom Eliot is said to have more or less identified with W. B. Yeats*) foretells as Yeats did in *Purgatory*, a play Eliot has greatly admired,

> the rending pain of re-enactment
> Of all that you have done, and been.

His utterance indeed is "tongued with fire beyond the language of the living"; no other Voice in Eliot's repertoire articulates with such authority. That he is the first apparition in the *Quartets* who comes close and speaks is a fact that underlines his authority; he is no such "dignified, invisible" presence as moved in the rose garden, nor a member of the dance you can see "if you do not come too close." He is "compound": Yeats, Mallarmé, Hamlet's father, Ezra Pound, Dante, Swift, Milton, "some dead master," "both one and many." He embodies also that simultaneity of the *literary* past which has been Eliot's theme since 1917; the "passage" that now

> presents no hindrance
> To the spirit unappeased and peregrine
> Between two worlds become much like each other

can be a passage of verse as well as the facile transition between Purgatory and a London ringed with fire:

> So I find words I never thought to speak
> In streets I never thought I should revisit
> When I left my body on a distant shore."†

He discloses a Gerontion's future: anaesthesia, acrimony, shame: these are

> the gifts reserved for age
> To set a crown upon your lifetime's effort,

---

*This information comes from Mr. Horace Gregory, who adds to it Eliot's emphasis on the fact that the ghost was also partly himself.

†There was a tradition that Dante visited Oxford about 1308. Swift, Yeats, and Pound of course were often in London.

and the "fruit of action" becomes indeed "shadow fruit." But he hints at the alternative to such a future:

> From wrong to wrong the exasperated spirit
> Proceeds, unless restored by that refining fire
> Where you must move in measure, like a dancer.

The third part of the poem absorbs such revenants into a "renewed, transfigured" pattern:

> These men, and those who opposed them
> And those whom they opposed
> Accept the constitution of silence
> And are folded in a single party.

To think of them

> is not to ring the bell backward
> Nor is it an incantation
> To summon the spectre of a Rose:

it is to bring them alive into our present consciousness: if we know more than they, they are that which we know, "united in the strife which divided them," like the community at Little Gidding and the Roundheads who scattered them. The fourth part celebrates the "refining fire," incendiary or pentecostal according to the use we make of it. The fifth, having united *East Coker's* "beginning" and "end," affirmed the possibility of words that do not

> strain
> Crack and sometimes break, under the burden,
> Under the tension,

and set to an easy rhythm our comings and goings and those of the dead, returns us for a moment to "a winter's afternoon, in a secluded chapel," before bringing us back with assurance to the "first world" *Burnt Norton* brushed against. The poet, totally effaced, can afford without distraction formally erotic images of fulfilment ("through the unknown, remembered gate"; "the crowned knot of fire"); can prevent the first world from sounding regressive and the laughter of the hidden children from appearing to complete a personal yearning, "the source of the longest river" from sounding trite, and "the voice of the hidden waterfall" from irritating us with "symbolic" vagueness.

> Quick now, here, now, always—
> A condition of complete simplicity
> (Costing not less than everything)
> And all shall be well and
> All manner of thing shall be well
> When the tongues of flame are in-folded
> Into the crowned knot of fire
> And the fire and the rose are one.

Any of these phrases, escaped from that masterly control, would be merely silly; but Eliot can even insert "all shall be well" into the climactic passage of his most extensive and demanding poem. The language, unprotected by formalities of diction, maintains commerce with deliquescent cliché, the speech of an age whose speech when sedate is commonly vapid, and these clichés not only never menace its decorum, they even seem transparent coinages. No one will say, "That is not what I meant at all," and no unnatural vices are fathered by this poetic heroism. "The poetry does not matter." These are the qualities that assure us of the new first world's durability. When it was glimpsed in *Burnt Norton* it was a precarious special thing, prompting contrast with

> the waste sad time
> Stretching before and after.

The finale of *Little Gidding* fends off nothing. It is a nearly unprecedented triumph of style.

VII. POSSUM BY GASLIGHT

Chronology
 The Family Reunion, 1939.
 Death of T. S. Eliot's first wife, 1947.
 The Cocktail Party, 1950.
 The Confidential Clerk, 1955.
 T. S. Eliot married to Valerie Fletcher, January 1957.
 The Elder Statesman, 1959.

PREPARED FACES

Q: Mr. Eliot, would you care to say what your new play will
be about?
A: My play deals with certain characters, and their relations
with one another and with themselves.

—Interview, c. 1948.

If, at about the age of thirty, a poet has devoted intellectual
passion to Francis Herbert Bradley's exorcism of the common-
sense world (reduced phase by phase to Appearance merely,
but capable of approximating Reality by a feat of self-trans-
cension), then we need not be surprised to find that poet, at
about the age of sixty, contriving plays. In the theatre we are
all Phenomenalists; it is the perfect Bradleyan form. A make-
believe world cut out of darkness by judicious prearrangement
of spotlights, in which periodically

With a hollow rumble of wings, with a movement of darkness on
darkness,
. . . we know that the hills and the trees, the distant panorama
And the bold imposing façade are all being rolled away;

in which salaried persons whose habitual selves are concealed
manipulate other selves equally makeshift through factitious,
imponderable psychic business; in which all is Appearance
mimicking for two hours a continuous Present (it will be
exactly repeated tomorrow night), yet enacting an ideal Transience (we have neither time nor will to deceive ourselves with

analysis), and presenting in terms of Immediate Experience whatever self-transcendence of the merely apparent it is capable of according us: this is the appointed milieu for drawing room existence, let alone plays, and when we encounter it in a play we need not even decide what meaning we are to give to the vexed term Imitation.

For the milieu of Eliot's plays—supposing it to exist—is like a play. Thus Edward Chamberlayne, in a speech by the Unidentified Guest, is reminded of how you look

> When you've dressed for a party
> And are going downstairs, with everything about you,
> Arranged to support you in the role you have chosen,

Thus the bewildered chorus at the Monchensey country house feel

> Like amateur actors in a dream when the curtain rises,
> to find themselves dressed for a different play, or having
> rehearsed the wrong parts.

Thus Sir Claude Mulhammer observes of an unwanted life in the City,

> It begins as a kind of make-believe
> And the make-believing makes it real.

Thus Lord Claverton (who comes to see himself as "the broken-down actor") does not flinch when he is told that

> . . . the difference between being an elder statesman
> And posing successfully as an elder statesman
> Is practically negligible.

For quotidian life, to which we are so much devoted, is an intricate ritual of appearances, like a cocktail party. Indeed, the transformation of this Prufrockian image of doom into an image of liberation is the main action of *The Cocktail Party*, which begins with a party failing and ends, on a note of expectancy, with a party beginning. Correspondingly, the main action of its successor, *The Confidential Clerk*, is the election, between alternative selves, of the one which accords with the largest array of verifiable facts. For the protagonists of the plays bustle with Bradleyan fuss about who one really is. Colby Simpkins finds that his new vocation as Sir Claude's Confidential Clerk has given him a new personality:

I'm not at all sure that I like the other person
That I feel myself becoming—though he fascinates me.
And yet from time to time, when I least expect it,
When my mind is cleared and empty, walking in the street
Or waking in the night, then the former person,
The person I used to be, returns to take possession. . . .

As for Edward Chamberlayne, reluctant host, he has "met himself"

as a middle-aged man
Beginning to know what it is to feel old.

He has been known to himself as a passionate lover, and must square this illusion with the unwelcome fact that he has never been in love with anybody. He changes before the eyes of his inamorata Celia,

I listened to your voice, that had always thrilled me,
And it become another voice—no, not a voice:
What I heard was only the noise of an insect,
Dry, endless, meaningless, inhuman—
You might have made it by scraping your legs together—

though she is careful to state that this is not a dwindling of *him*, but only "what was left of what I had thought you were . . . Something that I desperately wanted to exist."

She has seen only what we can see: a name, a voice, some mannerisms. That is all there ever is to see; and Eliot, far too intelligent to have rushed into theatre work without carefully pondering its nature, has taken as his point of dramatic leverage the irreducible fact that actions in the theatre are not analyzed but simply exhibited, at some distance and behind a set of conventions, like actions in a drawing-room. What the other characters know about the hero may differ in scope but not in kind from what the audience knows about him. *Prufrock* and *The Cocktail Party* are exercises in genres so radically different as to nullify any complaint about the "poetry" of the latter. Poetic drama, unlike dramatic monologue, shows us each of the characters as he appears from the outside, and shows him in that way alone. No one in the Eliot plays talks unless he is talking to someone else, and the author, as he once stated in response to a silly question about "a society without form," "intended to produce characters whose drawing-room behaviour was generally correct." So we see only what is normally seen, and what is normally seen is an invention.

A man's drawing-room self is in part other people's invention, in part his own; and the part that is his own is in turn partly a response to what he guesses other expect. Free him from that contraption, and in the third act he may do the most extraordinary things: repair an apparently hopeless marriage, or undertake "a care over the lives of humble people," or drop a financial career to play a church organ, or even die at peace. When he does this he has come to terms with some hitherto elusive Self,

> who does not speak,
> Who never talks, who cannot argue.

The means of freeing him from the contrived self is commonly a return of ghosts: the Eumenides, from beyond "the loop in time," or the vanished wife, or the woman who knows the secret of his parentage, or the people who have shared the past his contrived self has obliterated. The Elder Statesman finally refuses to flee from Gomez and Mrs. Carghill—

Because they are not real, Charles. They are merely ghosts:
Spectres from my past. They've always been with me
Though it was not till lately that I found the living persons
Whose ghosts tormented me, to be only human beings,
Malicious, petty, and I see myself emerging
From my spectral existence into something like reality.

As they become merely real so does he—

> In becoming no one he has become himself—

and it is the modest achievement of the play that we do not mistake anonymity for annihilation.

These plays of masked actors in Savile Row costumes, each work turning on the establishment of someone's moral identity, Eliot has reduced in the twenty years since *The Family Reunion* to a nearly ritual simplicity of means. The Eliot play, in fact, seems on the way to becoming a distinct dramatic genre, like the Shaw play or the Wilde play, in which a special language, a corresponding moral climate, and a whimsically melodramatic kind of plot irradiate one another's possibilities.

Everything depends on the language, as a look at *The Family Reunion* shows us. *The Family Reunion* is "poetic" enough; it abounds in the familiar Eliotic effects, phrases reverberatory without ascertainable core. Words throb as they do in *Prufrock* or *Gerontion;* Harry's splendid lines on the death of hope are as memorable as any the author of *The Hollow Men* has written:

> . . . The bright colour fades
> Together with the unrecapturable emotion,
> The glow upon the world, that never found its object;
> And the eye adjusts itself to a twilight
> Where the dead stone is seen to be batrachian,
> The aphyllous branch ophidian.

Verse of this kind specializes the play considerably; for while it adds an extra dimension to the drawing-room realities, it throws the responsibility for this dimension upon the language alone. If we are to believe in the man in the lounge suit speaking it, we have to accept the experience of losing touch with him occasionally while he becomes entranced and oracular. This comes about not because "people don't really talk poetry," but because Eliot's characteristic poetry doesn't imply a mind speaking, it implies a language spoken, plus a Voice. Seeking to adjust to the conversation of an empirical society the dream-heavy illuminations of his world made out of unquiet words, Eliot consequently arranged for the "poetical" parts of *The Family Reunion* to be spoken by a man half-crazed by contact with the literal Furies, a sibylline aunt, and a Chorus that actually does pass from a plane of badinage to a state of trance before the audience's eyes.

The verse of *The Family Reunion*, in fact, *encloses* everyone who speaks it. Harry, like Gerontion, is imprisoned with a view of life, speaking variations on the epigraph to *Prufrock*. "I am trying," he says desperately at one point, "to give you comparisons in a more familiar medium"; and he cries out to his family that they will understand less after he has explained. He is Lazarus come back to tell them all. But he has to use words when he talks to us; for *The Family Reunion*, a work which, like a much overpainted picture, bears on its surface the marks of more effort than anything else Eliot has published, is a rewriting of the long-unfinished *Sweeney Agonistes*, that play about a man encased by a private horror out of which his words gesture uselessly. The scale is now almost comically expanded. The income-level of the characters is raised several tax-brackets, the scene is a country house instead of a flat, the woman has been drowned in the Atlantic Ocean instead of a bathtub, and the Furies have pursued the culprit across Europe instead of through London. But it wasn't elbow-room the dramatist needed; the victory of getting the thing finished at last is rather moral than artistic. Palette-knife applications of Middletonian verse do not conceal the fact that the two-hour version is no more finished, in terms of significant action, than were the two fragments. Like all Eliot's poetry before *Ash-Wednesday*, the work contains a situation rather than a plot, and while the situation is strongly presented in Part I, the unravelling in Part II constantly stalls for time, and the denouement when it comes is arbitrary and enigmatic. Harry walks out (taking his chauffeur with him) to undertake

> A care over lives of humble people,
> The lesson of ignorance, of incurable diseases. . . .

It is rather like the end of *The Palace of Art*.

Because this first of the drawing-room plays is crammed

with intractable matter, and the succeeding ones contain less and less of the familiar Eliotic traffic with the viscera of language, they are sometimes regarded as a spent poet's hobby. On the contrary, they register the effort of one very cunning writer to devise a stage verse which shall *set the characters free*, and enable him to construct his plots around a theme of liberation. What is usually called poetry on the stage is rhetoric, and what rhetoric signifies we are in a position to know; T. S. Eliot spent one career dissociating it into moral components. Rhetoric clangs on the prison bars of self-dramatization. In *The Cocktail Party* rhetoric is gone, and *The Cocktail Party* is the first Eliot work (excepting *Ash-Wednesday*) in which anything happens. The situation expounded in Act I gets resolved into a new situation in Act II. That Act III is (as the author has himself said) an epilogue rather than a finale doesn't diminish the fact that Prufrock's hell has undergone transformation for the first time since it was posited in 1911. "That is not what I meant at all," says the Lady to Prufrock in his recurrent hallucination, "settling a pillow or throwing off a shawl, and turning toward the window." Lavinia Chamberlayne says to Edward,

. . . you kept on *saying* that you were in love with me—
I believe you were trying to persuade yourself you were.
I seemed always on the verge of some wonderful experience
And then it never happened. I wonder now
How you could have thought you were in love with me.

Edward can only answer,

Everybody told me that I was;
And they told me how well suited we were.

Throughout *The Waste Land*, in *Sweeney Agonistes* and in *The Family Reunion*, Prufrock, disguised as Sweeney and as Harry, drowned this woman over and over. The only thing that could happen was a deed of violence, which isn't an Aristotelian action but only an occurrence. In *The Cocktail Party* something happens at last. The "dead" woman is restored;

and then, as the doom Becket accepts looks from the outside like the one he was tempted to court, so Edward and Lavinia return from Harcourt-Reilly's office to a life which is superficially their former life, yet which no longer courts

> the final desolation
> Of solitude in the phantasmal world
> Of imagination, shuffling memories and desires.

Now this is possible because the verse is of a new kind. In Eliot's last plays the language has developed a quite inimitable explicitness, as though people were capable of saying what they wanted to.

> It will do you no harm to find yourself ridiculous.
> Resign yourself to be the fool you are.
> That's the best advice that *I* can give you.

Or,

> Your conscience was clear.
> I've very seldom heard people mention their consciences
> Except to observe that their consciences were clear.

This verse is neither a dense medium lying in wait for effects of full intensity and damping out anything slighter, nor is it apt to be set twittering by random trivialities. It is seldom quotable, nearly devoid of fine lines; dry, not desiccated; not prosaic because more explicit than prose. The characters make themselves understood to each other and to us with preternatural efficiency and wit, and as they enlighten one another they grow more and more separated before our eyes. This is why audiences are usually disquieted. For no defect of communication can be attributed to the language, and yet the total communication on which modern liberalism has staked its faith does not occur. The characters discover and affirm their own inalienable privacy, indistinguishable from identity. They do not advance toward a shared illumination; they do not all, once freed from the illusions with which the play concerns itself, do similar things or elect similar lives. And yet no one echoes Sweeney's complaint that he has to use words. It took Eliot twenty-five years to develop a language against which that imputation would not lie. It is the thing his verse does that prose cannot do; mere English prose cannot be so explicit.

Colloquial prose does not define its meaning, but refers to its meaning; and no prose defines emotional meanings. Prose sketches in what it can and then says, "You know what I mean." Hence prose, a system of reference to meanings already shared, draws interlocutors together, when the dramatist is representing them as understanding one another; and when they are represented as not understanding each other, that is because the language is defective. But a speech in verse can be as clear as a scientific law, its intelligibility residing in the structure of what is said, not in another's guess at its purport. So it is possible for the verse dramatist, if he understands this use of verse, to build up gradually a structure of meaning which clarifies to everyone on stage everything that can be formulated. What is then left unstated is simply each speaker's wordless experience of himself, the essential life in the possession of which he experiences both the freedom and the isolation of the finite centres. No one, in the late Eliot plays, makes a Laurentian fuss about this. It is simply so.

Clarity of discourse, then, is the function of the verse. It is secured by using only those components of poetry which can enhance the defining powers of colloquial speech: rhythm and syntax, brought to the assistance of images no more salient, though more tidily developed, than those that occur in enlightened speech. And clarity, once secured, determines the moral climate of the plays. Establishing as it does the separateness of the characters—each actor's part, speech by speech, a marvel of explicitness—it lends definition to Eliot's familiar theme, the difficulty of understanding that another person exists not simply as a figure in your inner drama, but in his own way, and the necessity of arriving at that understanding in order that both you and he may be free. As B. Kaghan remarks at the end of *The Confidential Clerk*,

You know, Claude, I think we all made the same mistake—
. . . We wanted Colby to be something he wasn't.

So they did: Sir Claude and Lady Elizabeth each separately and for different reasons wanted him for a son, Kaghan for a colleague, Lucasta for a lover. When he himself consults his inner identity, the dramatic and discussible counterpart of which is a revelation about his parentage, he discerns a second-rate organist, and that is the calling he elects.

Which brings us to the other principal component of Eliot's dramatic method: his unemphatic use of a structure of incidents in which one is not really expected to believe, thus throwing attention on to the invisible drama of volition and vocation. The plot provides, almost playfully, external and stageable points of reference for this essentially interior drama, and so solves the structural problem with which the author of *Murder in the Cathedral* was exercising himself. It coheres with the conspicuous neatness that sustains comedy, and it stays sufficiently trite not to deform the characters with grotesque preoccupations. They are preoccupied with their own problems, not extraordinary ones. The plot simply enables Eliot to resolve these problems on a stage.

We have seen in the play about Becket his ingenious effort to manœuvre the detective story into service as a frame of moral reference. In *The Family Reunion* he conscripted a Greek tragedy, Furies and all, with partial success. It was in *The Cocktail Party*, the play in which his invention runs highest, that he first hit upon a scheme of incident sufficiently odd to effect revelations and sufficiently trite not to solicit detailed credence. It is the psychiatric cure, presided over by his most interesting theatrical creation, Sir Henry Harcourt-Reilly. This figure prevents *The Cocktail Party* from being a play about psychiatry; indeed he invests the whole plot with his own evasiveness. He is nowhere identified as an alienist, and though the audience cannot help remarking in his office the requisite couch, it will also note that the patients sit upon chairs, and that only Sir Henry lies down, between interviews. "He bears," Eliot told an interviewer in 1949, "some slight resemblance to Heracles in Euripides' *Alcestis*"—scarcely a professional qualification. "He is also an exceptional doctor, who uses somewhat original methods. He is also a character invented by myself, and he is also Mr. Alec Guinness." Mr. Guinness is the last actor in the world to confer identity on a part; one senses Eliot's thorough delight at having so deftly outwitted expectation. He has even checkmated his commentators, for the song of the One-Eyed Riley has a source, and though not a literary source it has been repeatedly recognized, but no work of explication has ever succeeded in printing it. Reilly is a superb theatrical hoax. Certain members of the psychiatric profession even complained to the press that their mode of operation was being misrepresented. The neat unbelievable plot over which he presides, with its strange penumbra where frivolous people sustain a conspiracy of spiritual Guardianship, was the instrument exactly suited to Eliot's purposes, and when it was objected that it made the audience vaguely uncomfortable, he asked why they should not feel vaguely uncomfortable.

In *The Confidential Clerk*, the focus of discomfort is the plot's system of echoes from the popular literature of the nineteenth century. Various reviewers immediately noted analogies with *H.M.S. Pinafore* and *The Importance of Being Earnest*. A more pertinent antecedent seems to be *Great Expectations*. The retiring clerk, Eggerson, with his garden and "Mrs. E.," is no one if not Dickens' Wemmick with his fortifications and his "old 'un"; Colby is an uncorrupted Pip; Mrs. Guzzard is the most Dickensian *dea ex machina* imaginable, her transparently Dickensian surname suggesting that Eliot, far from wishing to conceal these analogies, is laying a good-humoured "period" wash over the action. He does this for the same reason that he undermines the psychiatry in the previous play, genially subverting a Victorian farce in order to secure a plot from which the characters can remain morally detached, which can engage their practical intelligences alone, and manœuvre them into position for the appropriate decisions, declarations, and self-discoveries. The plot of *The Elder Statesman*, for that matter, is equally Victorian. Out of its climax, the father's confession to his child, a skilful writer of gaslight melodrama would have drawn cascades of tears. So that it may maintain, like its two predecessors, that plane of ambivalent seriousness from which the predicament of the characters can be withdrawn, Eliot has thinned out brute motivation and conferred on the characters a luminous miracle-play simplicity. Charles and Monica are enclosed in a lovers' world which drains of oppressiveness the drawing-room's silver and mahogany, while Lord Claverton's universe of retrospect displaces the realities of an asylum where old men are sent to die. This simplest of Eliot's plays is the most personal of his works. The terms of the tender dedication to his wife Valerie—

> . . . The words mean what they say, but some have a further meaning
> For you and me only—

seem meant to inform us that we are very close, this time, to the Poet whom, he is confident, we have no chance of seeing. The public man—Eliot has been a public man—is removed from the scene for ever ("I shall not go far"); his daughter Monica, who seems to have stepped into the play from *Marina*, tells her lover (and the dedication has presented Eliot as a lover) that love has been a shield protecting both of them. They are not the persons we think we see, but "conscious of a new person, who is you and me together." Her father, we are given to understand, dies offstage ("He is under the beech tree. It is quiet and cold there.") Her last words are addressed to Charles:

> I feel utterly secure
> In you. I am a part of you. Now take me to my father.

The Invisible Poet, we sense after the curtain, has occupied the stage at length, and in more than one guise, in this one work in which we cannot persuade ourselves that we see him.

Eliot's long poetic career has been devoted to a determined effort at analysis and recovery: analysis of the moral implica-

tions that inhere unexamined in the poetic practices his generation received, and recovery of a tradition in which the intelligence can discriminate phases of emotional experience and put
poetry again at the service of a significant variety of human
concerns. If that effort has led him finally into a poetic drama
of which the language is the most unassuming feature, that is
not because he has relaxed his professional concern for language.
"Our effort," he wrote twenty years ago, "is not only to
explore the frontiers of the spirit, but as much to regain, under
very different conditions, what was known to men writing at
remote times and in alien languages." Yet "the poet must
start from where he is, and not from a point at which he be-
lieves the language to have been superior," and starting there
he learns that "a dramatic scene in modern dress and modern
speech differs in emotional quality from a similar scene set in
another time and place," but also that "emotions themselves
are constantly being lost; they can never be merely preserved,
but must always be rediscovered; and it is as much this endless
battle to regain civilization, in the midst of continuous outer
and inner change of history, as the struggle to conquer the
absolutely new, that is the occupation of the poet."

"A ceaseless care, a passionate and untiring devotion to
language, is the first conscious concern of the poet; it demands
study of how his language has been written, in both prose and
verse, in the past, and sensitiveness to the merits and short-
comings of the way in which it is spoken and written in his
own time."

Eliotic drama, assuming that any successors go on with it,
is presumably in the *Arden of Feversham* phase. There is temperamental appropriateness in his having chosen to wrestle with
the sort of rudimentary matters, ancillary to a possible
flourishing, that engaged, in a time as unlikely for the drama
as our own, numerous half-anonymous Elizabethans. He has
also availed himself of the privilege of reflecting that Shakespeare was the most invisible poet of all. When, at the 1949
Edinburgh Festival, Eliot was badgered with a list of written

questions, he supplied a distinguished precedent for his evasiveness:

> I should like to suggest to you a useful exercise. Imagine that you have just seen the first performance of *Hamlet*, and try to set down fourteen questions for Shakespeare to answer, parallel to these fourteen. Then consider whether it is not all for the best that Shakespeare never answered these questions, or if he did, that the answers have not been preserved.

INDEX

I. PEOPLE, PLACES AND EVENTS

INDEX

II. TITLES

Works by T. S. Eliot in Roman type, by other authors in italics. (Authors' names omitted in cases where the reader is assumed to know them: *Adonais*, *Hamlet*, etc.)

INDEX

INDEX